THE
LINEUP

The World's Greatest Crime Writers
Tell the Inside Story
of Their Greatest Detectives

EDITED BY OTTO PENZLER

Quercus

First published in Great Britain in 2010 by

Quercus
21 Bloomsbury Square
London
WC1A 2NS

A CIP catalogue record for this book is available
from the British Library

ISBN 978 1 84916 520 4 (HB)
ISBN 978 1 84916 521 1 (TPB)

Printed and bound in Great Britain by Clays Ltd, St Ives plc

10 9 8 7 6 5 4 3 2 1

For Rupert Holmes
Rightly known as the nicest man in show business—
and quite possibly the most talented

CONTENTS

CONTENTS

THE
LINEUP

INTRODUCTION

BY OTTO PENZLER

It is an unhappy fact, though no less true for its sadness, that independent bookstores in America (and soon, I'll wager, in the rest of the world) are in jeopardy.

There are many reasons for this, of course, as no large and dramatic changes ever seem to be caused by a single sudden event, except possibly the Big Bang.

It is easy, and necessary, to point to the proliferation of the big chains, like Barnes & Noble and Borders, which, in spite of their denials, have malevolently established many of their superstores as close as possible to well-established independent stores. They then offered astonishing discounts, advertised heavily, brought in comfortable easy chairs next to their coffee bars, and welcomed authors for readings in order to capture local book buyers. Inevitably, the established stores saw their customer base diminish and, ultimately unable to pay rents, salaries, insurance, utilities, and the myriad other bills shoved through the mail slot with the regularity of tides, they were forced to close their doors. Without exception, this occurrence is accompanied by the lamentations of many of the very same book buyers who abandoned these stores, seduced by the siren song of discounts. These discounts, of course, not to mention those padded easy chairs, dramatically diminish or go the way of the dodo bird as soon as the competition has had the last shovelful of dirt tossed on its grave.

The rise of Amazon.com and other online sites has also contributed to the demise of "brick and mortar" stores. With no expensive urban rents to slice away at profits, and fewer salaries and benefits to pay to employees, Amazon.com and its relatives have been so successful that several chains have found themselves in their own expanse of quicksand.

We have all seen the depressing, even chilling, statistics about the reading habits of Americans. A survey titled Reading at Risk, commissioned by the National Endowment for the Arts in 2007, found that 57 percent of our countrymen had not read a single book in a year. Just mull that over for a moment. Can you imagine going a full year and finding nothing—nothing!—that you needed or wanted to read? As someone who makes his living as a bookseller, editor, publisher, and author, I feel that maybe I didn't make the smartest career choice. Actually, it wasn't my first career choice, which was playing center field for the New York Yankees, but that's not really the point.

There's more. The average American reads five books a year. When you factor in students who are assigned a fair number of books, plus those of us who read many more than five, there are a lot of folks out there pulling the average down. It would be enough to make you laugh, if you don't weep, to learn that 27 percent of the pollsters admitted that *they* hadn't read a single book in the year. A pertinent quote, often attributed to Mark Twain, is "The man who does not read good books has no advantage over the man who cannot read them." If you want to shudder, the question that leaps to mind is whether those 57 percent of Americans don't want to read or can't read. Neither is an attractive option.

Not at all surprisingly, then, The Mysterious Bookshop, which

I opened on Friday the 13th of April, 1979, found itself in financial straits a few years ago. It had been struggling for a while, and the move from its first home in midtown Manhattan to hip downtown Tribeca did nothing to improve its circumstances. Not being wealthy, partially by accident of birth and the failure of my parents to leave me an obscene fortune, I was faced with the increasing difficulty of supporting a business that was bleeding money—some months a mere trickle, others a rushing, roaring hemorrhage.

To illustrate the level of desperation to which I had fallen, I called for a staff meeting. There are many reasons to risk the perils of going into business on your own, and one of the best is to avoid the meetings that seem to fill the days of those who toil in the corporate world. At this unprecedented event, I told the people who work with me of our situation, holding nothing back, and asked for ideas that might help us save the store (and, not to be blithely overlooked, their jobs).

A pertinent digression: Every year, I commission an original short story from one of the authors I know. The story has three requirements: it must have an element of mystery, it must be set during the Christmas season, and at least some of the action must transpire at The Mysterious Bookshop. We print the stories in handsome pamphlets and give them to our customers as a small Christmas present to thank them for their patronage.

Back to the meeting and the discussion of the sinking ship. Someone said that our clients really love those Christmas stories; maybe we could commission another story and give it away in the summertime. This seemed a nice idea, but counterproductive. We needed to find a way to *make* some money, not another way in which to *spend* it. When we broke up the meeting, I threatened to have another one but, in the meantime, asked everyone to keep thinking.

In the dead of night, as I waited for sleep to rescue me from worrying about the store, the pamphlet idea popped up again, and I came up with a twist. How would it be, I wondered with the optimism that three a.m. can induce, if I asked some of my author friends to write a biography, or profile, of their series character? We could then print them in handsome little pamphlets and give them to our customers—but only with a purchase. They would, naturally, love these profiles so much that they would come back every month to get the next one, and our sales would soar. The next day I got the cost estimate from my printer, and the idea suddenly seemed shaky. Let me rephrase that. The idea suddenly seemed stupid. Furthermore, I never ask writers to write for free. Adding the authors' fees to the printing cost made the whole thing prohibitive—until the mercenary niche of my brain, incredibly, shook off years of rust and provided another suggestion. For the collector market, produce 100 copies of each of the profiles in hardcover, ask the authors to sign them, and sell these very desirable limited-edition collector's items. And we did produce them, the authors signed them, and collectors bought them.

More than two years after initiating this series, we're still in business, which, against all odds, has picked up nicely. Many clients come in, call, or write each month to ask who will write the next profile, and then buy books in order to get a copy. The limited editions frequently sell out, covering all costs and even a little more. Many of the authors, beyond the reasonable call of friendship, have forgone their fees, generously calling it their contribution to the well-being of the bookshop.

Regrettably, not every reader of mystery fiction is a customer of The Mysterious Bookshop, so it made sense to bring these essays and stories to a wider readership by collecting them in a single volume with the broad distribution that Little, Brown can provide. This handsome volume, *The Lineup,* is the result. As for the profiles themselves, you are in for a rare pleasure. You will find that these remarkably talented and creative writers have taken many different and colorful approaches to telling readers previously unknown facts about their creations. There are short stories tucked into the biographies, interviews of the characters, revealing looks into the authors' lives and creative processes, and even frequent insights into the characters that came as revelations to their creators.

It is impossible for me to find words to express my gratitude to these wonderful writers, for their quick and positive response to a humble call for help. Take a look at the names of the contributors, and you will see the truth of the old adage that "the bigger they are, the nicer they are." As a mystery reader, you will find many of your favorite authors in these pages, and maybe you will also get a taste of someone you've not read before now, thereby gaining an opportunity to enjoy a whole new series about a character to whom you have just been introduced.

I do not *hope* you enjoy these splendid character sketches; I *know* you will.

KEN BRUEN

Born in 1951 in Galway, Ireland, the city in which he still makes his home, Ken Bruen had his first book published in 1992 and has been extremely prolific since then, producing seven novels in the Jack Taylor series, set in Galway; seven novels about Inspector Brant, set in England; ten stand-alone novels; and five short story collections, as well as uncollected stories. He was the editor of *Dublin Noir* (2006).

His lean, spare prose places him among the most original stylists in the history of crime fiction. His dark, hopelessly tragic, and violent tales have surprising bursts of absurd humor—moments that more accurately reflect the personality of the author.

Much loved by the mystery community, Bruen has been collecting honors and awards, including a Shamus Award from the Private Eye Writers of America for *The Guards,* which also received Edgar Allan Poe and Macavity award nominations for best novel of the year; and a Macavity for *The Killing of the Tinkers,* which was also nominated for an Anthony Award as best novel of the year.

JACK TAYLOR

BY KEN BRUEN

I'm always asked in interviews where this odd, grizzled, grumpy PI Taylor came from.

He is the world's worst detective. Cases get solved not because of him but despite him.

He's

Alcoholic

Addict

Rude

Obnoxious

And in very bad shape

And yet . . . Forster's famous words.

He gets the job done . . . somehow, and he so desperately wants to connect, even though he'd never admit it.

Only connect.

Jack does . . . usually when he least expects to.

His love of books has saved his sanity on so many occasions.

I said on a TV show recently, Jack hasn't drunk for nigh on three books, and they laughed.

Uproariously.

They would.

Three books . . .

And not a drink.

For them a joke. For Jack, total hell.

And the reviews say Jack is mellowing.

Like fuck.

They ain't seen *Cross* yet.

Or *Benediction*.

He's only warming up.

He will bow out on the final book . . . titled . . . *Amen*.

And no one can utter those words with quite such conviction as Jack.

When the end comes, and come it will, no one will be happier than Jack.

Yet . . .

The Guards . . . his first outing, he was drinking but still a little in control, and then . . .

His best friend turns out to be the real psycho and Jack literally drowns him, off Nimmo's Pier in the Claddagh.

In Galway, an almost mystical place for Irish people . . . Jack throws a bottle of really good booze in after his friend.

And heads for London.

New start.

The UK loves *Micks* so much.

Need I add it wasn't a success?

The sequel,

The Killing of the Tinkers.

They told me I couldn't write this.

My favorite caution.

This will kill your career.

My career has been killed so often, and I'm always told . . . Oh, my god, you

can't

write

this

. . . and some damn stubborn place in my bedraggled psyche, thought

Can't?

Then

Have to.

The Hackman Blues, the second crime novel I wrote (fourth published), I was dropped by my agent, my publisher,

because of it.

Said,

You let this be published, you're gone.

I did.

They were right.

I was gone.

As Derek Raymond said,

"I had the down escalator all to meself."

I continued to write, to teach, and to travel. Brief sojourn to learn Portuguese in a Brazilian jail, which helped the dark vision forming in me head.

I take fierce grief in Ireland from the literati, as I always say my influences are American.

The hard-boiled

masters and they were and remain thus.

I wrote a series of novels about UK cops, *out of more damn cheek* than anything else . . . a Mick writing about UK cops.

Did a stand-alone based on *Sunset Boulevard* and it sold well, but still I hadn't hit what it was that was fermenting in me mind, uncoiling like a snake. Did a doctorate in metaphysics and still . . . the vision hadn't clarified. I returned to Ireland in 2000 to find a new country.

We'd got rich.

The fook did that happen?

We went from Mass to Microsoft with no preparation, and suddenly, people were immigrating *to Ireland!*

What?

The village I grew up in had become a cool, trendy European city.

And bingo.

It all came together.

They said there were no Irish crime novels, as we'd no mean streets. . . . With the new prosperity, we'd also got . . . crack cocaine and all its outriders.

I had me Irish novel; it all jelled.

I grew up fascinated by the Guards . . . solid, beefy guys who took no shite from anyone, and I'd got a library ticket when I was ten years old, books being forbidden in our house.

My older beloved brother had died of alcoholism.

Write about the Guards.

Back in 2000, like the clergy, they were . . . forgive me, bulletproof, and still admired.

I figured, put it all in the blend, an alcoholic investigator, bounced from the Force, loves books and is totally conflicted by the old values of the Ireland he grew up in and this new

greedy mini-American country.

And he had to have a mouth on him . . . like all of the country.

It makes me smile now. Back then, the first book, there were no PIs in Ireland.

Just last week, seven years on, I checked the Yellow Pages, and we have twenty in Galway alone!

Business is brisk.

At the same time, I planned a series. Jack would be caught up in all the secrets Ireland had.

The priests, the Magdalen laundries, teenage suicides, the way the whole fabric of the country was changing.

The Magdalen Martyrs came out, by coincidence, just after the marvelous movie

The Magdalene Sisters.

Priest came out when all the horrendous scandals of the clergy emerged.

Good timing?

Pure luck or just bad karma.

I dunno.

The Guards, they told me, was the biggest mistake in a career littered with bad moves. . . . It was nominated for the Edgar®, won the Shamus, and sold to countries I'd never even heard of.

The Killing of the Tinkers won the Macavity.

But storms on the horizon, naturally.

I have a child with Down syndrome, and in *The Dramatist* guess what . . .

Yup.

Jack is responsible for the death of a child with . . . fill in the blank.

I never got such hate-filled e-mail.

"How could I?"

I did what you do.

I told the truth.

Always a real bad idea.

Said I'd always intended to kill her . . . almost did in book three but felt she wasn't involved enough yet in either Jack's or the readers' emotions.

How cold is that?

I gave up explaining that I was experiencing a parent's worst nightmare . . .

the loss of

a child.

Nope.

Didn't wash.

The sixth Jack . . . *Cross*, I went for broke and already, we've had all the shite about writers going too far and I was mentioned as the prime perp. . . . The crucifixion, a year before, in Belfast, they had done exactly what I described.

Jack's surname was a personal joke; Taylors Hill is the snotty area of Galway, a place

Jack would never have been allowed to visit.

I never expected Jack to go global. . . . In my view, he was too Irish, too parochial, too damn perverse to have a wide appeal.

But I wrote him as he was whispering in my ear, and the first book, it was like I knew him.

And I do.

Alas.

The alcoholism is based on my late brother, a man of true warm spirit, my best friend, and he died a vagrant in the Australian outback, so I knew of what I wrote.

And when they come back at me about Jack being so angry?

Gee, wonder where that comes from.

The Irish, we laugh and drink our merry way, fueled by Guinness and Jameson and

never a worry in the world.

What a load of bollocks!

I fucking hate that.

Alcoholism has destroyed the best and the finest of our race, as Jack is fond of quoting.

Most of our literature applauds the culture of drinking.

Jesus Wept.

I thought,

"What if there were a series of books showing the sheer havoc and misery that drink causes?"

Whoops.

Wouldn't play well if you wanted Irish Awards or the Irish Tourist Board to endorse you.

And they having serious Euros to invest in the *appropriate* Irish writer.

And you know, I said, like I've said to me cost so many times,

The fook with that.

Here's the irony. . . . Seven books in, the tourist board calls me, would I be open to showing Japanese tourists Jack's Galway?

If that isn't irony?

I was thinking, maybe have them beaten up with a hurly, get a real taste of Jack's city.

Our national sport is hurling, a cross between hockey and homicide, and it's fast, brutal, skillful, and I grew up with it.

A perfect hurly is made from ash, honed by an artisan, and sometimes has metal bands on the end.

It's a little like a Louisville slugger. I have two of those, sent to me by two of the best writers in mystery today.

A hurly has a swoosh like the slugger and that same lethal intent.

When I was in Texas last year and got to hit a few, they asked,

"Where did you learn to play ball?"

I didn't.

I played hurling.

I'm asked,

"How much of me is in Jack?'

The rage and reading.

Absolutely.

And . . . sure . . . some of the beatings.

The booze?

'Tis a sad tale, but I don't drink Guinness or, god forgive me, even Jameson.

. . . Horror, I drink Bud. . . .

Jack would indeed take a hurly to me.

The ordinary people of Galway, so beloved to Jack's heart, they shout at me from cars. . . . Jack has been a teetotaler for three books.

"Give the poor bastard a drink."

Writing Jack has been all I know of heaven and hell. It drains me to write him, and I hope to Christ he'll stop talking to me.

It's too personal, too harrowing.

I write another series on UK cops. . . . The main character is Brant, and writing those books is a vacation, a breeze . . . pure fun . . . or a short story . . . more time in the sun, but Jack . . .

Otto Penzler once said to me,

"Bruen, what is it with you, you get us to love characters and then you kill them?"

Indeed.

I read on one of those blog discussions, the big no-no is . . . don't kill a child.

Gotcha.

Let me go classical here a moment, a little learned, or pseudo, if you prefer, or as our Irish teenagers in their new American tones say,

"Like, whatever."

There is a quote from Aeschylus that is the real motivation behind Jack Taylor, at least for me. It best helps me write him.

> *Pain that cannot forget*
> *Falls drop by drop*
> *Upon the heart*
> *And in our own despair,*
> *Against our will,*
> *There comes wisdom*
> *Through the awful*
> *Grace of God*

The key word for me there is always . . . *awful*.

With Jack, I wanted to see just how much suffering you can inflict on one human being

Till he finally breaks.

Alcohol

Cocaine

Despair

Depression

Betrayal

Suicide

Murder

Jack's been there.

Did quit smoking, though.

Not that he's happy with it.

And those lists?

I've been asked so often,

"What's with the bloody lists?"

I've studied chaos, damn, lived it most of me life, and one response to it is to make lists.

Try to impose order on a world spinning more and more out of control.

The later books, the lists got dropped, editorial decision more than anything else.

And quoting other mystery writers.

Because I love to. Not just my favorites, but also ones less known that maybe readers might pick up.

In *Priest,* I changed direction, went with simply Pascal's *Pensées.* Jack steals it from a library in a mental hospital. Nothing else quite seemed to fit the mood of the book.

While I was planning the series, a couple of things were crystal clear in my head.

Jack would always go down the dark streets of the history we'd

kept under wraps, like the Magdalen laundries. I grew up right beside them and knew firsthand of the horrors therein.

It was an Irish series, so there had to be a priest, a recurring
character, but I didn't want your lovable Barry Fitzgerald gom-
been of *The Quiet Man*. I wanted a flawed human version to
whom priesthood was simply a job, and one he didn't especially
care for.

When I was a child, the country was so poor, for many the only
hope of education was by joining the priesthood. Callow youths,
like cannon fodder, they went, as it was their *mothers' wish*.

What an awful burden to lay on any child. No wonder they went
nuts.

Fr. Malachy would always be Jack's nemesis and, like the best of
enemies, they even joined uneasy forces for *Priest*.

I knew from the off that this series was going to get me into all
sorts of shite in Ireland and so went completely for broke.

Jack's mother.

Like Italians and the other Europeans, we love our mothers. . . .
Never no mind she might be the biggest bitch who ever walked the
planet, Irish boys love *their mammy*.

Fook that.

Jack loathed his mother and never tried to hide it. She was everything that is worst about our country.

Pious

Sanctimonious

A hypocrite

And a mouth on her

And worst of all . . . long-suffering, though she instigated most of
the suffering.

Jack was having none of it, took her on from the get-go, and
it seemed natural her staunchest ally would be Fr. Malachy . . . a
match made only in the malice of Ireland.

Naturally, readers presumed Jack's mother was based on my own, as if even I have that kind of cojones.

My mother was once asked what she thought of the series, said,

"I never read him."

Nor did she.

Ever.

Bitter?

Not really.

I grew up in a house where books and reading were regarded as not only a waste of time but a waste of money.

God forbid you ever waste money.

My mother, Lord rest her, said,

"Ken lives in a separate room from the rest of us."

She was right.

By one of those odd coincidences, when Jack's mother had a stroke, so did mine, so all that Jack experienced then is based on what I was going through.

It's been eerie with the series like that.

The Killing of the Tinkers, I had a young psycho beheading swans. The swans are to Galway what the apes are to Gibraltar, though a little more attractive to look at.

My publisher was horrified, said,

"You can't do that!"

Notice how often that crops up in my career.

You can't.

You daren't.

You shouldn't.

I refused to back down, and just before the book was published, some lunatic began disemboweling the swans.

I sent my publisher the article, and he said,

"Okay . . . long as it's not you doing it."

I confuse people, not deliberately, but they read the books, thank god! (How Irish is that?) with the darkness, ferocity, brutality, and then they meet me and I'm mellow, easy to be with, and they're a tad bewildered.

A tad

is my nod to my UK readers, the two of them.

I reserve my murderous intent for my work.

Which brings me along to the violence I've been crucified for.

I never dwell on it, but it's there, explicit, and no doubt about what happens. It's ugly, fast, and very intense.

As all violence is.

Last November, I was at a book launch. A guy walked up and broke my jaw with a hurly.

Now, that is one very bad book review.

Will Jack do similar?

Already has.

Many times.

And that led me to the accusations of being pro-vigilante, a fascist, a supporter of all kinds of violent organizations.

You live in Galway, as I do, every single day, our latest horror, some thug walks free after raping an old lady, a seventy-nine-year-old nun, and the perp walks free, is given therapy, and in one ludicrous case, sent to Spain for a holiday.

I would love to say this is Irish exaggeration, but even in the past two years, my own personal history, a drunk driver who killed someone dear to my heart walked free because of personal problems.

The old people in Ireland used to say,

"Me blood boils."

Jesus.

Mine wept . . . freaking buckets.

So, I put it on Jack.

Let him deal with it.

And he does.

Usually with a hurly.

Jack believes as I do.

"Law is for the courts; justice is administered in alleys."

Controversial?

Of course.

In a society where there are no longer consequences, a hurly is a good edge.

One of me best friends, a doctor, has fretted for years about my views on so-called justice and the tone of my books.

He was, he said, my friend,

"Despite your, um . . . odd ideas."

Three weeks ago, his daughter was very seriously mugged and he came round, not looking for solace, but for my hurly.

When I put Jack out there, I figured maybe three books, and lo and behold, I'm on number seven. . . .

The bastard won't go away.

Cross, the sixth, went another direction, had to if the series was to stay fresh and challenging.

More of a thriller element than any of the previous. It also showed the dying of the Celtic Tiger. We were plunging into recession after eight years of living it on the hog, and *hog* is the perfect term. It made us, indeed, greedy at the trough, and suddenly, they were taking it away. The sheen was off the tiger and we were . . . fook, in maybe financial trouble.

We reacted like any child that you spoil and then take away the toys. We reacted very, very badly.

Still do.

And Jack, no longer shopping in charity shops, might have to return to them.

And,

He's getting old.

Losing his hearing.

Has the limp.

You ask,

Jesus, how much longer can he go on?

Indeed.

Would the only woman in his life, Ridge . . . and of course, the only constant female in Jack's life, who's gay . . .

take over the series?

No.

She doesn't even read that much.

When should a series end?

Simple.

When it's stale.

When you are no longer all that bothered by what happens to the main character. Jack is way past his sell-by date and if he gets through one more book, no one will be more surprised—or relieved—than me.

I've been truly amazed by the response to Jack.

The New York Times said he was as likely to give you a slap in the mouth as give five Euros to a homeless person.

I kind of liked that.

Brian Widenmouth, a fine online reviewer, suggested that Jack was already dead! . . . and this was all in look-back. Long as he didn't think I was dead too.

An Irish reviewer said I must have been a cop . . . had to be.

And you have to mention the movie.

In limbo hell.

Fookit.

The first serious offer wanted a happy ending. . . .

And I said,

"Happy?"

I don't do fooking happy.

Shite, *I don't even do nice anymore!*

Then the casting . . . Now, that was fun.

My mate of over twenty years David Soul was keen but couldn't quite get that Galway accent.

My only suggestion, and you know how much they take notice of the writer's idea.

Yeah.

Right in the bin.

But I always saw it being shot in black-and-white.

Color . . . in Jack's life?

Naw, he'd reach for the hurly.

The first offer to film *The Guards* was from a UK company, and they wanted it to be shot in Brighton, with Brighton Pier substituting for Nimmo's Pier, a recurrent landmark in the series. Not only is it in the Claddagh, but it's literally the last outpost before America and also the scene of Jack's first real murderous act, the drowning of his erstwhile friend.

I couldn't agree. The number of actors, etc., in Galway who could sure use the work would never forgive me. And *The Guards* is such a Galway novel.

The bookstores:

Kennys,

Charlie Byrne's,

Dubray's.

All pivotal to Jack's daily life.

And the pubs, like McSwiggan's, where a tree literally grows in the center of the pub, the question arising, Which came first, the tree or the pub?

As negotiations went back and forth, a ferocious storm hit Brighton and washed away the pier.

God spoke, if not last, at least loudest.

Jack would have loved the irony.

Next serious offer, they wanted a happy ending.

What?

And sink the whole series on the very first book?

I don't do happy, as I've said, and neither, by Christ, does Jack.

Research?

I was assured by the son of a retired top Guard that I must have been a cop, and this has frequently come up. I take it as a compliment and I think, too, the fact that I was a security guard at the Twin Towers has muddied the truth.

The title of my new stand-alone, *Once Were Cops,* will only cloud it further.

I'm very good friends with a Ban Garda, a female Guard, and all of Ridge, her attitudes, comes from this source.

A nice sidebar, I decided to have the Ban Garda in my books wear tiny pearl earrings, and I'm not saying it's a direct result, but recently, I notice they are indeed wearing said items.

In the beginning with Ridge, even I wasn't entirely sure why she was so hostile and combative, and I woke one morning and knew.

She was gay.

Not that I'm saying being gay means the above, but being gay in a strict, traditional, macho organization like the Guards will certainly embitter you.

In the new Jack, *Benediction,* he comes up against gay bashing, and yet again I had to battle to keep one particular scene, against the cry of it not being realistic.

You guessed it, not one hundred yards from my home, a young gay man was beaten into a coma by gay haters and no, I wasn't involved.

Superintendent Clancy, Jack's former partner in the Guards and great friend, is now his bitter enemy, and they regularly collide, with Jack taking the worst of it.

The final showdown, if such it is, comes in the newest Jack, the eventual head-to-head that has been simmering for six books.

As I wrote that scene, one song would not leave my head:

Springsteen's "The Price You Pay."

For a time, Thomas Merton and a pint were all Jack seemed to need, not always in that order, but you get the drift.

Jack soured on Merton, as he did on so many others.

In *The Guards,* Jack comments that he is so laden down with deaths, he feels like an old cemetery. Just about anyone who gets close to him is getting buried.

I was delighted that St. Martin's, when they began the American publications, never asked for the language or tone to be Americanized. They went with all the Irish-ism's, and I am so grateful for the chance they took on that.

A question I'm rarely asked and would have seemed obvious:

What do I think of the Guards?

I have the height of respect for them. They are still unarmed, and the new breed of criminal is armed to the teeth.

Every weekend, when the young folk go on the piss, young girls go into the water, usually in the canals and usually about three in the morning. Young Guards plunge into that freezing water and rescue them.

And how do the Guards feel about me?

Mmmmm . . .

When *The Killing of the Tinkers* was published, a parcel came through my door, a solid silver Zippo with the Garda insignia on it and a note that read,

"We don't always approve of what you write,

but keep it up."

It's not exactly an endorsement, but, you know, it sure made my day. And what impressed me most?

It was primed, fueled, flinted.

You might say,

Good to go. . . .

As is Jack, for one more run at it.

Or, perhaps . . . limp at it.

LEE CHILD

Lee Child was born in 1954 in Coventry, England. His family soon moved to Birmingham, where he went to the same high school that J. R. R. Tolkien once attended. He received a formal English education, reading Latin, Greek, and Old English, then attended law school in Sheffield. After working in the theater, he began an eighteen-year career with Granada Television in Manchester. When he was made redundant due to restructuring, he embarked on a fiction-writing career.

Jack Reacher, who has been featured in all of Child's novels, made his first appearance in 1997 in *Killing Floor*, which was an immediate success, winning both the Anthony and Barry awards for best first novel of the year. The series has increased in popularity each year, with foreign rights selling widely around the world, while making regular appearances on major bestseller lists everywhere. *One Shot*, Child's 2005 novel, is in development with Paramount Pictures.

The James Bond–ish Child drives a supercharged Jaguar and divides his time between the south of France and Manhattan, where he has become an enthusiastic fan of the New York Yankees. He is married and has a daughter.

JACK REACHER

BY LEE CHILD

How far back should I go with this? Reacher made his first appearance in print on March 17, 1997—Saint Patrick's Day—when Putnam published *Killing Floor* in the US, which was Reacher's—and my—debut. But I can trace his genesis backward at least to New Year's Eve 1988. Back then I worked for a commercial television station in Manchester, England. I was eleven years into a career as a presentation director, which was a little like an air traffic controller for the network airwaves. In February of 1988, the UK commercial network had started twenty-four-hour broadcasting. For a year before that, management had been talking about how to man the new expanded commitment. None of us really wanted to work nights. Management didn't really want to hire extra people. End of story. Stalemate. Impasse.

What broke it was the offer of a huge raise. We took it, and by New Year's Eve we were ten fat and happy months into the new contract. I went to a party but didn't feel much like celebrating. Not that I wasn't content in the short term—I sleep better by day than night, and I like being up and about when the world is quiet and lonely, and for sure I was having a ball with the new salary. But I knew in my bones that management resented the raise, and that the new contract was in fact the beginning of the end. Sooner or later, we would all be fired in revenge. I felt it was only a matter of time. Nobody agreed with me except one woman.

At the party, in a quiet moment, she asked me, "What are you going to do when this is all over?"

I said, "I'm going to write books."

Why that answer? And why then?

I had always been an insatiable reader. All genres, all the time, but very unstructured. I naturally gravitated toward crime, adventure, and thrillers, but for a long time in the UK we lacked genre stores and fan magazines, and of course the Internet hadn't started yet, so there was no effective network capable of leading a reader from one thing to the next. As a result, I had come across some very obscure stuff while being completely ignorant of many major figures. For instance, in February of 1988—while the ink was still drying on our new TV contracts—I took a vacation in the Yucatan. I flew back via Miami and picked up John D. MacDonald's *The Lonely Silver Rain* at the bookstall in the airport. I had never heard of MacDonald or Travis McGee. I read the book on the plane back to London and loved it.

I was back in the States at Easter that year and bought every McGee title I could find, which added up to about a linear yard's worth.

Nobody needs me to sing MacDonald's praises, but that yard of books did more for me than provide excellent entertainment. For some reason the McGee books spoke to me like textbooks. I felt I could see what MacDonald was doing, and why, and how, as if I could see the skeleton beneath the skin. I read them all that summer, and by New Year's Eve I was completely sure that when the ax fell, I wanted to do what MacDonald had done. I could stay in the entertainment business but work for myself in the world of books.

It took six years for the ax to fall. But fall it did, and so it came time to make good on that earlier ambition. I went to W.H. Smith's store in the Manchester Arndale mall—which the IRA destroyed a year later—and bought three legal pads, a pencil, a pencil sharpener, and an eraser. The bill was a penny under four pounds.

(I read Ngaio Marsh's essay in Otto Penzler's 1978 book *The Great Detectives,* and she reports doing very much the same thing, except that 1931 prices were radically lower than 1994's, and she didn't buy an eraser—maybe she already had one, or was more self-confident than I was.) Then I sat down with my purchases and let years of half-formed thoughts take shape. But not just six years of thoughts—now I have to take the process back another thirty years or so, to the point when my reading habit first took hold.

I had found that I liked some things in books and disliked other things. I had always been drawn to outlaws. I liked cleverness and ingenuity. I liked the promise of intriguing revelations. I disliked a hero who was generally smart but did something stupid three-quarters of the way through the book, merely to set up the last part of the action. Detectives on the trail who walked into rooms and got hit over the head from behind just didn't do it for me. And I liked winners. I was vaguely uneasy with the normal story arc that has a guy lose, lose, lose before he wins in the end. I liked to see something done spectacularly well. In sports, I liked crushing victories rather than ninth-inning nail-biters.

Some of my reading was directed, of course, in school. I was part of probably the last generation ever to receive a classical English education. I read Latin and Greek and Old English, all the ancient myths and medieval sagas and poems. I met the "knight errant" at its source.

Then I took a law degree at university. I never intended to be a lawyer, but the subject knit together all my nonfiction interests—history, politics, economics, sociology . . . and language. Legal language strives for concision and avoids ambiguity wherever possible.

The result is inevitably dull, but all that striving and avoiding really teaches a person how to write.

Then I went to work in the theater, which back then featured plenty of experimental theater, some of it good, most of it awful, and I developed a growing contempt for those who saw their minimal audiences as badges of honor.

"The public is too stupid to understand us," they would say.

I hated that attitude. To me, entertainment was a transaction. You do it, they watch it, then it exists. Like a Zen question: If you put on a show and nobody comes, have you in fact put on a show at all?

So for me, the audience mattered from the start. Which helped me thrive in television. And along the way, I discovered I *was* the audience. We were generally doing quality mass-market entertainment, but even so, some guys were conscious of slumming. Not me.

G. K. Chesterton once said of Charles Dickens, "Dickens didn't write what people wanted. Dickens *wanted* what people wanted." I would never compare myself to Charles Dickens, but I know exactly what Chesterton meant.

So, at thirty-nine years of age, after maybe thirty-five years of conscious experience, I sat down and opened the first of my three legal pads on my dining room table and lined up my pencil and sharpener and eraser and . . . thought some more, and came up with three specific conclusions.

First: Character is king. There are probably fewer than six books every century remembered specifically for their plots. People remember characters. Same with television. Who remembers the Lone Ranger? Everybody. Who remembers any actual Lone Ranger story lines? Nobody.

So my lead character had to carry the whole weight . . . and there was a lot of weight to carry. Remember, I was broke and out of work.

Second conclusion: If you can see a bandwagon, it's too late to get on. I think the person who said that to me was talking about investment issues—as if I had anything to invest—but it seemed an excellent motto for entertainment as well. It's a crowded field. Why do what everyone else is doing?

So I was going to have to do something a little different. It seemed to me that the mystery series that were then well under way—and most that were just starting out—were, when carefully analyzed, soap operas. (Which to me is not a derogatory term. . . . Soap opera is an incredibly powerful narrative engine, and soap operas had put food on my table for eighteen years. Lots of it, and high quality.) Lead characters were primus inter pares in a repertory cast, locations were fixed and significant, employment was fixed and significant. In other words, series heroes had partners, friends, jobs, apartments, favorite bars, favorite restaurants, neighbors, family, even dogs and cats. They jogged, worked out, had pastimes. They had bills to pay and issues to resolve.

If you can see a bandwagon, it's too late to get on. I was going to have to avoid all that stuff.

But, the third conclusion, and the most confounding: You can't design a character too specifically. I knew in my bones that to think too carefully would produce a laundry list of imagined qualities and virtues and would result in a flat, boring, cardboard character. I would be consulting a mental checklist: "I need to satisfy *this* demographic . . . check . . . and please *these* people . . . check . . ." until I had a guy with all the spark and life beaten out of him. So I quite self-consciously pushed that thirty-five-year-old soup of ideas and influences into the distant background and decided to relax and see what would come along.

Jack Reacher came along.

I was interested in dislocation and alienation, and I had noticed that people who have spent their lives in the military have trouble adjusting to civilian life afterward. It's like moving to a different planet. So I wrote a character who had been first a military brat, then a military officer, and was now plunged unwillingly into the civilian world. And because the books would be broadly crime novels, I made him an ex–military cop, in order to give him plausible familiarity with investigative procedures and forensics and so on.

Those twin decisions gave him a double layer of alienation. First, his transition from the rough, tough world of the army made him a fish out of water in civilian life, which situation was then further reinforced by any law enforcement officer's separation from the rest of the population.

And he was American. I'm British. But by that point I had been a regular visitor to the United States for twenty years—my wife is from New York—and I felt I knew the country pretty well, at least as well as I could expect an alienated ex-military drifter to know it. And it's easier to be rootless and alienated in a giant country like America. Alienation on a tiny crowded island like Britain is of a different order, almost wholly psychological rather than physical or literal.

I like reading the internal, claustrophobic British crime books, but I didn't want to write them. I wanted big, rangy plots, big landscapes, big skies.

His status as a former officer happened instinctively. Looking back, I clearly wanted to tap into the medieval knight errant paradigm, and a knight errant has to have been a knight in the first place. I thought a West Point history and a rank of major would be suitable.

In literary terms it was an important choice, but later I realized it has plausibility issues. His whole personality, approach, and implied past experiences make it much more likely that in the real world he would have been a warrant officer, not a commissioned officer.

But to me it was crucial that he should have a certain nobility—which is a strange thing to say about a guy who goes around busting heads as frequently and thoroughly as Jack Reacher does, but it is clear from subsequent reaction that his "white hat" status depends heavily on our images of and assumptions about rank. (And his "white hat" status has tempted readers to classify the series as a set of modern-day Westerns, which is convincing in terms of feel and structure.)

Some of the novels are just like *Shane* or a Zane Grey story or a Lone Ranger episode—lonely, embattled community has a problem; mysterious stranger rides in off the range, solves the problem, rides off into the sunset—but I have never been a fan or even a reader of Westerns. What is happening there is that Westerns too have strong roots in the medieval knight errant sagas.

As in much of evolution, if B isn't descended directly from A, then they both shared a common ancestor much further back.

At first he wasn't called Jack Reacher. In fact, he wasn't called anything at all. The part of writing that I find most difficult is coming up with character names. My books are heavily populated with stationery brands and other authors, because when I need to name someone I tend to look around my office helplessly until my eye alights on the front of a notebook or the spine of a book on my shelves.

Once or twice I stared out my window until a neighbor walked past, or I thought back to the last clerk's name badge I saw in a store. . . . All kinds of people get their names in my books, most of them unwittingly. But obviously the main character's name is very important to get right. With luck it will appear in many books and even be talked about in other contexts.

I started writing with no clear idea of the name. The first book was written in the first person, which meant he didn't need a name until someone else asked what it was, which didn't happen for thirty or so manuscript pages. Then a police detective asked, "Name?" I put my pencil down and thought. The best I could come up with was Franklin, as I recall. But I wasn't happy with it.

Then I went shopping. Part of the problem of not having a day job was, well, I didn't have a day job, and my wife therefore assumed that after many years of solo struggle, she now had help with chores. So she asked me to go to the supermarket with her, to carry stuff home. I'm a big guy; she's a small woman.

She was also a worried woman, although she was hiding it well. Our life savings were disappearing, and regular paychecks were merely distant memories.

In the supermarket—and this is a common experience for tall men—a little old lady approached me and said, "You're a nice tall gentleman, so would you reach that can for me?" My wife said to me, "If this writing thing doesn't work out, you can always be a reacher in a supermarket." I thought, Great name! And I used it, and I smile now when I read Internet commentary imagining I specified the name for its forward-going, striving, progressive implications.

His first name came from conclusion number two—don't do what the others are doing. There was a miniature rash at the time of characters with cute or complex first names. So I looked for the simplest and plainest name I could find. I chose Jack, and not as a diminutive for John, either. It's just Jack. (One of my grandfathers was called Harry, which most people assumed was a diminutive for Henry, but it wasn't. Harry was on his birth certificate.)

In my third book, *Tripwire*, there's a passage that starts: "Reacher had been named Jack by his father, who was a plain New Hampshire Yankee with an implacable horror of anything fancy."

I wanted to underpin Reacher's blunt and straightforward manner with a blunt and straightforward name. I didn't think the character would have worked with, say, MacNaughten Lawrence for a name. Still don't. Even though the first name could have been abbreviated to "Mac" on nearly all occasions, the hidden truth on his official papers would have implied something that I didn't want implied.

So, he's an ex–military officer, he's American, he's alienated, he struggles to participate effectively in civilian society, and he has a plain name.

And he's huge.

He's six feet five inches tall, and around two hundred fifty pounds, all of it muscle. In *Tripwire,* after he's been doing physical labor in the sun for a spell, he's described as looking "like a condom stuffed with walnuts." No one in his right mind would mess with him.

I had in mind the kind of intimidating physical presence that pro footballers have, relaxed, utterly sure of themselves, but in Reacher's case with a barely visible hint of danger. (In fact, in *One Shot,* he admits to having played football for Army while at West Point, but that his career was limited to only one game. "Why?" someone asks. "Were you injured?" "No," he replies. "I was too violent.")

His physical presence is another offshoot of conclusion number two—don't do what the others are doing. For a long time what the others had been doing was making their protagonists more and more flawed and vulnerable. Way back, it had been a welcome development to move away from the uniformly lantern-jawed he-men that had crowded the genre. Heroes became smaller, realistically afraid, physically unexceptional.

On the emotional side, they became battered. They were alcoholics, recovering alcoholics, divorced recovering alcoholics, divorced recovering alcoholics living in cabins in the woods and traumatized by professional mistakes. Literal and metaphorical bullets were lodged near hearts. There was an overwhelming feeling of incipient failure and melancholy.

As with all trends, this one was started by inspired pioneers and then overdone by imitators. By the time I started writing, I was tired of it. I wanted to start over with an old-fashioned hero who had no problems and no issues, and didn't go in for navel gazing. His physical competence is really an expression of his mental competence too. He's a fully functioning person.

And I thought it would be interesting to reverse the paradigm in terms of physical vulnerability. Usually, a book's hero comes up against people he needs to be afraid of.

What if, I asked myself, the hero is the toughest SOB in the valley, and others need to be afraid of him? In my fourth book, *Running Blind,* an FBI agent called Blake threatens to leak Reacher's name to a violent psychopath called Petrosian.

Blake thinks it's an effective motivator—and in real life and most books it would be. But Reacher just says: "Look at me, Blake. Get real. There's maybe ten people on the planet I need to be scared of. Extremely unlikely this guy Petrosian happens to be one of them."

I was trying to discover whether drama was possible without the usual David-versus-Goliath structure. I wondered, would Goliath-versus-Goliath work?

I have a fan and a friend who works in the gaudy world of pro wrestling—worked, actually, because he's retired now. You'll be shocked (shocked!) to hear that their bouts are heavily scripted and rehearsed, even to the extent of having story conferences. My friend's major concern is that the wrestling paradigm always has the designated good guy lose, and lose, and lose, before winning in the final round. It was hard for him to come to terms with the absence of a battered underdog. But I always wanted Reacher to be the overdog.

Because I was following my instincts. Remember, "Dickens *wanted* what the audience wanted." I *was* the audience. I wanted the kind of vicarious satisfaction that comes from seeing bad guys getting their heads handed to them by a wrong-righter even bigger and harder than them. I thought, Isn't that what fiction is for? Because the existence of fiction is a curious thing.

Language evolved way back when leisure was simply unheard of. Language was all about survival and cooperation and the dissemination of facts in pursuit of literally life-and-death issues. For most of our existence language has been for telling the truth. Then fiction started up, and we started burning brain cells on stories about things that didn't happen to people who didn't exist. Why? The only answer can be that humans deeply, deeply desired it. They needed the consolation. Real life is rarely satisfactory.

The transaction is clearly apparent in romantic fiction. In real life, you sit on the subway and you see a beautiful girl. Truth is, you aren't going to dinner with her, you aren't taking her home, you aren't going to live happily ever after. In fact, you aren't even going to talk to her. But in a novel, all that good stuff happens. It's a way to live vicariously.

Same for crime fiction. In real life, your house gets burgled or your car gets ripped off, they aren't going to find the bad guys, and you aren't going to get your stuff back. Someone bullies or disrespects you at work or in school or in a relationship, there isn't much you can do about it. But something can be done about it in a book, and people enjoy watching it happen. They love it. It's closure, albeit also vicarious.

So I wanted Reacher to do what we all want to do ourselves—stand strong and unafraid, never back off, never back down, come up with the smart replies. I thought of all the situations that we—timid, uncertain, scared, worried, humiliated—find ourselves in and imagined a kind of therapeutic consolation in seeing our wildest dreams acted out on the page.

So Reacher always wins.

Which is theoretically a problem. He's a plain, uncomplicated man who breezes through life without evident trouble. Shouldn't he be boring?

In theory, yes. But readers don't agree. Because actually he has plenty of minor problems. He's awkward in civilian society. He gets around his difficulties by assembling a series of eccentricities that border on the weird. If he doesn't know how something works, he just doesn't participate. He doesn't have a cell phone, doesn't understand text messaging, doesn't grasp e-mail. He doesn't do laundry. He buys cheap clothes, junks them three or four days later, and buys more. To him, that's a rigorously rational solution to an evident problem. To us, it's almost autistic.

The contrast between his narrow and highly developed skills and his general helplessness humanizes him. It gives him dimension. He has enough problems to make him interesting, but, crucially, he himself doesn't *know* he has these problems. He thinks he's fine. He thinks he's normal. Hence interest without the whiny self-awareness of the bullet-lodged-near-the-heart guys.

What motivates him?

He has no need for or interest in employment. He's not a proactive do-gooder. So why does he get involved in things? Well, partly because of noblesse oblige, a French chivalric concept that means "nobility obligates," which mandates honorable, generous, and responsible behavior because of high rank or birth.

Reacher had the rank and the skills, and he feels a slightly Marxist obligation "from he who has, to him who needs." Again, that attitude predates the twentieth century by a long way. It shows up in nineteenth-century Western heroes, and thirteenth-century European heroes, all the way back to the Greeks and, we can be sure, much further back into oral traditions where no written records exist. Added to which, in Reacher's case, is a cantankerousness that provokes him.

In *Persuader,* during a flashback to his military days, he is asked why he became an MP when he could have chosen any other branch of the service. He gives a vague answer, along the lines of wanting to look after the little guy.

His questioner is skeptical. She says, disbelievingly, "You care about the little guy?"

"Not really," Reacher admits. "I don't really care about the little guy. I just hate the big guy. I hate big smug people who think they can get away with things."

That's what motivates him. The world is full of unfairness and injustice. He can't intervene everywhere. He needs to sense a sneering, arrogant, manipulative opponent in the shadows. Then he'll go to work. Partly because he himself is arrogant.

In a sense, each book is a contest between Reacher's arrogance and his opponent's. Arrogance is not an attractive attribute, but I don't hide Reacher's because I think the greatest mistake a series writer can make is to get too chummy with his main character. I aim to like Reacher just a little less than I hope you will. Because basically a book is a simple psychological transaction.

"I'm the main character," the main character announces.

The reader asks: "Am I going to like you?"

There are several possible answers to that question. The worst is: "Yes, you really are, and I'll tell you why!"

But Reacher answers: "You might or you might not, and either way is fine with me."

Because, as an author, I believe that kind of insouciant self-confidence forms a more enduring bond.

Does it?

MICHAEL CONNELLY

Born in 1956, Michael Connelly grew up in Pennsylvania, attended the University of Florida (graduating in 1980), and went to work as a journalist in Daytona Beach and Fort Lauderdale, Florida, mainly on the crime beat. After he was short-listed for a Pulitzer Prize for feature writing, he moved to the *Los Angeles Times* as a police reporter. A few years later, his first novel about Hieronymus (generally known as Harry) Bosch, *The Black Echo,* was published. Based in part on a real crime, it won the Edgar Allan Poe Award from the Mystery Writers of America for best first novel.

Fourteen more Bosch novels have followed as the LAPD detective became one of the most popular and loved characters of contemporary detective fiction and his creator became one of the bestselling mystery writers in the world. In addition to the Bosch series, Connelly has produced such bestselling stand-alone novels as *The Poet* (1996), *Blood Work* (1998) (filmed in 2002 with Clint Eastwood as director and star), *Void Moon* (2000), *Chasing the Dime* (2002), *The Lincoln Lawyer* (2005), which was nominated for a best novel Edgar®, *The Brass Verdict* (2008), and *The Scarecrow* (2009).

In 2003 and 2004, Connelly became the first author to serve as president of the Mystery Writers of America for two years. He served as the guest editor for *The Best American Mystery Stories 2002*. Translated into thirty-five languages, he has won the major mystery-writing awards in several countries (Japan, France, Italy) as well as in the United States.

He lives in Tampa, Florida, with his wife and daughter.

HIERONYMUS BOSCH

BY MICHAEL CONNELLY

A few years ago I was on a book tour that took me to Bryn Mawr, on the Main Line outside Philadelphia. I got in early and had some free time before my reading, so I steered the rental car west to the small town of Devon. At least it was a small town in the mid-1960s, when I lived there as a boy with my family.

By staying close to the railroad line I was able to find Highland Avenue without difficulty. It was here that my family lived in a middle-class neighborhood close to the tracks. Our house was a two-story white colonial that my father, a contractor, had designed and built.

I stopped the car in front of 321 Highland, but I didn't get out. I just sat behind the wheel and looked up at the house for a while. Things had changed about the place, but many things were still the same. My eyes were drawn to the upper window that belonged to the bedroom I had shared with one of my brothers.

It was in that room that I would lie on the top bunk at night and look out through the window. I could see the lights through the woods across the street and hear the rumble of the freight trains that intermittently chugged by. I could also cast my eyes into the front yard and, through the shadows of the night, make out the mouth of the tunnel that was down there. The tunnel that would often invade my dreams as a boy. The tunnel in which I believe Harry Bosch was born.

The house was on a piece of sloping land, which meant that when I visited friends who lived behind us, I had to go out the back door and climb a steep hill to get to their yards. If I went out the front door to the street, the lawn dropped down into a gulley that led to a brick-lined drainage tunnel that went under Highland Avenue and into the woods across the street. The tunnel was old and filled with mud and fallen brick-and-mortar rubble. Gnarled roots had broken through from overhead and crept down like hands ready to grab you. Spiderwebs clung to these roots in silvery patterns that caught the light that leaked down from above. The tunnel smelled as damp as a flooded basement.

It was an unspoken rite of passage in my neighborhood that every young boy had to go through the tunnel. On his own, holding no one's hand, and not turning back or chickening out. Those who weren't up to it faced certain peer group banishments and the attendant verbal abuse. The tunnel was the crucible that separated the boys from the men. And nobody wanted to be a sissy.

You knew who had been through the tunnel and who had not. There wasn't a neighborhood list in which names were checked off. It wasn't even spoken about. It was just one of the things you knew as a boy in that neighborhood. You knew who wore the invisible badge of courage that would soon open the door to manhood, and who had chickened out.

All memories of childhood are exaggerated in some fashion. It was said that if you were down in there when the trash truck passed by up above, the roots swayed and the tunnel rumbled like an earthquake. It was also said that if you called out from the middle of the tunnel, your voice made a perfect echo in both directions. I cannot be sure of the tunnel's dimensions, but my honest guess is that it was no more than five feet high and forty feet from entrance to exit. But to a ten-year-old it didn't matter. Whatever the measurements were, they were the dimensions of fear.

As the time for me to go through drew near, I thought about the tunnel a lot. It was summer, and I knew that before the season's end, before school began again, I had to prove myself. I had to pass through that tunnel. At night on the top bunk, I could see it down there waiting for me.

The dreams started that summer. Nightmares, really. Intense and dark, with me always alone. It was always the same scene: I entered the tunnel, ready for the challenge, but a few steps in, the brick walls suddenly started to contract. Then, rippling violently in front of me, up out of the mud, a giant tongue lashed about at me.

And then I would wake up just as I realized I had stepped into the mouth of a great waiting beast.

I didn't have to go to an analyst then or now to know why the dream had manifested or what it was about. It interrupted my sleep often that summer and then disappeared once I made the journey through the tunnel. Strangely, I have no memory of my actual passage. I cannot confirm the spiderwebs. But I can confirm that I made it and, once through, became one of the boys who taunted those who had not yet passed the test.

———

A few years later, my family had moved from Highland Avenue in suburban Philadelphia to Twenty-sixth Avenue in Fort Lauderdale, Florida, as my father chased a series of jobs in the sun. The Vietnam War was the backdrop to life then. I was in high school and not a good student, so I paid attention to Vietnam because I thought it could be my destiny. I remember the principal on the loudspeaker in the classroom calling for a moment of silence and prayer in memory of a former student who had been killed over there. William Fennel.

I didn't know him, but years later I would look his name up on the wall of the memorial in Washington, DC.

One summer I remember my father talking about a man he worked with in a real-estate office. He said the man had to wear a full beard to cover facial scarring from wounds he'd received while he was a soldier in Vietnam. He told my father he had been something they called a tunnel rat. His job was to go into the underground labyrinths where the enemy hid and waited.

The man refused to tell my father all the details, but my teenage imagination filled in the story and was possibly more powerful than the truth. It seemed to me that no war assignment could be more frightening or dangerous than being a tunnel rat. And that summer, after so many years, the dream came back to me. Once more I dreamed of being in the mouth of the underground monster.

———

Soon after high school I knew I wanted to be a writer. I loved reading detective stories, and those were what I wanted to write. I went to journalism school in college and hoped that a job at a newspaper would teach me the craft of writing while at the same time giving me entrée into the world I wanted to write about: the police department. For several years after college I lived and worked in Florida and tried to write a couple of detective novels on the side. They didn't work. They are about men who specialize in finding runaways but who themselves have run away from things in their own lives. Sure, I learned more about writing and the form of the detective novel as I moved from one draft to the next, but the manuscripts never got past the bottom drawer of my desk. I remain the only one who has ever read them.

At thirty years old, I knew I had it in me to take one more shot at a novel. But I gave myself an ultimatum. If the book didn't work and was not published, I would shelve my aspirations and rededicate myself to my career as a journalist. In preparation for taking final aim at my goal, I decided to shake everything up in my life. I sent out résumés to California, three thousand miles away, the land of my literary heroes—Raymond Chandler, Ross Macdonald, and Joseph Wambaugh. It was my conviction that I had to start this novel and stage this part of my journey in Los Angeles.

On the day I interviewed for a job as a police reporter at the *Los Angeles Times,* the editor handed me the Metro section and pointed to a story bannered across the top. He gave me fifteen minutes to read it and tell him how I would follow up the story. It was a test. He wanted to see how well and how fast I could think on my feet.

The story was about a bold bank heist. Thieves had cleverly used the city's labyrinthine storm water tunnel system to move under downtown and into close proximity of the target bank. They then drilled through the wall of the city tunnel and dug their own line to a position directly beneath the bank's safe-deposit vault. They went up and in and spent a night in the vault drilling open boxes and bagging their contents. Then they got away.

Whatever I told the editor must have impressed him. I got the job and moved to Los Angeles. Soon after starting on the police beat, I was allowed to sit in on a detective squad briefing on the unsolved tunnel caper. The case investigators showed photographs that depicted the thieves' route through the tunnels. It was a dark and shadowy netherworld and eerily reminiscent of the mysterious tunnel I had dreamed of when I was a kid.

———

My plan had been to spend a year or two getting to know Los Angeles before daring to write about this huge, sprawling, and intriguing place my heroes had trodden and known so well. But that night after the police briefing, I went into the spare bedroom of the apartment I shared with my wife by the 101 freeway and started writing. I'd had an epiphany: I would write about a detective who has a recurring dream of tunnels, who has experience in those tunnels, and whose past informs his present. Now the tendrils of my life were coming together, and I felt that at last I had the true baseline for a character and story that could travel the distance and be published, and live on in readers' imaginations.

I called him Pierce. I had read something, somewhere, in which Raymond Chandler had described the fictional detective as someone who must be willing and able to pierce all veils and layers of society. My detective would be such a man, and so I called him Pierce.

I wrote with the window open most of the time and wanted to play music that would filter out the disruptive noise of the nearby freeway. I grew up on rock and roll, but as a writer I found that music with lyrics could intrude upon the writing process in its own way. I was going to write about a detective who was alone in the world, so I gravitated toward music that invoked loneliness in me. Jazz. More to the point, the sound of the jazz saxophone. I started with the essentials—John Coltrane, Sonny Rollins, Wayne Shorter—and branched out from there. Along the way I read a piece in *Time* magazine about a musician named Frank Morgan, a protégé of Charlie Parker's who had overcome heroin addiction and imprisonment to record again after thirty years. It was in Frank Morgan's alto sax that I found the soundtrack of my detective. In his sad but uplifting ballad "Lullaby," written by pianist George Cables, I discovered my detective's anthem. For many years I played that song at the start of each writing day.

My detective, like Frank Morgan, was to be a survivor, a man who overcomes his past to ensure his present—and his future. So I chose his music carefully. Pierce would listen to music created by artists who had overcome great obstacles in order to make it. Whether it was beating drug addiction, fighting racism, surmounting poverty, or rising above medical disability, the jazz musicians I drew inspiration from were survivors. And I gave the whole playlist to Detective Pierce.

By day I was a news reporter on the crime beat. By night and weekend I was an amateur novelist trying to finally make it happen. I viewed my day job as research for the night shift. It was as if I were dropping into a gold mine, down a tunnel where I could look for whatever glittered. The sights and sounds of police stations and jails, the cop slang, the internal politics. I would come out each day and bury the gold in my book that night.

Most of the real detectives I knew were veterans of military service, about half of them Vietnam vets. A lot of them smoked, a symptom of the addictive personality I had come to believe was a necessary dimension of a good detective. I remember once sitting at a detective's desk while he smoked a cigarette, the No Smoking sign hanging on the wall right behind his head. Though I had never smoked myself, I made Pierce a smoker. Though I had escaped going to Vietnam, because the war ended as I turned eighteen, I made Pierce a Vietnam vet. I made him a tunnel rat who still dreamed of the tunnel and was always searching for that light at its end.

The aspects of character continued to fall into place as I wrote the first draft of a novel that would feature Pierce investigating the murder of a man who had been a fellow tunnel rat and who might have been involved in the tunnel heist of a Los Angeles bank.

The real tunnel heist I based the story on took place in 1987, the year I came to Los Angeles. The year is also notable because it was when the novel *The Black Dahlia* by James Ellroy was published. Although the book impressed me, I was more taken at the time with the author's history, which I'd read about in a profile in a local magazine. Ellroy's mother was murdered when he was a boy. He struggled to overcome that life-altering crime, and many other personal demons, enough to write *The Black Dahlia* and several other novels before it.

I thought the psychology was intriguing. In my amateur analysis it looked to me that Ellroy was working out whatever damage had been visited upon him by his mother's murder by writing stories about detectives who avenge victims and solve murders—especially of women.

I decided to apply the same psychology to Pierce. I gave him a history similar to Ellroy's. When Pierce is a boy, his mother is murdered. Since he doesn't know his father, the crime not only takes away his one loving parent, but also relegates the boy to the world of foster homes and state youth facilities. The boy survives his upbringing and becomes a man in Vietnam, where his job is to go into the tunnels to seek the enemy. From there he comes home to one more flawed institution: the police department. The soldier becomes a detective who repeatedly avenges his mother's death by solving murders—especially of women.

It is the cornerstone of the character. The trauma of his youth becomes the driving force behind the detective. It is the aspect that will allow every case he takes on to become personal.

I did not know Ellroy when I borrowed from his past for my fictional detective. Years later, though, when I prepared to write a novel in which my detective would investigate his mother's long-unsolved murder, I sent the author a letter. I explained my story idea to him. I knew that Ellroy had a plan to write a nonfiction account of his mother's unsolved murder. I asked if he thought my novel would be too much of an encroachment. His response came by way of a late-night phone call several weeks later. "Unfortunately, I don't have a franchise on murdered mothers," he said. "Good luck with your book."

My plan for Pierce was simple. I wanted to acknowledge my mentors and use what they had taught me to mold something that was my own. Chandler, Macdonald, Wambaugh, also James Lee Burke, Lawrence Block, and Thomas Harris. I wanted to combine elements of the characters who were outsiders with the traits of those characters who were on the inside. Pierce would be an outsider with an insider's job. He'd face political and bureaucratic obstacles at every turn. He'd be good at his job but flawed in the way he carried it out. At times he'd be his own worst enemy. He'd feel as though he were always on a solitary mission—alone in the tunnel—even though he might have a partner and be part of an organization that was thousands strong. He'd be a seeker of true justice, not just closure on a case.

Detective Pierce would be built to be as relentless as a bullet, a self-reliant loner who stood alone, who could not be gotten to. Nothing would come between him and his mission, and nothing short of death could stop him from getting the job done.

My goal was to create a character whom readers would find impossible to love on all levels, who in fact was capable of doing things that the readers might find objectionable. But, at the end of the day, my guy would be the kind of detective whom readers would want on the case if it was ever them or a loved one lying on the stainless steel table in the morgue.

I put none of this down on paper. I just carried it in the pockets of my imagination, and when I was ready I set to work on the story. From early on I titled it *The Black Echo*. Abstract and mysterious, the phrase also conjured up some of the fear I remembered from the fateful passage through the tunnel beneath Highland Avenue.

I caught a lucky break while I was writing *The Black Echo*. I came across a book called *The Tunnels of Cu Chi*. Written by Tom Mangold and John Penycate, the book is a harrowing account of the real experiences of the tunnel rats of the Vietnam War. It was only after I read this book that Pierce's background as a tunnel rat and his recurring dreams fully took shape. That book stayed on my desk as I wrote *The Black Echo*. And, almost twenty years later, it is still within reach of where I write today. It is easily as scary and claustrophobia inducing as a Stephen King novel. But *Cu Chi* is true. It makes a ten-year-old's anxieties about crawling through a forty-foot drainage tunnel seem like, well, child's play.

———

When I went to college at the University of Florida, my intention was to major in building-construction sciences. I wanted to be a builder, like my father. But I wasn't there long before I realized that I wanted to build stories instead of houses. While shifting to journalism and creative writing, I took a good number of art history and humanities classes as well. In one of those classes, the professor had the students examine the work of the fifteenth-century Flemish painter Hieronymus Bosch.

Bosch's work was unfamiliar to me until I saw it in that class. Simply put, it is the stuff of nightmares, an exploration of the wages of sin and of a world gone wrong. The paintings, full of dark, hellish landscapes of torture and debauchery, are about chaos and its consequences. Fires burn out of control in a dark underworld. Birdlike monsters torture and maim the sinners of society. Horned owls sit and judge from the mouths of damp tunnels. Man is depicted again and again as embracing evil, as being the instigator of his own downfall.

Bosch's masterpiece triptych, *The Garden of Earthly Delights*, shows Adam and Eve in the Garden of Eden in the first panel. In the second is the chaos that ensues from their choosing corporeal temptation over spiritual life. And in the third panel are the tortures of a wildly punishing hell.

Anyone who has taken the time to study the Bosch paintings comes away with an indelible imprint of the work on his or her mind. The mark of a true artist, I believe, is to create something that lives on in another's imagination. Hieronymus Bosch certainly accomplished this. His work has lived in my imagination from the moment I saw it. After all, I could clearly see a kinship between some of Bosch's monsters and the behemoth of my own dream.

It was while working on the second draft of *The Black Echo* that I was reminded of the painter I had studied in college fifteen years before. I can't remember today what prompted the connection. But some reference to the painter made me remember the class and the paintings. And I was struck by another revelation. After all, what was a murder scene but a world gone wrong? What was a homicide investigation about but chaos and its consequences? In a moment I knew I must change the name of my detective. Whether readers were familiar with the painter Hieronymus Bosch did not matter to me. I was writing about a man who every day ventured into the human abyss, whose job took him across landscapes of chaos and its consequences. I was writing the story of a man who confronted horrific evil among men and who all the while wrestled with his own dark currents. From that day on he became Detective Hieronymus Bosch.

———

The name Hieronymus is the Latin source of the name Jerome. By that measure, Detective Hieronymus Bosch should perhaps go by Jerry for short. But I went with Harry instead, choosing it as a nod to Dirty Harry Callahan and Harry Caul, two detectives from films that were important to me in my evolution as a storyteller. My hope is that Harry Bosch shares a kinship with those two Harrys, as well as with the characters created by the hugely influential writers listed as inspirations earlier.

———

With a name, a history, and a mission, Harry Bosch seemed to lack only a code. Every detective, private or public, in the annals of crime fiction has a personal code by which he or she makes a stand. Raymond Chandler wrote an essay about it: "Down these mean streets a man must go . . ."

I decided to keep it short. I wanted Bosch to have a code that would be telling of his status as someone who for much of his life was on the outside looking in. I wanted him to have a code that would not let him forget his origins and that would plant him firmly on the side of the underdog. I wanted Bosch to operate with a code of conduct and fairness that would not allow him to suffer fools lightly or leave him beholden to the powerful and rich. He would operate fairly and never use his position to his personal advantage. He would understand that he must give his best effort on each case no matter who the victim may be or where the clues may lead.

Everybody counts or nobody counts.

This would be his code.

―――

The creative fulfillment that comes from writing a series of novels with a returning character is that the biography of that character continually evolves. The series moves forward at the same time it moves backward. New cases, new missions, carry the reader forward. But strewn throughout the stories are the glittering nuggets of history that take the reader into the past.

So, too, Harry Bosch evolves. The man built to be relentless and bulletproof now shows he is vulnerable. In recent years he has discovered a daughter, a piece of history that in many ways turns all that came before it upside down. Through her, Harry can be gotten to. It changes things, especially him.

Through fifteen novels I would say that Harry Bosch has mellowed. He is still an outsider with an insider's job. He still won't suffer fools lightly or accept bureaucracy when it gets between him and the completion of the mission. But he has a greater sense of himself and more knowledge of human nature. His mission has made him a man who is both hopeful and cynical. He knows what true justice is and has more insight into redemption. He has a better understanding of the frailties that lead to the many different kinds of human corruption.

In *Angels Flight,* the sixth book in the series, Harry opens a pack of matches and finds a fortune printed on the inside flap. It reads: *Happy is the man who finds refuge in himself.* For Bosch it is a hint of what is to come. Harry pursues his mission at the same time he seeks refuge and continues to find it in himself. That makes his a biography still in progress.

———

The house my father built on Highland Avenue may still be standing, but the tunnel is long gone. The day I escaped from the book tour and drove out there, it was the first thing I noticed. The sloping property had been resculpted in the years since my family left. The drainage gulley had been filled and the front lawn leveled. The woods that were across the street were gone as well, replaced by a well-manicured subdivision.

Maybe it's true that you can't go home again. But not finding the tunnel that day didn't bother me. I was thankful for what it had given me. An early test of character and a memory that would live on in my imagination. If I am lucky, the character who came out of that tunnel will live just as long.

JOHN CONNOLLY

Born in Dublin, Ireland, in 1968, John Connolly received a BA in English from Trinity College in Dublin, then an MA in journalism from Dublin City University, taking a job as a freelance journalist for the *Irish Times,* which he did for five years; he continues to contribute articles from time to time. He has also worked as a bartender, a waiter, a government official, and at London's famous Harrod's department store.

His first novel, *Every Dead Thing* (1999), introduced Charlie Parker, the dark ex-cop who has starred in most of his subsequent work. It achieved the virtually inconceivable double honor of winning a Shamus Award from the Private Eye Writers of America and being nominated for the Bram Stoker Award by the Horror Writers Association. Crossing genres in the same work of fiction has been historically both risky and difficult, but Connolly has managed it with a rare ability to plot brilliantly while writing original and distinguished prose.

In addition to the Charlie Parker books, Connolly has produced the stand-alone suspense novel *Bad Men* (2003); a collection of horror tales, *Nocturnes* (2004); and a noncrime novel, *The Book of Lost Things* (2006). One of the stories in *Nocturnes,* "The New Daughter," serves as the partial basis for a forthcoming film with that title starring Kevin Costner and Ivana Baquero. His most recent books are *The Gates,* "a strange book for strange young people," and *The Lovers,* a Charlie Parker novel.

John Connolly lives in Dublin and, sometimes, in Maine.

CHARLIE PARKER

BY JOHN CONNOLLY

I

I never met Belinda Pereira. By the time I heard her name spoken for the first time, she was already dead. But on the night that she was killed, I stood outside her apartment in the rain, and I listened as a detective described the circumstances of her death. She was twenty-six years old. Were it not for her, I don't think I would be writing the books I write. In a way, they are an attempt to make sense of her murder, and for that reason they all fail.

Because there was no sense to her murder.

Dublin is a peculiar city. It closes down for the Christmas season and doesn't really find its stride again until early in the New Year. When I worked as a journalist, Christmas was a period during which most staff journalists preferred not to work. It wasn't simply that they wanted to spend time with their families, as most people do at that time of year, or to leave the grim winter weather behind and head for somewhere warmer; it was because nothing much really happened in Ireland at Christmas. During the Troubles, even the terrorists would call a brief cease-fire beginning about December

24, so they could stay at home and pretend to be ordinary men and women without blood on their hands.

But I was a freelance journalist, and I worked whatever hours I was offered because I was afraid that if I turned them down, I would never be given work again. By 1996, I had essentially been a full-time freelancer for the *Irish Times* newspaper in Dublin for three years, and had graduated from education and assorted features to regular shifts in the newsroom, which was how I came to be working on December 28, when Belinda died.

One of the tasks newsroom journalists are required to do is to call the police or the fire department and ask if anything newsworthy has happened. These calls are usually made every hour because, personal sources apart, it is not the place of the police and the fire department to take the initiative in informing journalists of interesting events. In fact, the office of the *Irish Times* could have been on fire, and the fire department wouldn't have called us to let us know. That was just the way things were.

So, on the night of December 28, I made my final call to the press office of the Garda Síochána, as the Irish police are called. I was about to go home, and I was expecting nothing different from what I'd been told a number of times already that day: all is quiet.

But that was not what I was told. Instead, the officer informed me that a young woman's body had been found in an apartment at Mellor Court, on the north side of the city not far from the newspaper's offices on D'Olier Street. She had been badly beaten, so the gardaí were treating it as a suspicious death. And, since there was nobody else in the sparsely staffed newsroom who was free, and as I had made the call, the story was mine.

This was something of a mixed blessing. On any ordinary news day, the crime correspondent or a more senior reporter would have been assigned to the story, but as it was Christmas, I was as good as it was going to get for the newspaper. It would be a front-page story, and an above-the-fold byline, which all journalists love. On the other hand, I had already been working for nine or ten hours, and it was raining outside. It would be a long night.

I walked down to Mellor Court, and there I did all of the things that give journalists a bad name: I stopped people going into the apartment building to ask if they knew anything of what had occurred; I talked to the security guard who was manning the door of a nearby convenience store; and then, when my efforts had come to nothing, I simply waited in the rain for someone from the gardaí to emerge and tell me what was happening.

When the detective in charge did eventually come out, he looked pale and shaken. No formal identification of the body had been made, he said. A passport had been found in the apartment, and a preliminary identification had been made from that, but the victim had been so badly beaten that there was no way as yet of being sure she was the girl in the passport photo. All he could say for now was that she was not an Irish national, and she was dead.

I went back to the newspaper office and wrote up the story. Later that night, the girl's identity was revealed: her name was Belinda Pereira, a child of Sri Lankan parents living in London.

Dublin, at that time, was not a very violent city. In fact, Ireland still has one of the lowest homicide rates in Europe, although gangland killings have inflated that figure in recent years, and we have become increasingly inured to casual homicide. But in 1996, Belinda Pereira's death was shocking to the Irish public. Here was a young woman, far from home, who had been brutally murdered, and at Christmas too, a season of peace. It was felt that the person or persons responsible for her death should be found and punished. Her murder was headline news in every Irish newspaper.

Then, a few days after her death, it emerged that Belinda Pereira had come to Dublin to work as a prostitute. It wasn't the first time that she had done so, and she had also worked as a call girl in England. A convent-educated schoolgirl, she was studying to be a beautician in London. Prostitution appeared to be a way to supplement her income. In addition, there were reports that her parents had decided to separate, and her mother wanted to return to Sri Lanka. A week's work in Dublin would have allowed Belinda to earn the money to help her mother get home.

When the details of her lifestyle were revealed, public attitudes toward her death changed. I think people made two judgments upon her. The first was that her murder was not as terrible as it had first seemed, and was certainly not as tragic as it might have been had she worked as, say, a nurse or a secretary. The second was that she had asked for what had happened to her. After all, she was working as a prostitute. She should have expected to meet people who were less morally scrupulous than the norm. In fact, she was obviously less morally scrupulous than many other young women. She had put herself in harm's way, and she had suffered for it. It was her own fault.

I did not feel that way. Perhaps it was because she was young—two years younger than I was—and beautiful. It might have been because it was the first murder I had ever covered, and I had not yet grown used to such matters. Whatever the reasons, I believed that there was nothing this young woman could have done in life to merit the terrible death that was visited upon her. In fact, there was nothing that very many of us could do to deserve such an end. When the tabloid newspapers began routinely to refer to her as "the Sri Lankan hooker Belinda Pereira," I felt ashamed and angry. That was what she had been reduced to: a foreign hooker. Such casual dismissal of her life was the first step on the road from caring about what happened to her to not caring at all.

And so Belinda Pereira's death stayed with me, even as the public gradually forgot about her.

II

I have always written.

That sounds like a rather arch statement to make, but it's true. When I was a young boy I began reading Enid Blyton books, struggling phonetically with unfamiliar words. (As a consequence, I believed for many years that the word *cupboard* was pronounced "cup-board" instead of "cubbard.") The next natural step seemed to be to tell stories of my own. I was addicted to Ron Ely's *Tarzan* TV series and the adventures of Casey Jones, both of which were shown on television in Ireland on Saturday mornings, so they became the subjects of my first stories. I was six. My teacher, Mrs. Foley, would pay me five pence for each tale I submitted, so I was, I suppose, a hack from an early age.

I read voraciously, as all writers should. Like many boys, I flirted with the horror genre and then, in my early teens, I read my first mystery novel. Each summer, my father would take us to spend two weeks with my grandmother in Ballylongford, a small village in County Kerry. She had bookshelves that would be regularly raided and refilled by visiting relatives, and at the beginning of each vacation my father would engage in the solemn ritual of the Choosing of the Book. Only on vacation would my father read a novel, preferring newspapers for the rest of the year, so the selection of the right book was of paramount importance to him. (He once chose *I, Claudius*, which was a grave error, as it took him two years to finish, a mistake he never repeated.)

That summer, my father chose a book entitled *Let's Hear It for the Deaf Man*, by Ed McBain. I think he chose it because it was short, and after the *I, Claudius* debacle, short was good. One day, he put it aside to tackle the newspaper, and intrigued by the title, I began reading. That book became the first, and only, book over which my father and I fought for possession. Thereafter, I read every single Ed

McBain book I could find. It was my introduction to the genre of which I would ultimately become a small part.

I met McBain, whose real name was Evan Hunter, shortly before he died. There had been a misunderstanding between us early in my career when, as a means of paying homage to him, I had given some characters in my first novel names that echoed his own work. There was a Fat Ollie, and an Evan Baines—awkward, I know, but well-intentioned. McBain was incensed, misinterpreting it as an act of theft. Years later, when we met at last, I explained to him the reason for what I had done and subsequently received a gracious and apologetic e-mail in reply. It was a great relief. It's possible that I might not have ended up writing what I do had it not been for him, and I did not want him to think ill of me.

Now that I come to think of it, my encounters with my literary idols have usually involved a dollop of mild humiliation for me. When interviewing James Lee Burke in Montana, I managed to get lost for a time in the Great Rattlesnake Wilderness while out for a walk with him, and was eventually found by his neighbor's dogs. I interviewed Stephen King, and managed to cause my pile of first editions, ready to be signed, to fall on his foot. Sometimes I wonder if it's really safe to allow me out on my own.

I studied English at university, and one option was a course in detective fiction. It was to be a defining choice for me, as it introduced me to the work of Ross Macdonald. Although it would be another five years before I began writing my first novel, it owes its genesis to that course. I hunted down every book by Macdonald I could find, which, in those pre-Internet days, meant scouring used-book stores for British paperback editions with fantastically unsuitable covers, usually featuring women in various states of undress. I even found a first edition of *Find a Victim* from 1954 on my parents' bookshelf at home. It had come from a lending library in the American Midwest. I have no idea how it ended up in my parents' possession.

After college, I entered journalism, mainly because I liked writing and I could see few other ways in which I could be paid to write. Inevitably, perhaps, I grew frustrated with journalism. I wanted to write fiction, and newspapers tend to disapprove of the urge toward the fictitious in their reporters.

So one evening I sat down at my computer at home and began writing about a man driving toward a cemetery, flowers on the backseat of his car, his mind filled with memories of his dead wife and child.

He was Charlie Parker, and it was the beginning of *Every Dead Thing*.

III

In 1996, I had already completed the first half of what would eventually become my first novel. I had been very influenced by two writers mentioned earlier, James Lee Burke and Ross Macdonald. Burke's influence was stylistic and linguistic, while Macdonald's was more difficult to pinpoint. It was thematic, perhaps, or even philosophical. His detective, Lew Archer, was profoundly empathetic. Archer himself says at one point, "I hear voices crying in the night, and I go see what's the matter." I loved that about Archer: his inability to remain silent or inactive while another was suffering. It has always seemed to me that empathy is one of the greatest of human emotions, the capacity to feel another's pain as one's own and, as a consequence, to work to take that pain away. For me, evil is the absence of empathy.

The Irish philosopher-politician Edmund Burke once wrote, "All that is necessary for the triumph of evil is that good men do nothing." At some level, that is what the best of mystery fiction is about: the refusal of good men and women to do nothing in the face of evil, even at considerable cost to themselves, because a failure to intervene makes one complicit in what occurs.

Macdonald's novels are also fascinated by the idea of the sins of the fathers being visited on the sons, of one generation suffering for the sins of its predecessors. Macdonald understood that suffering is frequently not earned or deserved. People suffer through no fault of their own. They suffer because they are vulnerable or oppressed. They suffer because they are in the wrong place at the wrong time. They suffer because they are the wrong color, or creed, or sex. They suffer because they can be made to suffer.

It seemed to me that there was a distinction between the outlook of Macdonald (and some of his peers) and that of certain British crime writers of a similar vintage. If one reads the classic "Golden Age" British crime novels, one again and again encounters individuals who suffer and die because they are bad. Few nice people die in Agatha Christie's novels. Most of them are adulterers, or thieves, or blackmailers. They bring their deaths upon themselves. We are not asked to feel pity for them or empathy. Their killers have to be found and punished as a matter of social order rather than because the murders they have committed diminish us all as human beings, or as an effort at recompense for the deaths of innocents. Even Dorothy L. Sayers, whose awareness of a moral universe ruled by God could hardly be in doubt, is not immune to cold-heartedness. In *The Nine Tailors,* death comes to a thief in the form of divine retribution. Even God is not merciful in the face of criminal behavior.

I think that something of Macdonald's intensely humane view of people and how they suffer influenced my reaction to Belinda Pereira's death. As a consequence, the novel on which I was working began to change. Its central character, the private detective Charlie Parker, became a being defined not simply by anger and the desire for revenge, but by his own sufferings. Because he has suffered, he is unwilling to allow others to suffer in turn. It is his capacity for empathy that ultimately ensures he does not destroy himself with selfishness and grief, or allow himself to be destroyed by the man he is hunting, the killer of his wife and child.

The novel had always begun with its prologue. That was the first part of it I wrote, and although it went through many revisions, the essence remained the same. I wanted to write about a man who loses everything and who struggles to survive, to remain human in the aftermath. There was a kind of awful liberation, I thought, in having one's worst nightmares come to pass. Once someone had endured loss on that level, it seemed to me that very little could ever hurt him to a similar degree again. I gave him the name Charlie Parker because I liked the connotations of flight, freedom, and spirituality that came with the nickname Bird, the moniker given to the jazz musician with whom he shared this name, especially for a man so mired in mortality. In subsequent novels, the nickname was largely dispensed with. I didn't want readers to think it was a gimmick, because it was not meant to be.

Yet Parker was still in the process of being formed, even when that first novel was completed and eventually published in 1999, and Belinda Pereira was still hovering in the background, battered and bloodied. By that time, the investigation into her death had ground to a halt.

IV

Let's return for a moment to Macdonald, who, as well as being a great novelist (the greatest mystery novelist of his age, I would argue, greater even than Chandler), was also a generous and perceptive critic. In an essay on James M. Cain, Macdonald wrote, "A first novel can be a kind of index to an author's ensuing work."

First novels are frequently criticized for including rather too much material. In part, this is a consequence of a writer's belief that he or she may never have the opportunity to publish a novel again, and therefore everything that seems even mildly important or relevant should be included in what may be that single published work. Also, first novels tend to represent the sum total of a writer's knowledge and experience up to that stage in his or her life. To put it another way, it takes a lifetime to write a first novel, and then a contract gives one a year to write a second.

Macdonald offers a different perspective on the first novel. It is an introduction to a writer, and to that writer's obsessions. Not every subject or theme may be dealt with in depth in that first work, or examined in great detail, but they will recur later in the writer's career, and a passing reference in a first novel may become the core of a later book. (That has certainly been my experience as a writer. The novel I'm currently working on, *The Lovers,* deals with an incident that is barely described in *Every Dead Thing,* and I have very consciously crafted the Parker books as a sequence of novels, each one building upon what has happened earlier.)

The seeds of what Parker would become were sown in *Every Dead Thing,* but it was only over the course of the subsequent books that they bore fruit, a not uncommon characteristic of detective series. The first signs of this are apparent in *Dark Hollow,* my second novel, and the book in which I decided to deal explicitly with my feelings about the Belinda Pereira case. In the novel, Parker is required to view the body of a young woman, Rita Ferris, who has been murdered in her apartment. He forces himself to imagine her final moments, an act of painful empathy but one that is necessary for him, a small service for the dead. Later, it becomes clear that Rita has been working as a prostitute to supplement her income and support her child, but Parker keeps that knowledge to himself until he has to divulge it. He does not want her to be judged and discarded because of this one aspect of her life.

In *Dark Hollow,* the person responsible for the death of Rita Ferris is found, and a degree of punishment is meted out. In real life,

Belinda Pereira's killer has not been found. It has been suggested that two pimps from Monaghan, a county in the north of Ireland, were responsible, but if they were, there is not enough evidence to bring them to trial. A public appeal by the Garda Síochána in 2005 for new information led nowhere.

I wonder sometimes if part of the appeal of mystery fiction is its capacity to give us answers and solutions that we don't always get in real life. In real life, the guilty go unpunished. In real life, a young woman can be beaten with a hammer until she is beyond identification, and her killer or killers can retreat into the shadows, never to be found. But in mystery fiction, a man of some goodness, however compromised he may be, can choose to act on behalf of the victim and achieve a measure of justice. No matter how dark such fiction may appear to be, it is never entirely without hope.

V

Why, then, given the nature and setting of Belinda Pereira's murder, did I not choose to set *Dark Hollow* in Ireland? Why is Charlie Parker not Irish?

Like most writers, I began writing what I read, and what I read was largely American fiction, and not exclusively mystery fiction either. I had never been very attracted to the British model, and mystery fiction has never really been part of the Irish literary tradition.

That latter observation may be worth closer examination, given the surge in production of Irish crime fiction in recent years. Nobody has ever been able to come up with a single compelling reason why Irish writers chose not to investigate the possibilities of crime fiction for many years, even while English and Scottish writers pursued them with a vengeance. The dearth of Irish crime fiction is, I suspect, a consequence of a number of factors, some literary and some social.

To begin with, Ireland was a rural society, and it was G. K. Chesterton who noted that crime fiction functions better in urban rather than rural settings, that it is, on one level, tied up with the poetry of urban life. Ireland was also not a very violent society, terrorism apart. I realize, of course, that the use of the term "terrorism apart" is a little like saying that Einstein didn't achieve much scientifically, "the Theory of Relativity apart." Terrorism cast a shadow over modern Irish life for the best part of three decades, and its influence extended far beyond the bombings and shootings that took place in Northern Ireland and, on occasion, in the South. One might argue that it would be difficult to write about crime in Ireland and *not* touch upon the subject of terrorism, which may be why so many writers chose instead to neglect the genre entirely.

There are exceptions: Eugene McEldowney's *A Kind of Homecoming,* for example, or Eoin McNamee's *Resurrection Man,* which dealt with the Protestant killers known as the "Shankill Butchers," although McNamee might well dispute the description of *Resurrection Man* as a crime novel. Perhaps, too, there was a sense that mystery fiction was simply not up to the task of tackling the subject of terrorism, particularly terrorism that was ongoing and so close to home. The wounds were too raw, and fresh ones were being inflicted every day. Even Irish literary fiction seemed to struggle with the enormity of what was happening on our small island.

Finally, there has long been a strong antirationalist tradition in Irish literature, which found its expression in, among others, the great Anglo-Irish gothic novels: Charles Maturin's *Melmoth the Wanderer,* Sheridan Le Fanu's *Uncle Silas,* Bram Stoker's *Dracula,* Oscar Wilde's *The Picture of Dorian Gray;* the fantasy fiction of Mervyn Wall (the two Fursey books); and the surreal visions of Flann O'Brien (*At Swim-Two-Birds; The Third Policeman,* itself a kind of anticrime novel). By contrast, crime fiction, in its most conservative form, is intensely rationalist in outlook. Think of Poe's Dupin, Christie's Poirot, and Conan Doyle's Sherlock Holmes, each of whom places great store by the processes of ratiocination. Philosophically, this is at odds with the Irish outlook, one that for many years placed a greater emphasis on an artistic rather than a scientific response to the world.

Quite simply, I did not see an Irish literary tradition of which I wanted to be a part. It also seemed that Irish literature was concerned primarily with the nature of being Irish, itself not unreasonable given that we are a young state, but I had no interest in writing about the nature of Irishness. There were two options, then: to import elements of the American crime novel into the Irish realm, which I did not feel would work, or to bring a European perspective to the American crime novel, which was the path I chose.

Since then, Irish crime fiction has begun to flourish (a result of the changes in Irish society over the past decade, among other things), but it is interesting that Irish readers still prefer to read crime novels set elsewhere. We remain uncomfortable with crime fiction as a means of examining Irish society, and I suspect that Irish writers will continue to find a more sympathetic audience in the United States than they will at home for some time to come.

VI

From the moment that I began writing *Every Dead Thing,* there were supernatural elements in the novel. The supernatural touches to my books are frequently criticized by the more conservative elements in the genre, those who would like to see mystery fiction set in aspic somewhere between the birth of Sherlock Holmes and the last appearance of Hercule Poirot. It is, I suppose, the side of the mystery community that I find most depressing, this reluctance to countenance experimentation, particularly when it comes to the intermingling of genres. Yet, in so many aspects of art and culture, it is through precisely this kind of experimentation that new and interesting forms emerge.

Anthony Cox, in a dedication to his fellow writer Milward Kennedy, stated that he himself wished to produce a novel that "breaks every rule of the austere club to which we both belong." Cox was writing in 1930. Almost seventy years later, I had something of the same urge, but in my case there were specific rules I wished to break, if only because I did not accept their validity. One was a rule of structure, which explains the peculiar "hourglass" form of *Every Dead Thing,* in which a crime that is committed, and solved, in the first half of the novel feeds into the larger mystery tackled in the second half. Another was to do with the supernatural and the metaphysical.

I wanted Charlie Parker to be haunted, but not haunted in the manner most commonly found in mystery fiction, where "haunted" tends to be a euphemism for "brooding," "drinks a bit," or "stares into space a lot." I wondered what might happen if a man believed himself *literally* to be haunted, if his guilt and grief were tormenting him to such a degree that he was unable to determine if the visions of the dead he encountered were real or merely manifestations of his troubled psyche.

There were some literary influences at work here, particularly the early-twentieth-century ghost stories of English writers like M. R. James. It's possible, too, that something of that Irish antirationalist tradition had also crept in. Then, of course, there are my own Catholic origins, which seemed to find an echo in the themes of reparation and redemption that are so much a part of the mystery fiction I love.

For me, the supernatural serves a number of functions in my novels. To begin with, it suggests a deeper understanding of the word *mystery* and its religious origins—a mystery as the Greeks would have understood it, or as the writers of the medieval mystery plays, which were versions of Bible stories, would have interpreted it. The curious thing about mystery novels is that generally they are not very mysterious at all. What seems beyond understanding at the start is usually explicable in quite simple terms by the end: the butler did it. I hoped to restore something of that older sense of mystery in my work, and the supernatural touches suggested a means of doing so. They also function as indicators of a larger moral universe, and in that sense they are as much metaphysical as supernatural. (Even here, though, there are antecedents. Chesterton, in the Father Brown stories, introduced a strong metaphysical element to the genre. What gave Father Brown his insights into crime was an "understanding of sin," of the nature of the human soul.)

Perhaps at the heart of my difficulties with the structures and rules of the classical crime story is the simple fact that I don't share the beliefs on which they are based. The world is not rational and intelligible. Order is fragile, a thin crust upon the underlying chaos. Any answers we get will be partial at best and at worst will simply give rise to further, deeper doubts. It is interesting that the classical detective story exerted such a strong influence on the postmodern novel. In the latter, writers found a means of antiliterary expression, a way to react against the weight and expectations of an older, restrictive literary tradition, but the classical story also provided them with something to disprove: the rationalist belief that the mind can solve everything. When just one or two details of the mystery novel are twisted, the opposite becomes the case, and the world that is revealed is both more frightening and more real as a consequence.

Thus, we have Nabokov writing *Despair,* or the genre experiments of Borges. Thomas Pynchon can produce *The Crying of Lot 49,* a Californian anti–detective novel that leaves us awaiting a moment of revelation that does not come. There is no explanation at the end, because there cannot be.

Sometimes I envy literary writers that freedom: the freedom not to explain. Ultimately, crime readers expect a solution, however partial, to the mystery with which they have been presented in the course of the book, and writers in the genre have a certain obligation to fulfill that expectation. Literary writers have no such obligation.

Yet there are ways of subverting those expectations, even within the genre, so that some questions can remain unanswered or are, in fact, rendered more interesting by the fact that they are unanswerable. Thus, for me, the supernatural represents my small effort at genre subversion.

VII

After the publication of *Dark Hollow,* one of Belinda Pereira's relatives got in touch with me. He had read the book not knowing that one of the characters was based on Belinda, and had only discovered the connection when he saw an interview I gave about the novel and its origins. He wrote to tell me that he did not object to Belinda's being remembered in that way, and he gave me a little background into what happened to her family following her death. Her parents did not know that their daughter had sometimes worked as a prostitute. By the time her mother managed to return to Sri Lanka, the news of Belinda's death, and the circumstances surrounding it, had reached there. The family was disgraced. Her mother, he told me, never recovered from Belinda's death. She contracted cancer and died without ever seeing a measure of justice achieved for her lost child.

The novelist John Gardner once wrote that there are two choices open to the writer who lives in a world in which there are pits filled with the skulls of children. The first is to gaze into one of those pits and write about what one sees. The other, the one that I have made, is to write about how one can endure a world where there are pits filled with the skulls of children; the skulls of children and the bodies of young women who die far from home at the hands of violent men.

And so I created Charlie Parker, and through him I try to understand that world, and present a version of it in which one might live, and in which justice is attainable not only in the next life but in this one too.

ROBERT CRAIS

Born in Louisiana in 1953, Robert Crais moved to Hollywood in 1976, becoming one of the most successful television writers of the time. In addition to scripts for such hugely successful series as *Hill Street Blues, Cagney & Lacey, L.A. Law,* and *Miami Vice,* he wrote numerous pilots and made-for-television movies and miniseries. He was nominated for an Emmy for his work on *Hill Street Blues*. After an active decade of writing and producing TV programs, he quit to become a full-time novelist.

His first novel, *The Monkey's Raincoat,* introduced Elvis Cole, with elements of his own life forming the basis of the story. It was nominated for an Edgar Allan Poe Award, won the Anthony and Macavity awards, and was named one of the 100 favorite mysteries of the century by the Independent Mystery Booksellers Association. Although never planning the novel to be the first of a series, Crais realized that he had produced something special—an interesting and powerful character who served as a surrogate for himself, and through whom he could comment on topics of the day. Joe Pike, Cole's sidekick, developed as the series progressed, becoming a formidable personality in his own right. Crais became a perennial bestseller with the publication of *L.A. Requiem* in 1999—one of the most beautifully conceived and written private-detective stories of all time.

In addition to the Elvis Cole series, Crais has written three stand-alone thrillers: *Demolition Angel* (2000), *Hostage* (2001), and *The Two-Minute Rule* (2006). *Hostage* was filmed in 2005, with Bruce Willis starring as the former Los Angeles SWAT negotiator Jeff Talley.

Crais lives in Los Angeles, California, with his wife, Pat.

ELVIS COLE AND JOE PIKE

BY ROBERT CRAIS

Elvis Cole and Joe Pike are twenty years old as I write this in 2007. They came to life in my first published novel, *The Monkey's Raincoat*, in 1987. Twenty years is a long time. I had no idea they would be with me for twenty years. I hadn't planned on creating a series (I thought *The Monkey's Raincoat* would be a one-shot) and certainly did not expect these two characters of mine to become so successful both in the United States and abroad (at this writing, Elvis and Joe are published in forty countries around the world). Aspiring writers certainly hope for this kind of good fortune, and dream about it, but only a fool would expect it. Yet here we are twenty years later, me, Elvis, and Joe. And you.

If you're reading this, you probably groove on my guys and maybe even snap up my new books as soon as they come out. And then you move on to a new book by Mike Connelly or T. Jefferson Parker or Lee Child, or any of the scores of other terrific writers currently plowing the crime fiction fields, and a whole new set of characters are in your head. But get this—

Elvis and Joe never leave me. Elvis Cole and Joe Pike have been in my head every day for these past twenty years, and likely will be every day for the rest of my life. When I'm writing the current book, I'm thinking about the next, one book leading to another as sure as a stream flows downhill. And even when I'm writing a stand-alone in which Elvis and Joe do not appear, they are still behind the trees in my head, knowing their turn will come again soon, and I am always aware of them.

Part 1: Making the Climb with Elvis Cole

Elvis Cole and I were near the top of Mount Lee where the service road ends at the big communication station they have above the Hollywood sign. Then we climbed higher. When you reach the station, you are in a chain-link-and-concertina-wire box designed to protect the sign and the communication station, but the north side of the box is a steep, rocky shoulder with a narrow path cut to the peak. I followed Cole up, busting through brittle waist-high brush to a small clearing at the top of the mountain. Up there, we were above the fence and the video cameras and the motion detectors. We were alone at the top of Los Angeles.

Cole brushed the sweat from his eyes, then stood with his hands on his hips, looking out at our city. It had been a long, fast hike up the hill. I was sucking air like an iron lung, but he wasn't even breathing hard.

Cole said, "Some view."

"Where's Pike?"

"I left a message on his cell, said we'd be coming up here, but I never heard back. You know how he is. Might be down there right now, watching us. He'd do that just to see if we could spot him."

Cole studied the surrounding canyons, their cut ridges furred with pale gray chaparral and scrub oak. Spotting Pike would be like spotting a flea lost in hair, but I figured Cole could do it if anyone could.

I said, "You see him?"

Cole pointed.

"Sure. Right there."

"Where?"

"Right there. He's waving."

I followed his finger toward a blur of dead brush, then, out of the corner of my eye caught Elvis Cole smiling.

I said, "Funny. Make fun of the writer. Ha ha."

Cole offered his bottle of water, but I had my own. We drank, washing away the steep hike up from Griffith Park before I gazed out at the city. I never got tired of the view from that high place. The City of Angels spread south below us in a flat plain all the way to the Channel Islands and Santa Catalina. Skyscraper islands broke the surface to mark downtown, the Miracle Mile, Century City, and the Wilshire Corridor. Behind us, the San Fernando Valley ran north into a head-on collision with the Verdugo, San Gabriel, and the Santa Susana Mountains. The top of Los Angeles was a good place to talk. We did that sometimes. Often. Like we were doing that day.

Cole said, "Want to ask you something."

"Listen, if it's about the Dodgers tickets . . ."

I had great season tickets and laid off ten or twelve games to Cole every year. Gratis. He used my seats to trade for information. In Los Angeles, choice Dodgers seats worked better than a court order.

Cole raised a hand, stopping me.

"Not the Dodgers. I've been wondering about our relationship, me and you. I want to ask you something."

"If you want more games just say so."

He wanted more Dodgers tickets. I can read him like a book.

"Don't get pissy. Even if I did, you're making more dough off my cases than I do. Look at how many e-mails you get through the website, people asking how come I always work for free."

"You don't work for free. Peter Alan Nelsen paid you a load."

"And how long ago was that, *Lullaby Town*?"

"Jonathan Greene paid you up front in *Sunset Express*. So did Jody Taylor in *Voodoo River*. Besides, I've only chronicled ten of your cases. . . ."

Cole widened his eyes, making a big deal.

"Chronicled. Am I being *chronicled?*"

"I only cover your interesting cases. Our readers wouldn't care about the boring dogs you work to pay the bills."

"So my day-to-day is too dull to be *chronicled?*"

"If it's not the tickets, then what?"

Cole had more of his water, then tucked the bottle into a pocket on his cargo shorts. He considered the city for another moment, then took off his sunglasses to look at me.

"Why me?"

"Why you what?"

"You could chronicle cops or lawyers or architects, but you chronicle me. I've been wondering why."

Cole had never asked that before, though I often thought about it. He was right: I could have written any type of fiction, from dark fantasies to so-called literary fiction to Westerns. The choice was mine, but I had chosen to write about Elvis Cole, a private investigator who lived and worked in Los Angeles. I had my reasons, and weighed their values and importance again with each new book.

I said, "You represent hope."

Cole stared at me with an expression that said he got it but maybe didn't agree with it. Or like it. I tried to explain.

"Why didn't you become a police officer?"

"That how we're going to play this? I ask a question, you answer with a question?"

"Bear with me. It's true I could write other things, but it's also true you could have chosen a different line of work. You're relatively bright—"

"Thank you too much."

"You could have become a police officer."

"Too many bosses. Way I work now, it's like being a writer. I don't have to salute. I'm not staring up the ass of a command structure."

"Ha. Writer."

"Think about it—if I worked Hollywood Robbery, all I would see are robberies in Hollywood. Devonshire Sex Crimes, nothing but sex crimes in Devonshire. Me being freelance, I can do whatever I want. Like you."

"Not like me. All I do is make up stories. You put yourself on the line for people in need. That makes you more. Especially because of who you are."

Cole frowned at me.

"Like how?"

"You're ordinary."

"This is a compliment?"

"If you were a cop or an FBI agent, you would be part of an enormous bureaucratic system. You would have the full weight and authority of that system behind you. Even if I had cast you as a man struggling against the system from within, you would still be part of a team. You would have power. I didn't want that."

I tipped my head toward the city and the millions of people spread across that great flat plane, continuing.

"You're on your own. Like me. Like them. You're one of us, so, I think, you're a metaphor for us."

"What do you mean, us? You're a bestselling novelist."

"I wasn't always a novelist, and these books about you didn't start out as bestsellers. We've come a long way, brother."

Cole grunted his agreement, then adjusted his cap. The late-morning sun was bright. Cole was wearing the faded blue Dodgers cap he wore when hiking or running or driving around with the top down. So was I. We often dressed alike.

When he finished with the cap, he said, "So how does that make me Mr. Hopeful?"

"Didn't say you're Mr. Hopeful. I said you represent hope. To me and to people like me. Look at it. . . ."

I waved at the city.

"Those people down there, me, most folks—all we have is ourselves. The tranny drops a week before Christmas, some dip keys the new car, the rent jacks up, and we're left wondering how we're going to make it. That would be where you come in."

"I don't do transmissions."

"All you have is yourself."

"I have Pike."

"You know what I mean. A lone character who faces the dark side in this crazy world inspires me. If you can survive, then I can survive. If you can persevere, then those people down there can make a difference in their own lives. You see?"

"Bro, do not oversell this. I'm just trying to hang on like everyone else."

"That's why you're worth writing about. You've had what most people would call a pretty tough life; so has Pike. You could have become cynical and despairing. You could have given up on yourself, and people, and sit around moaning about how bad you have it and how life is shit, but you don't."

Cole slowly shook his head. His voice was quiet.

"No. I won't do that."

"That's what I love about you. That's why you represent hope. You hang on to yourself with the humor and the Jiminy Cricket stuff and that damned cat, and the determination with which you help people become better than they are, just the way you've become better than you were. If you can hang on, I can hang on. If you can beat the odds, then I can beat the odds. Through you, I get to see the world as a better place, so maybe our readers feel the same way. You give me hope, man, and I believe hope is worth encouraging. Hence, the books."

Cole stared at the city as he thought it through.

"It sounds like you're trying to convince yourself."

"Maybe that's why I'm drawn to crime fiction—I get to work through my fears. Maybe I need you to reassure me."

Cole didn't look pleased.

"Like I'm what, some kind of hero?"

"People need heroes, bro. Always have and always will. Heroes give us the hope."

Cole still didn't look happy with me, like he knew I had dodged the hero question.

He said, "Life isn't fair."

"No, but I guess, down deep, I think it should be."

Cole nodded.

"Me too. Gotta tell you, though, all this makes me uncomfortable. Like I have some standard to live up to."

"Don't freak out. Watching you live it through makes you worth writing about."

He stared at the city again.

"Do people really think you look like me?" Cole asked.

"Ha."

"You don't look anything like me."

"I kinda think I look like Pike."

"Writers."

"Have I answered your question? Let's head back. Unlike one of us, I'm real. My legs are getting stiff."

He frowned.

"You keep saying I'm fictional. Has it occurred to you that maybe I'm real and you're the fiction?"

"It's my name on the books."

"Uh-huh. So if I'm just someone you imagined, and here you are talking to me, maybe you're crazy."

What can you say to something like that?

Cole said, "Maybe you're a figment of my need to be *chronicled*. Maybe I'm writing books about a guy who writes books about a private investigator."

"Who would write about a guy who spends all day typing? Talk about yawn."

"You joke about me calling myself the World's Greatest Detective. Maybe I'm not joking. Maybe I need to be famous so badly I've imagined there's a guy writing books about me and that guy is you. Think about it."

Cole will say things like this with a straight face.

I said, "Elvis Cole, Mentally Ill Detective?"

"I can't believe people think you look like me."

"Listen. Let's start back. My legs."

Los Angeles spread out before us in all directions as far as we could see. Down below, other hikers were coming up the trail. We made our way back through brush that was dry and brittle from the heat. I looked for Pike, thinking he might be watching us, but I did not see him.

Cole said, "You think I could have a few extra games this year?"

I knew it. He's like that.

Part 2: Pike's Way

The sunglasses, twenty-four/seven. The empty, humorless expression. The sleeveless sweatshirt. The arrow tattoos that move him forward. The silence.

Ladies and gentlemen, I give you Joe Pike.

I first saw Joe Pike at the Florida Drive-in Theater in Baton Rouge, Louisiana. Would have been the late '60s, one of those triple-bill nights southern drive-ins are famous for. Me, I would have been a kid, carted to the drive-in by my mom to get me out of the house, or maybe alone, having snuck across the marshy fields and cane reeds on foot to slip between the rows of cars. I remembered him years later when I was creating the characters and story that would become *The Monkey's Raincoat*. Gunfighter eyes peered out of a face burned dark by the sun, so cold they went beyond cold into the empty void of deep space. The thin, humorless lips. Your worst nightmare if he paints you with his rattlesnake gaze. Clint Eastwood. *A Fistful of Dollars. For a Few Dollars More. The Good, the Bad, and the Ugly.* A walking can of whup ass. I could have left it there, but I never leave well enough alone.

Mr. Eastwood, the God Priest of manliness back in the day, was *not* the flash-image inspiration for Joe Pike—he was what I imagined when I first imagined Elvis Cole. In those early days of thinking about Elvis, I envisioned Cole as the stereotypical loner, and those first notions were as clichéd as they come. Cole listened to moody jazz. He had an apartment in Hollywood with a window looking out at a neon sign. He smoked, liked cheap bourbon in a shot glass, and was big on smoking and sipping the bourbon as he watched the neon sign blink. Yawn. When I came to my senses a few days later, I dropped all that and created the character you know as Elvis Cole.

Even as I developed Cole (and the themes worth spending a year of my life writing about), I knew I wanted Cole to have a friend. Butch and Sundance. Batman and Robin. Lucky Jack Aubrey and Stephen Maturin. Thelma and Louise. Spenser and Hawk. Spade and Archer (even though Archer was dead). Before I wrote *The Monkey's Raincoat*, I wrote a lot of television, and watched even more. *Cagney & Lacey. Miami Vice* with Crockett and Tubbs. These friendships had always inspired me (both as a reader and a writer). Cole was not going to be part of a formal organization like the police—I identified more closely with an outsider who did not have the power and authority that come with the badge—but I also had no interest in writing about a character who was so disaffected that he was empty of friends. Elvis Cole needed a friend. Note that I am using the word *friend,* not *partner*. The human stuff of friendship was—and is—important in all of this.

That image of the man with no name appeared, but that's where it ended. The image reappeared but quickly changed. The narrowed eyes and sharp-cut jaw evolved within Elvis Cole's house in the Hollywood hills and became something much more compelling. I was once aboard a ship in the South Pacific where the water was seventeen thousand feet deep. Water that deep grows dark as it swallows the light. It is bottomless. When you see a shadow move in that darkness, the hair will stand up on the back of your neck. You know all the way down in your DNA that something dangerous swims in those waters. I was drawn to it. Out there at sea, I leaned across the rail again and again, trying to see into the depths. I still do, only now the water is Pike.

For a piece like this, I find it easier to describe Elvis Cole than Joe Pike. Armchair psychologists will no doubt pipe up with the certain opinions that this is because I identify more with Cole or that he is my alter ego (he isn't), but I think it is less a factor of identification than understanding. Pike is an iceberg, and I am trying to understand the parts of him beneath the water. Careless swimmers have disturbed the silt. The waters are murky, the shadows indistinct and shifting, the darkness increases as the water deepens, and Pike is a very deep presence.

Listen. I wanted the fun and kickass good time of this enigmatic character—the twitch is there for you to enjoy—but Pike and Cole were always more. My fiction is about underdogs. And because I want there to be justice in this world, underdogs must have heroes . . . or they must become heroes. In many ways, the more I thought about Elvis, and who he was, and how he came to be Elvis, the more I thought he might have taken another road that could have led him to become someone like Pike. Elvis has chosen to engage life; Pike, in many ways, has stepped outside it. Somewhere in his past, he became "other."

Once upon a time for, I guess, advertising purposes, a publisher dubbed Joe Pike a "sociopath." He isn't. I once thought of Elvis and Joe as a kind of yin and yang, a view that has been echoed by more than a few readers and reviewers. They are not. Nor is Pike simply Elvis Cole's assassin; a handy-dandy, guilty-pleasure author's device for getting Cole out of the morally queasy side waters of dropping the hammer on bad guys without benefit of judge, jury, constitutional protections, or hand-wringing after-action remorse. Pike is Pike. Like Elvis Cole, he is an underdog who has turned himself into a hero.

My books are about self-creation. I'm big on that. You can either be the victim of your past or rise above it. Both Elvis and Joe have done just that, but having risen isn't a done-deal, over-and-out, now-I-can-relax kind of thing. Having risen, you have to maintain, because that whole "rising" business, well, it's an ongoing process.

And there lies a key difference between Elvis and Joe. I suspect Joe Pike thinks about this stuff. I also suspect that Elvis Cole doesn't—he just lives it, as natural to him as breathing or saying funny things, until "forced" to voice his philosophies in order to set a client straight.

Their example is the example of choices made. Cole doggedly embracing the "normal" and aggressively cultivating those parts of himself that consciously resist the darkness of his own experience—the Disney icons, the science-fiction films he enjoyed as a boy, the relaxed and comfortable attire (Hawaiian shirts and sneakers), the quippy, self-effacing sense of humor. These are the proud standards telling you this man is living life on his own terms. His very job—private investigator—tells you he holds himself apart. Cole is, at the end of the day, the product of these lifestyle choices. He would be a great guy to have a beer or catch a Dodgers game with.

Joe Pike is a conscious representative of our righteous rage at injustice. He is what happens when society fails.

The product of abusive childhood violence, Pike learned early that if you want justice, you must look to yourself. Pike was an only child living with his mother and a violent, alcoholic father at the edge of a small town. He and his mother suffered regular beatings from his father. Society did not save him—not the police, friends, or neighbors. No Eastwood-like hero rode into town to save Mrs. Pike and her young son. Joe learned his father's lesson well. No one will save you, so you had better save yourself. You don't wring your hands or try to "handle" a bully. You deal with a bully by employing an overwhelming physical response. Presented with a threat, you confront it head-on. Pike's philosophy (and his rage) was boiled to its primal base: dominate or be dominated. So Pike set about preparing himself to control his environment, and does.

The seeds of this was the rage he felt at his own helplessness, I think, but Pike's rage is not mindless. He knows that some part of himself was lost (probably in childhood), and he has spent much of his adult life, I think, learning to deal with his "otherness" and maybe even trying to give life to that dead part of himself. To think he is mindless—floating in the dark waters like his namesake fish, all cortical activity and no forebrain—would be a mistake.

Though I know many things about Pike, he is still a mystery obscured by the deep water. When Pike is within himself and seemingly disconnected from his surroundings, he has pulled back from the outer world to a place I describe as "the green world"—a natural, primal world where he feels safe. On the face of it, the green world represents the safety of the forest where he hid from his father. But the green world also represents the primitive nature of Pike's character. We are one with, and part of, that nature. We are the animals in the forest, whether that forest is a leafy green glade or the sprawling city of Los Angeles. Our animal natures are revealed in either place.

Pike would probably tell you, if he thought it was worth spending the breath, that he has accepted the responsibility for his own security. Pike doesn't give a lot of due to what we call "black-letter law." Pike has a very strict moral and ethical code, but it is a code independent of written statutes.

When Larkin Conner Barkley asks him, in *The Watchman,* whether he feels remorse at having killed men, Pike is able to answer without hesitation.

"No."

And he doesn't. He has accepted a certain matter-of-factness about these things. If a man threatens you, you put him down. It is the natural order. No sense worrying about it, so he doesn't. These are not feelings or thoughts that Pike would share, so I'm not sure even Elvis knows how far away Pike goes when he goes to that green world. It's as if Pike has settled into a temporary moment of transcendental calm like a Zen warrior, divorced from the chaos around him but at peace with it. We can't see his thoughts in that deep water, and might not understand them even if we could.

The space between us and how Pike sees the world is part of his mystery. His lack of emotion suggests an inner landscape that has been carpet-bombed and left as barren as the desert surrounding Tikrit. It also suggests an emptiness waiting to be filled, and therein lies his tragic nature and the uniqueness of his friendship with Cole. Pike recognizes that Cole's inner landscape is teeming with life. Pike admires this life and wonders at its depth and complexity, and would sacrifice himself without hesitation for his friend. This is not something a sociopath would do.

This is the stuff of heroes. These books are heroic fiction with liberal doses of myth and adventure, but I hope they are more than escapist fantasy. Though these are crime novels, the "crime novel" is simply the canvas upon which I have chosen to paint, and my subject matter, I believe, is larger than guns, gunfighting, macho posturing, and the relative thrills of wing chun arm traps and high-velocity action sequences, though these things are certainly part of these books, and I hope you enjoy them. I do!

I write about people. My thrill of accomplishment doesn't come from the blind-side plot twist, but from that nuance of character that touches you, moves you, involves you, and, I hope, surprises you—not with the "aha!" of an unexpected plot reveal, but with the resonance of human understanding.

People always ask me where Joe and Elvis came from. Here's the answer:

You are Joe Pike.

You are Elvis Cole.

Meaning that some part of you identifies with some part of them, so much so that in that instant of identification, you are them and can understand them. Pike's loneliness. Cole's longing. And in that moment what I am writing about isn't just action and clues, but fully realized human beings.

JEFFERY DEAVER

Born outside Chicago in 1950, Jeffery Deaver received a journalism degree from the University of Missouri and became a journalist, then got a law degree from Fordham University and practiced for several years. A poet, he also wrote songs and performed them around the country.

The author of twenty-five novels and two short-story collections, Deaver has been translated into twenty-five languages and is a perennial bestseller in America and elsewhere. Among his many honors and nominations are six Edgar Allan Poe Award nominations, three Ellery Queen Readers Awards for best short story of the year, the 2001 W.H. Smith Thumping Good Read Award for *The Empty Chair*, and the 2004 Ian Fleming Steel Dagger Award from the Crime Writers' Association for *Garden of Beasts*.

In addition to his popular and critically acclaimed series about the brilliant quadriplegic detective Lincoln Rhyme, he has written more than a dozen nonseries suspense novels.

His first Lincoln Rhyme novel, *The Bone Collector*, was filmed by Universal in 1999 and starred Denzel Washington and Angelina Jolie. A nonseries novel, *A Maiden's Grave*, was an HBO movie retitled *Dead Silence* that starred James Garner and Marlee Matlin.

Deaver lives in Chapel Hill, North Carolina.

LINCOLN RHYME

BY JEFFERY DEAVER

MEMORANDUM

From: Robert McNulty, Chief of Department, New York City
                      Police Department

To: Inspector Frederick Fielding
       Deputy Inspector William Boylston
       Captain Alonzo Carrega
       Captain Ruth Gillespie
       Captain Sam Morris
       Sergeant Leo Williams
       Lieutenant Detective Diego Sanchez
       Lieutenant Detective Carl Sibiewski
       Lieutenant Detective Lon Sellitto
       Detective Antwan Brown
       Detective Eddie Yu
       Detective Peter Antonini
       Detective Amelia Sachs
       Detective Mel Cooper
       Police Officer Ronald Pulaski

CC: Sergeant Amy Mandel

Re: Lincoln Rhyme News Release

In light of the recent tragic events, our Public Information department has prepared the following release for news organizations around the country. As you are someone who has in the past worked with Lincoln Rhyme, we are sending you a draft of this document for review. If you wish to make any changes or additions, please send them by 1030 hours Friday to Sgt. Amy Mandel, the office of the Deputy Commissioner of Public Information, One Police Plaza, Room 1320.

Please note the time and place of the memorial service.

* * * FOR IMMEDIATE RELEASE * * *

New York City—Capt. Lincoln Henry Rhyme (Ret.), internationally known forensic scientist, died yesterday of gunshot wounds following an attack by a murder suspect he had been pursuing for more than a year.

The assailant, whose name is unknown but who goes by the nickname the Watchmaker, gained entrance to Capt. Rhyme's Central Park West town house, shot him twice, and escaped. The assailant's condition is unknown. He was believed to have been wounded by NYPD detective Amelia Sachs, who was present at the time. An extensive manhunt is under way in the metropolitan area.

Capt. Rhyme was pronounced dead at the scene.

"This is a terrible loss," said Police Commissioner Harold T. Stanton, "one that will be felt throughout the department, indeed throughout the entire city. Capt. Rhyme has been instrumental in bringing to justice many criminals who would not have been apprehended if not for his brilliance. The security of our city is now diminished due to this heinous crime."

For years Capt. Rhyme had been commanding officer of the unit that supervised the NYPD crime scene operation.

It was, in fact, while he was searching a scene in a subway tunnel undergoing construction work that he was struck by a falling beam, which broke his spine. He was rendered a C-4 quadriplegic, paralyzed from the neck down, able to move only one finger of his left hand and his shoulders and head. Though he was initially on a ventilator, his condition stabilized and he was able to breathe without assistance.

He retired on disability but continued to consult as a private "criminalist," or forensic scientist, working primarily for the NYPD, though also for the Federal Bureau of Investigation, the Department of Homeland Security, the Bureau of Alcohol, Tobacco, Firearms, and Explosives, and the Central Intelligence Agency, among others, as well as many international law-enforcement agencies.

Lincoln Rhyme was born in the suburbs of Chicago. His father was a research scientist who held various positions with manufacturing corporations and at Argonne National Laboratory. His mother was a homemaker and occasional teacher. The family lived in various towns in the northern Illinois area. In high school, Capt. Rhyme was on the varsity track-and-field team and president of the science club and the classics club. He was valedictorian of his high school graduating class. Capt. Rhyme was graduated from the University of Illinois at Champagne-Urbana, receiving dual degrees in chemistry and history. He went on to study geology, mechanical engineering, and forensic science at the graduate level.

Capt. Rhyme turned down lucrative offers to work in the

private sector or in academia and chose instead to specialize in crime scene work.

He said in an interview that theoretical science had no interest for him. He wanted to put his talents to practical use. "I couldn't be a karate expert who spends all his time in the monastery or practice hall. I'd be itching to get out on the street."

Some friends believed an incident in his past, possibly a crime of some sort, steered him to law enforcement, but none was able to say what that might have been.

Capt. Rhyme attended the NYPD Police Academy in Manhattan and joined the force as an officer in the crime scene unit. He quickly rose through the division and was eventually named commanding officer of the division overseeing the unit while still a captain, usually a position held by an officer with the higher rank of deputy inspector.

Capt. Rhyme took forensic science in New York City to a new level. He fought for budget increases to buy state-of-the-art equipment, evidence-collection gear, and computers. He personally created a number of databases of "samples," such as motor oils, gasoline, dirt, insects, animal droppings, and construction materials, against which his officers could compare trace evidence from crime scenes and thus identify and locate the perpetrator with unprecedented speed. He would wander through the streets of the city at all hours, collecting such materials.

He developed new approaches to searching crime scenes (for which he coined the now-common term "walking the grid"). He instituted the practice of using a single officer to examine scenes, believing that a solo searcher could achieve a better understanding of the crime and the perpetrator than a group of officers could.

FBI Special Agent Frederick Dellray, who worked with Capt. Rhyme frequently, said, "When it came to physical evidence, there was not a soul in the country who was better. No, make that the world. I mean, he was the one we brought in to set up our Physical Evidence Response Team. Nobody from Washington or Quantico, nope. We picked *him*. I mean, this's a guy solved a case 'cause he found a fleck of cow manure from the eighteen hundreds. He couldn't tell you who Britney Spears is or who won *American Idol,* but, it came to evidence, that man knew f***ing everything."

Although most senior crime scene officers are content to leave the actual searches and lab work to underlings, Capt. Rhyme would have none of that. Even as a captain, he searched scenes, gathered samples, and did much of the analysis himself.

"When we were partnered," said Lt. Lon Sellitto, "he was a lot of times first officer at the scene and would insist on searching it himself, even if it was hot."

A "hot" crime scene is one at which an armed and dangerous perpetrator might still be present.

"I remember one time," Lt. Sellitto recalled, "he was running a scene and the perp comes back with a gun, starts shooting. Lincoln dives under cover and returns fire, but he was mad about the whole thing—every time he fired, he said, he was contaminating the scene. I told him later, 'Geez, Linc, you shoot the guy, you're not gonna have to *worry* about the scene.' He didn't laugh."

When asked once about his fastidious approach to forensic work, Capt. Rhyme cited Locard's Principle, which was named after the early French criminalist Edmond Locard, who stated that in every crime there is some exchange between the criminal and the victim, or the criminal and the scene, though the trace might be extremely difficult to find.

As Capt. Rhyme put it: "Often the only thing that will stop a vicious killer is a microscopic bit of dust, a hair, a fiber, a sloughed-off skin cell, a coffee stain. If you're lazy or stupid and miss that cell or fiber, well, how're you going to explain that to the family of the next victim?"

Capt. Rhyme insisted on employees' total devotion to their job, and once fired an officer for using the toilet beside the bedroom where a murder had occurred.

Still, he rewarded hard work and loyalty. A former protégé reported that on more than one occasion, Capt. Rhyme would berate senior police officials to secure raises or promotions for his people. Or he would adamantly, and loudly, defend his team's judgments about handling cases.

In several instances Capt. Rhyme himself ordered senior police officials, reporters, and even a deputy mayor arrested when their presence threatened to contaminate or interfere with a crime scene.

In addition to gathering and analyzing evidence, Capt. Rhyme enjoyed testifying in court against those whose arrests he had participated in.

Bernard Rothstein, a well-known criminal-defense lawyer who has represented many organized-crime figures, recalled several cases in which Capt. Rhyme testified. "If I saw that Rhyme had done the forensic work in a case against one of my clients, I'd think, brother, I am *not* looking forward to that cross-examination. You can punch holes in the testimony of most crime scene cops when they get up on the stand. But Lincoln Rhyme? He'd punch holes in *you*."

After his accident at the subway crime scene, Rhyme converted a parlor in his Central Park West town house into a forensic lab, one that was as well equipped as those in many small cities.

Det. Melvin Cooper, an NYPD crime scene officer who often worked with Capt. Rhyme and did much of his laboratory work for him, recalled one of the first cases run out of his town house. "It was a big homicide, and we had a bunch of evidence. We cranked up the gas chromatograph, the scanning electron microscope, and the mass spectrometer. Some other instruments too. Then I turned on a table lamp, and that was the last straw. It blew out the electricity. I don't mean just his town house. I mean the entire block and a lot of Central Park too. Took us nearly an hour to get back on line."

Despite his injury, Capt. Rhyme was not active in disability rights organizations. He once told a reporter, "I'm a white male who lives in New York City, is six feet tall, weighs 182 pounds, has dark hair, and is disabled. Those are all conditions that have, to a greater or lesser degree, affected my career as a criminalist. I don't focus on any of them. My purpose in life is to find the truth behind crimes. Everything else is secondary. In other words, I'm a criminalist who, by the way, happens to be disabled."

Ironically, largely because of this attitude, Capt. Rhyme has been held out by many advocates as an example of the new disabled movement, in which individuals are given neither to self-pity nor to exploiting or obsessing over their condition.

"Lincoln Rhyme stood for the proposition that the disabled are human beings first, with the same talents and passions—and shortcomings—as everyone else," said Sonja Wente, director of the Spinal Cord Injury Awareness Center. "He avoided both the pedestal and the soapbox."

Capt. Rhyme himself observed in a recent interview, "The line between the disabled and the nondisabled is shrinking. Computers, video cameras, high-definition monitors, biometric devices, and voice-recognition software have moved my life closer to that of somebody who's fully able-bodied, while the same technology is creating a more sedentary, housebound life for those who have no disability whatsoever. From what I've read, I lead a more active life than a lot of people nowadays."

Nonetheless, Capt. Rhyme did not simply accept his disability; he fought hard to maintain his ability to live as normal a life as he could and, in fact, to improve his condition.

"Lincoln engaged in a daily regimen of exercises on various machinery, including a stationary bike and a treadmill," said Thom Reston, his personal aide and caregiver for a number of years. "I was always saying slow down, take it easy, watch your blood pressure." The aide added, laughing, "He ignored me."

In fact, in recent years, Reston said, the exercise paid off, and Capt. Rhyme was able to regain some use of his extremities and some sensation, a feat that spinal-cord doctors described as a rare achievement.

Capt. Rhyme was not only a practicing criminalist; throughout his tenure at the NYPD, he was in demand as a teacher and lecturer. After his accident, when traveling became more difficult, he continued to lecture on occasion at John Jay School of Criminal Justice and Fordham University in New York City. He wrote about forensic issues, and his articles have appeared in, among others, *Forensic Science Review, The New Scotland Yard Forensic Investigation Annual, American College of Forensic Examiners Jour-*

nal, *Report of the American Society of Crime Lab Directors,* and *The Journal of the International Institute of Forensic Science.*

He authored two books: a text on forensic science used by thousands of police departments and law-enforcement agencies around the world, and a popular nonfiction book, *The Scenes of the Crime,* about sites in New York City where unsolved murders occurred. The book is still in print.

Capt. Rhyme was himself the subject of a series of best-selling popular novels, which recounted some of his better-known cases, including *The Bone Collector,* about a serial kidnapper; *The Stone Monkey,* recounting the hunt for a Chinese "snakehead," or human smuggler; and *The Twelfth Card,* in which he and Det. Amelia Sachs, who worked with him often, investigated a crime that occurred just after the Civil War.

Publicly dismissive of the novels, he stated in interviews that he thought the books merely trivial "entertainments," good for reading on airplanes or at the beach, but little else.

Privately, though, he was delighted to be the subject of the series, keeping an autographed set on his shelves. Visitors reported that he would often make them sit silently and listen to passages he particularly liked on CD.

"Lincoln and his ego were never far apart," joked Mr. Reston.

Capt. Rhyme was divorced from his wife, Blaine Chapman Rhyme, twelve years ago. They had no children. He is survived by his partner, Det. Sachs; his aunt, Jeanette Hanson; and four cousins, Arthur Rhyme, Marie Rhyme-Sloane, Richard Hanson, and Margaret Hanson.

A memorial service for Capt. Rhyme will be held at 7:00

p.m., Monday, at the New York Society for Ethical Culture, 2 West 64th Street, at Central Park West, New York, NY. Det. Sachs has asked that, in lieu of flowers, donations be made to a charitable organization for the benefit of children with spinal-cord injuries or disease.

————

The first floor of the town house on Central Park West was quiet, dark. The lights were off, and little of the dusk light from outside penetrated the curtains in the east-facing room.

What had once been a quaint Victorian parlor was now filled with laboratory equipment, shelves, cabinets, office chairs, electronic devices. On examining tables were plastic and paper bags, and tubes and boxes containing evidence. They were in no particular order.

The atmosphere here was of a workplace whose otherwise busy pulse had been stopped cold.

Tall, red-haired Amelia Sachs stood in the corner, beside frumpy Lon Sellitto. They both wore black suits.

Her eyes gazed down at Lincoln Rhyme's obituary.

Sellitto glanced down at it. "Weird, hm?"

She gave a faint, unhappy laugh, then shook her head.

"I felt exactly the same way. Hard enough to think about the *idea,* you know, without seeing it in black-and-white."

"Yeah, I guess that's it."

Sellitto looked at his watch. "Well, it's about time."

The hour was close to seven p.m., Monday, when the obit announced the memorial service was about to start.

"Ready?"

"As I'll ever be."

The two shared a glance, left the town house. Sachs locked the door. She glanced up at Lincoln Rhyme's darkened bedroom, outside of which falcons nested on the ledge. She and Sellitto started down the street toward the Society for Ethical Culture, which was just a short walk away.

———

Amelia Sachs returned to the town house, accompanied by a group of other officers.

Casual observers might have thought that the cops were returning from the memorial service for a reception at the home of the deceased.

But they'd have been wrong. The hour was merely 7:20, which wouldn't have allowed nearly enough time for a proper service, even for someone as unspiritual as Lincoln Rhyme. And a closer look at the officers would have revealed that they had their weapons drawn and were whispering into microphones held in hands or protruding from headsets.

The dozen officers split into two groups, and on word from Lon Sellitto at a nearby command post, one sped through the front door, another jogged around back.

Amelia Sachs, not surprisingly, was the first one through the front door.

The lights flashed on and she crouched in the doorway, ignoring the painful griping of arthritic joints as she trained her Glock on an astonished man in a suit and dark blue shirt, bending over an evidence table. He was surprised in the act of picking up a plastic bag in his latex-gloved fingers.

"Freeze," Sachs barked, and he did, noting undoubtedly the steadiness of her hand holding the pistol and the look in her eye that explained she was more than prepared to fire it.

"I—"

"Hands on your head."

The solidly built middle-aged man sighed in disgust, dropped the bag, and complied. "Look, I can explain."

Sachs wondered how often she'd heard that in her years as a cop, at moments just like this.

"Cuff him, search him," she barked to young, spiky-haired Ron Pulaski and the other officers on the takedown team. "He's a cop. Remember, he might have two weapons."

They relieved the man of his service Glock and, yep, a backup in an ankle holster, then cuffed him.

"You don't understand."

Sachs had heard that quite a bit too.

"Detective Peter Antonini, you're under arrest for murder." She offered up the mantra of the *Miranda* warning, then asked, "Do you wish to waive your right to remain silent?"

"No, I sure as hell don't."

"There's not much he needs to say anyway," said a new voice in the room. Lincoln Rhyme wheeled his TDX wheelchair out of the small elevator that connected the lab with the upstairs bedroom. He nodded at the examination table. "Looks like the evidence tells it all."

———

"You?" Antonini gasped. "You're . . . you were dead."

"I thought you wanted to remain silent," Rhyme reminded him, enjoying the look of absolute astonishment on the guilty man's face.

The criminalist wheeled to the evidence table and looked over what the officers had pulled from Antonini's pocket—Baggies of hair and dirt and other trace evidence, which he had intended to substitute for the evidence sitting on the table, evidence the officer believed would convict him of murder.

"You son of a bitch."

"He keeps talking," Rhyme said, amused. "What's the point of *Miranda?*"

At which point detective second-class Peter Antonini, attached to Major Cases, did indeed fall silent as Sachs called Sellitto in the command van and told him about the successful takedown. Sellitto would in turn relay the news to the brass at One Police Plaza.

You were dead. . . .

Rhyme's phony death and the obituary had been a last-ditch effort to solve a series of crimes that cut to the heart of the NYPD, crimes that might have gone unnoticed if not for an offhand observation made by Ron Pulaski a week before.

The young officer was in the lab helping Sellitto and Rhyme on a murder investigation in Lower Manhattan, when a supervisor called with the news that the suspect had shot himself. Rhyme found the death troubling; he wanted closure in his cases, sure, but resolution by suicide was inelegant. It didn't allow for complete explanations, and Lincoln Rhyme detested unanswered questions.

It was then that Pulaski had frowned and said, "Another one?"

"Whatta you mean?" Sellitto had barked.

"One of our suspects dying before he gets collared. That's happened before. Those two others. Remember, sir?"

"No, I don't."

"Tell us, Pulaski," Rhyme had encouraged.

"About two months, that Hidalgo woman, she was killed in a mugging."

Rhyme remembered. A woman being investigated for attempted murder—beating her young child nearly to death—was found dead, killed during an apparent robbery. The evidence had initially suggested that Maria Hidalgo was guilty of beating the child, but after her death it was found that she was innocent. Her ex-husband had had some kind of psychotic break and attacked the child. Sadly, she'd died before she could be vindicated.

The other case, Pulaski had reminded them, involved an Arab American who'd gotten into a fight with some non-Muslim men and killed one of them. Rhyme and Sellitto were looking into the politically charged case, when the suspect had fallen in his bathtub and drowned. Rhyme later determined that the Muslim *had* killed the victim, but under circumstances that suggested manslaughter or even negligent homicide, not murder.

He, too, died before the facts had come out.

"Kinda strange," Sellitto had said, then nodded at Pulaski. "Good thinking, kid."

Rhyme had said, "Yeah, *too* strange. Pulaski, do me favor and check out if there're any other cases like those—where suspects under investigation got offed or committed suicide."

A few days later, Pulaski came back with the results: There were seven cases in which suspects had died while out on bail or before they'd been officially arrested. The means of death were suicide, accident, and random mugging.

Sellitto and Rhyme wondered if maybe a rogue cop was taking justice into his own hands—getting details on the progress of cases, deciding the suspects were guilty, and executing them himself, avoiding the risk that the suspects might get off at trial.

The detective and Rhyme understood the terrible damage this could cause the department if true—a murderer in their midst using NYPD resources to facilitate his crimes. They talked to Chief of Department McNulty and were given carte blanche to get to the truth.

Amelia Sachs, Pulaski, and Sellitto interviewed friends and family of the suspects and witnesses nearby at the time they had died. From these accounts, it appeared that a middle-aged white man had been seen with many of the suspects just before their deaths. Several witnesses thought the man had displayed a gold shield; he was therefore a detective. The killer clearly knew Rhyme, since three of the victims were apparently murdered while the criminalist was running their cases. He and Sachs came up with a list of white detectives, aged thirty-five to fifty-five, he'd worked with over the past six months.

They surreptitiously checked the detectives' whereabouts at the times of the killings, eventually clearing all but twelve.

Rhyme opened an official investigation into the most recent case—the fake suicide that Pulaski had commented on. The scene was pretty cold and hadn't been well preserved—being only a suicide—but Amelia Sachs came up with a few clues that gave some hope of finding the killer. A few clothing fibers that didn't match anything in the victim's apartment, tool marks that might have come from jimmying a window, and traces of unusual cooking oil. Those weren't helpful in finding the killer's identity, but something else she found suggested where he might live: traces of loam-rich soil that turned out to be unique to the banks of the Hudson River, some of which contained "white gas," kerosene used in boats.

So it was possible that the rogue cop lived near the river in Manhattan, the Bronx, Westchester, or New Jersey.

This narrowed the list to four detectives: from the Bronx, Diego Sanchez; from New Jersey, Carl Sibiewski; from Westchester, Peter Antonini and Eddie Yu.

But there the case stalled. The evidence wasn't strong enough to get a warrant to search their houses for the clothing fibers, tools, cooking oil, and guns.

They needed to flush him out. And Rhyme had an idea how.

The killer would know that Rhyme was investigating the suicide—it was an official case—and would know that the criminalist had some evidence. They decided to give him the perfect opportunity to steal it or replace it with something implicating someone else.

So Rhyme arranged his own death and had the chief send out the memo about it to a number of officers, including the four suspects (the others were told of the ploy, and they agreed to play along). The memo would mention the memorial service, implying that at that time the lab would be unoccupied.

Sellitto set up a search-and-surveillance team outside the town house, and while Rhyme remained in his bedroom, Sachs and Sellitto played the good mourners and left, giving the perp a chance to break in and show himself.

Which he oh so courteously had done, using a screwdriver that appeared to be the same one that had left marks on the windows of prior victims' residences.

Rhyme now ordered, "Get a warrant. I want all the clothes in his house, cooking oils and soil samples, other tools too. And any guns. Send 'em to ballistics."

As he was led to the door, Peter Antonini pulled away roughly from one of the officers holding him and spun to face Rhyme and Sachs. "You think the system works. You think justice is served." His eyes were mad with rage. "But it doesn't. I've been a cop long enough to know how screwed up it all is. You know how many guilty people get off every day? Murderers, child abusers, wife beaters . . . I'm sick of it!"

Amelia Sachs responded. "And what about those *innocent* ones you killed? *Our* system would have worked for them. Yours didn't."

"Acceptable losses," he said coolly. "Sacrifices have to be made."

Rhyme sighed. He found rants tedious. "It's time you left, Detective Antonini. Get him downtown."

The escorts led him out the door.

"Thom, if you don't mind, it's cocktail hour. Well past it, in fact."

A few moments later, as Thom was fastening a cup of single-malt scotch to Rhyme's chair, Lon Sellitto walked into the room. He squinted at Rhyme. "You don't even look *sick*. Let alone dead."

"Funny. Have a drink."

The chunky detective pursed his lips, then said, "You know how many calories're in whiskey?"

"Less than a doughnut, I'll bet."

Sellitto cocked his head, meaning good point, and took the glass Thom offered. Sachs declined, as did Pulaski.

The rumpled detective sipped the whiskey. "Chief of department's on his way. Wants to thank you. Press officer too."

"Oh, great," Rhyme muttered. "Just what I need. A bunch of sappy-eyed *grateful* visitors. Hell. I liked being dead better."

"Linc, got a question. Why'd you pick the Watchmaker to do the deed?"

"Because he's the only credible perp I could think of." Rhyme had recently foiled an elaborate murder plot by the professional killer, who'd threatened Rhyme's life before disappearing. "Everybody on the force knows he *wants* to kill me." The criminalist took a long sip of the smoky liquor. "And he's probably one of the few men in the world who could."

An uneasy silence followed that sobering comment, and Pulaski apparently felt the need to fill it. "Hey, Detective Rhyme, is this all accurate?" A nod at the memo that contained his obituary.

"Of course it is," Rhyme said, as if the comment were absurd. "It had to be—in case the killer knew something about me. Otherwise he might think something was up."

"Oh, sure. I guess."

"And by the way, do you always get your superior officers' attention with 'hey'?"

"Sorry. I—"

"Relax, rookie. I'm a civilian, not your superior. But it's something to ponder."

"I'll keep it in mind, sir."

Sachs sat next to Rhyme and put her hand on his—the right one, which had some motion and sensation. She squeezed his fingers. "Gave me kind of a pause." Looking down at the sheet. "Lon and I were talking about it."

It had given Rhyme some pause too. He felt the breeze from death's wings nearly every day, closer than to most people. He'd learned to ignore the presence. But seeing the account in black-and-white had been a bit startling.

"Whatta you gonna do with it?" Sellitto asked, glancing down at the paper.

"Save it, of course. Such beautiful prose, such pithy journalism . . . Besides, it's going to come in handy someday."

Sellitto barked a laugh. "Hell, Linc, you're gonna live forever. You know what they say. Only the good die young."

COLIN DEXTER

Born in Lincolnshire, England, in 1930, Colin Dexter graduated from Cambridge University and spent most of his professional life as an educator in his beloved Oxford. He came comparatively late to crime writing, being already in his forties when he attempted his first novel, *Last Bus to Woodstock,* which was accepted by the second publisher to which it was sent. It introduced Inspector Morse, the somewhat curmudgeonly senior officer in the Criminal Investigator Department with the Thames Valley Police, and Sergeant Lewis, who appeared in every one of Dexter's thirteen novels and most of the short stories collected in *Morse's Greatest Mystery and Other Stories* (1993).

Among his numerous awards are Gold Daggers from the British Crime Writers' Association for *The Wench Is Dead* (1989) and *The Way Through the Woods* (1992) and the Cartier Diamond Dagger for lifetime achievement, presented to him in 1997.

The hugely successful *Inspector Morse* television series, produced by ITV in England and shown in the United States on PBS, was based on the books and additional stories; it starred John Thaw and Kevin Whateley, running for thirty-three episodes from 1987 to 2000. Like Alfred Hitchcock did in his films, Colin Dexter made brief cameo appearances in most of the episodes.

INSPECTOR MORSE

BY COLIN DEXTER

Perhaps (I hope) the most sensible way for me to write about Chief Inspector Morse is to try to answer some of the many questions that have been put to me most frequently by audiences and correspondents. Then, at least, I can believe that my answers will be focused upon things in which people seem genuinely interested.

But first, a few brief words about myself. The whole of my working life was spent in education: first, as a teacher of Latin and Greek in English grammar schools; second, with increasing deafness blighting my life, as a senior administrative officer with the Oxford Delegacy of Local Examinations, in charge of Latin, Greek, Ancient History, and English.

Well, here goes!

What emboldened you to enlist in the rather crowded ranks of the crime-writing fraternity?

It is not unknown, even in midsummer, for the heavens to open in North Wales; and there are few things more dispiriting than to sit in a guesthouse with the rain streaming in rivulets down the windows, and with offspring affirming that every other father somehow manages to locate a splendid resort, with blue skies and warm seas, for the annual family holiday. That was my situation one Saturday afternoon in August 1973. Having rather nervously asserted that we were *not* planning a premature return to Oxford, I shut myself up in the narrow confines of the kitchen with a biro and a pad of ruled paper—with only a very vague idea of what I was intending to do. I had already finished reading the two paperback detective stories left by previous guests, and I figured that if I tried hard, I might possibly do almost as well in the genre myself. So for a couple of hours I tried *very* hard, resulting in how many paragraphs, I cannot recall. I doubt more than two or three. It was, however, that all-important start: *Initium est dimidium facti* (the beginning is one half of the deed), as the Roman proverb has it.

Had I any reason other than vanity for wishing to see my name on the jacket of a detective story? Not money, certainly, since I was fortunate enough to enjoy a well-paid university post, annually climbing a little higher up the salary scale. If, as Dr. Johnson remarked—in an uncharacteristically cynical vein—"no man but a blockhead ever wrote except for money," then I was one of the blockheads. And not because I thought I had anything of criminological, psychological, or sociological import to communicate to my fellow man. I had just one simple aim in mind—an aim to which I have always held firm in my subsequent writings: to tell a story that would entertain whatever readers might be coming my way.

It would be pleasing to report that later on that August Saturday afternoon the sun broke through the lowering clouds. Yet, as I recall, it didn't. What I can report is that my first work of fiction, *Last Bus to Woodstock,* originated on that day, and was finally published by Macmillan in 1975. It featured a detective named Morse. "Just call me Morse!" as he was to say so many times when some delicious and desirable woman asked him for his Christian name. And that is how I shall refer to him throughout this article.

Which crime writers and what kind of crime writing have influenced you?

First memories for me are of Sexton Blake and Tinker, then Edgar Wallace ("King of Thriller Writers"), with his racy and uncluttered style. Next Agatha Christie, pulling the wool over my eyes from page one in myriad imaginative and ingenious plots, and almost invariably baffling the delighted reader until the last chapter, last page, last paragraph.

And she more than any other writer determined the direction of my writing, with an emphasis more on "who" perpetrated the dreadful deed, rather than "why" or "how." For some "dreadful deed" it had to be, since no reader will be overlong enthralled by the theft of a tin of salmon from the supermarket. It was Christie, then, who motivated my eagerness for surprise endings in the Morse novels. Other writers of course were influential, and like most teenagers I was a great fan of Father Brown and Sherlock Holmes. But more important, I should mention John Dickson Carr (Carter Dickson), with his wonderfully "impossible" locked-room puzzles. I was never able to write such a mystery for Morse to solve, but again it was the "puzzle" element that delighted me so hugely. And it is not unfitting that in his book *Bloody Murder,* Julian Symons writes of "the puzzles set by Colin Dexter," gently adding that "perhaps it is churlish to wish that motives and behaviour were a touch nearer reality." So often have I listened to some of my crime-writing colleagues arguing about the respective merits of "plot" versus "characterization." But I have always viewed such discussions as somewhat phony, since the totality of a good story subsumes them both, and the greatest accolade that any of us can hope for is to hear one's partner's plea from a room downstairs: "I'll be up in a few minutes, darling. Just let me finish this chapter first."

Furthermore, in this connection, there is little doubt in my mind that Homer and Ovid would have been the top earners in Hollywood. One other major influence: I had long envied the ability of some few writers, Simenon and Chandler in particular, to establish in their novels a curiously pleasing ambience of a city, a street, a bistro, etc. And I have ever hoped that the physical sense of Oxford, and the very spirit of the city, has permeated the pages in which Morse is summoned to so many (mostly fatal) scenes. Perhaps my one wholly legitimate claim to notoriety is that single-handedly I have made Oxford the murder capital of the UK—and probably of the EU.

What sort of man was Morse? Was he like you?

Of Morse's physical presence, I had very little idea. I had assumed, I suppose, that (unlike me) he measured up to the height specification for the police force; that his incurable addiction to real ale and single-malt scotch whiskey was gradually but inevitably adding a few inches to his girth; that unlike his creator he had a good head of hair; that to the world at large he paraded no deformities. He was in no way likely to be confused with the description I once gave of myself to a Finnish journalist: "short, fat, bald, and deaf," on which the lady in question congratulated me warmly, saying that because of this she had recognized me "immediately"!

Morse's other qualities? Well, unless one is a genius, which I am not, a writer will tend in many respects to be semi-autobiographical in the delineation of the character and temperament of the detective hero. As such, Morse changes very little throughout the novels, betraying the same qualities displayed in my first and, and as I thought at the time, my only one. He was, and remained, a sensitive and sometimes strangely vulnerable man; always a bit of a loner by nature; strongly attracted to beautiful women (often the crooks); dedicated to alcohol; and almost always on the verge of giving up nicotine. In politics, ever on the Left, feeling himself congenitally incapable of voting for the Tory party; a "high-church atheist" (as

I called him), yet with a deep love for the Methodist Hymnal, the King James Bible, the church music of Byrd, Tallis, Purcell, etc., the sight of candles, and the smell of incense. Finally, like me, he would have given his hobbies in *Who's Who* as reading the poets, crosswords, and Wagner.

And what of his negative qualities? He was quite unwilling to give thanks to any of his hardworking underlings (especially Lewis) and had little or no respect for most of his superior officers. He was unorthodox, with little knowledge of police procedure and only minimal respect for forensic pathology. He was often pig-headed and impatient, a man with alpha-plus acumen, normally six furlongs ahead of the whole field during any investigation but so often running on the wrong racecourse. And has there ever been a fictional detective so desperately mean with money?

On this latter point, I was encouraged by my editors to *exemplify* any fault rather than merely stating it. And I think that readers began to expect such exemplification in each novel. For example, in *The Remorseful Day*, the pair of detectives are the first customers in the bar of Oxford's Randolph Hotel at 11:00 a.m., and Lewis's eyebrows are raised a few millimeters when, throwing the car keys to him, Morse suggests that it's high time he, Morse, bought the drinks: a large Glenfiddich for himself and half a pint of orange juice for Lewis—only for the unfortunate barmaid to tell Morse that she cannot find sufficient change so early on for the fifty-pound note proffered. Whereupon, patting his presumably empty pockets, Morse asks his sergeant if by any chance he has some appropriate small change on his person. (Here, I must admit, I had little difficulty in finding exemplars, with advanced symptoms of this odious trait, among a few of the Oxford dons I worked with.) But let me insert a caveat. Mrs. Valerie Lewis (alas killed in a hit-and-run accident) always knew whenever her husband had been selected as Morse's lieutenant: there was a perceptible change in his step—if less change in his pocket.

How did you get your first Morse novel published?

I have ever maintained that luck, good and bad, plays a considerably larger part in our lives than most people are prepared to acknowledge. It was not always so. The Romans, for example, as well as regularly pouring their libations and sacrificing animals to their traditional pantheon, were also very careful to appease and to seek the approval of the goddess of good luck (Fortuna). We can all accept that a little talent and a lot of hard graft are indispensable concomitants in any worthy enterprise. But what a blessing if the gods collectively are occasionally smiling on us! As they were, after a few early frowns, upon me.

I had my manuscript typed up, with just the one heavily corrected and smudged carbon copy, and asked around for the best bets among the publishing houses. Collins, Gollancz, and Macmillan, in that order, topped the list. I had no agent (still haven't) and I posted the typescript to Collins—from whom, after a chivvying letter from me, I received a letter about four months later. It was a pleasantly argued letter of the kind that so many hopeful, budding authors have come to know only too well: an "if-ever-you-write-anything-else" kind of letter. A rejection letter. So, leaving out my second choice, I parceled up *Last Bus to Woodstock* once more and sent it to Macmillan, a publishing house with, as I learned, an increasingly prestigious crime list.

Within forty-eight hours I received a phone call from the senior crime editor there, Lord Hardinge of Penshurst, asking me to get up to London posthaste. He had read my novel and was prepared to publish it without further ado (and without alteration!), "warts and all." Later I learned that he had been suffering from a serious bout of flu at the time and had requested that any new stories should be brought to his bedside. Whether or not his illness was impairing his judgment in any way, I just don't know. What I do know is that the gods were smiling benevolently on me that particular weekend. Incidentally, when I say that I have never had an agent, that is strictly true. But I have ever stuck with Macmillan. And for over thirty years now, successive crime editors—George Hardinge, Hilary Hale, Maria Rejt, and Beverley Cousins—have handled my literary affairs wonderfully well. I have been, let me repeat it, a very lucky writer.

How did you come up with the names of Morse and Lewis?

Strangely enough, I spent eighteen months in the Royal Signals Regiment doing my National Service, and became a high-speed Morse code operator, serving most of the time in West Germany (1948–50). That, however, had nothing to do with Chief Inspector Morse, whom I named after Sir Jeremy Morse, a man with as sweet and clear a brain as I have known. He was a former chairman of Lloyds Bank; key member of the Bank of England and the IMF; Fellow of All Souls, Oxford; Warden of Winchester College, etc., etc., regularly parading his genius in chess problems and crossword puzzles. Indeed, it was in the crossword world where, as early as the mid-1950s, we became keen competitors—and later good friends. And when I wished to introduce a detective-hero of consummate mental caliber, the surname was staring me in the face, was it not?

What of his strange first name? In *The Wench Is Dead,* Morse was taken to hospital in Oxford, where from his sickbed he was to solve a murder mystery of well over a hundred years standing. To add, as I trust, a measure of verisimilitude to the situation, I had a medical chart fixed to the bottom of his bed, chiefly recording the regular functioning or nonfunctioning of his bladder and bowels. The chart was headed "Mr. E. Morse." Now, there are many men's first names beginning with *E,* from Eamon to Ezra, and I had no idea at all which one was Morse's. Understandably so, really, since first-name terms were a bit of a rarity in my day. At school I was "Dexter (ii)," with my older brother "Dexter (i)"; in the army I was "922 Dexter," the last three digits of my army number; as a schoolmaster I was just

"Dexter" to my colleagues and "Sir" to my pupils; and at Oxford, in correspondence to the many hundreds of examiners for whom I was responsible, it was ever "Dear Jones," "Dear Smith," etc., with "Dear Miss/Mrs. Whatever" for the ladies.

But just "Morse" was not going to be wholly satisfactory henceforth, since some of the leading bookmakers had produced a list of odds, with Ernest, I believe, a common favorite. So I had to come up with something, and I did. In previous novels I had informed my readers that Morse's mother was a Quaker and that his father's great hero was Captain Cook. An examination of the New England Quaker lists threw up a variety of names—not just the familiar Faith, Hope, and Charity, but others, also enshrining comparable Christian virtues. And it was my wife, Dorothy, who discovered Determination Davies, and (yes!) Endeavour Jones. Things were settled then. "It is now Endeavour Morse," wrote a correspondent to *The Times,* "endeavour more shall be so"! I broke the news at the end of *Death Is Now My Neighbor,* whereupon Lewis was heard to mumble, "You poor sod, sir."

What about Lewis? Like that of Morse, his surname was taken from one of my favorite crossword rivals, Dorothy Taylor, who used the nom de guerre "Mrs. B. Lewis" when entering crossword competitions. Lewis is a good name for a Welshman, and Lewis was a Welshman when I first wrote of him; roughly the same age as Morse too. ITV's decision to make him a younger man with a Geordie accent was taken without consultation with me, and indeed without my knowledge. Yet I did not remonstrate, nor, as it happens, should I have done so. After viewing the first TV episode of *Morse,* "The Dead of Jericho," I realized that the casting of Kevin Whately as Lewis was a happy triumph, effecting a semisurrogate father-son relationship between the two detectives. In subsequent Morse novels, I solved the obvious discrepancy in the most cowardly of all ways—I ignored it completely, never giving further physical descriptions of Sergeant Lewis. His first name, though? In the television episode

"Promised Land," Lewis (not Morse!) joined the Aussie lager boys joyously, and the matey Oz culture naturally necessitated a first name. Robbie, we decided, was as appropriate as any.

How and why did Morse make it to TV?

In the 1980s, the Independent Television Corporation (ITV) was looking for a new detective series, and simultaneously it appeared that many viewers wanted less violence, fewer gunfights, and (please!) no more car chases. Several of the imported American crime programs were coming to the end of their runs, and perhaps the stage was being set for a quieter, more cerebral breed of detective series, where brains were likely to be a better bet than brawn. The Zeitgeist was definitely changing. But there were some early doubts about whether Morse could and should fit the bill. It may well be, as someone pointed out at the time, that as well as being "more everything else," such a program might also turn out to be more tedious. "Dexter's idea of dramatic confrontation," I read, "is a couple of Classics dons arguing about Aristotle outside the Ashmolean." Fortunately for me, two very gifted men, each with huge experience in the TV world, were very much pro Morse. After reading some of my novels, both agreed that the beautiful city of Oxford would be an ideal setting for a series of murders, solved by a lugubrious Wagnerian and his solid (never stolid!) sidekick.

At a meeting in a north Oxford pub, The Friar Bacon, Kenny McBain, Anthony Minghella, Julian Mitchell, and I drank a few pints of beer together and talked of many things . . . of which I remember only one with clarity. When I suggested that after lunch I would with the greatest pleasure show them around a few of the murder sites in Oxford that I had already used, McBain smiled and declined my offer: "We've already visited them, Colin." After lunch, half launched upon the shores of light was *Inspector Morse* that day.

Thereafter, the whole machinery of the televisual requirements began to fall into place: the casting, the film scripts, the locations, the schedules, the directors, the producers, etc. The biggest item of contention, as I recall, was the proposed one-night, two-hour, prime-time programming. I had thought that this was asking a little too much of our likely audience. I was wrong. But again, as with the books, I was extremely lucky. Things can of course so often go sadly awry, and several of my crime-writing colleagues have not experienced the good fortune of which I was continuously aware in ITV's treatment of *Inspector Morse*.

Wherein lay this good fortune? First and foremost, it was undoubtedly in the casting of John Thaw and Kevin Whately as Morse and Lewis, with much of the credit for this resting with Ted Childs, the executive producer of all thirty-three episodes. Second, with the string of distinguished screenplay writers, directors, and producers ITV was able to enlist in the making of the thirty-three *Inspector Morse* episodes filmed. Third, with the sheer technical brilliance of the camera crews, who somehow seemed perpetually enthused and exhilarated by the beauties of Oxford. Indeed, Oxford itself from the outset assumed a leading role in the series, with audiences a little disappointed when the main body of the action was filmed in Australia or Italy or elsewhere. Fourth was the wonderful array of talent among supporting actors and actresses, both established media stars and newcomers, from Sir John Gielgud in *The Twilight of the Gods* to Elizabeth Hurley in *Last Seen Wearing*. To the best of my knowledge, no one ever refused an invitation to take a part in the series, and on visits to Oxford, actors as diverse as Ken Dodd and Charlton Heston lightheartedly informed the *Oxford Mail* that they had only the one remaining ambition in life: to be selected for a minor part in one of the programs. Fifth (and more of this anon), in Barrington Pheloung we had a musical genius. Finally, I must mention the contagious camaraderie engendered among the film crews by such a wise and experienced producer as Chris Burt.

For a brief while let me dwell separately on one of these factors—Oxford.

Morse's city, described passim, lived in, and murdered in, is not *only* the city of the great men—scholars, historians, poets, scientists, doctors, churchmen, etc.—whose portraits hang proudly in many of the college dining halls used in the Morse episodes. Oxford is, and always was, a city of "Town" as well as "Gown." And one of my proudest possessions is the following citation: "The Lord Mayor and Oxford City Council place on record their appreciation of the literary talents of Colin Dexter, who has been the most visual and the most watched novelist of our City. We are extremely grateful that in his novels he has shown our City as having a distinct and separate identity from its famous University."

I was a bit like Morse myself: quite certainly *in* the university but not wholly *of* the university. And whilst I am indulging in some self-gratification, let me admit to feeling a warm glow (forgive me!) on reading the words of the distinguished novelist and critic Malcolm Bradbury: "Oxford generally imagines it is famous for dreaming spires, British prime ministers (and American presidents), Matthew Arnold, John Ruskin, Cardinal Newman, and Evelyn Waugh. But it is surely Dexter's Oxford that has laid the strongest imprint over the contemporary city, and it is the Morse Tour that draws a great proportion of its visitors." All a bit over the top, I agree.

What sort of problems arose with the adaptation of the Morse novels to the TV series?

Each medium, written novel and televised version of it, has its own distinctive strengths—and weaknesses. In a crime novel, a writer can get away with anything, can literally get away with murder, or multiple murders (as I know perfectly well). And if I wish to write, "Lewis decided to risk jumping down the twenty-foot wall, and happily landed uninjured," there is no problem. On TV, however, he would either break his leg(s) or call in a stuntman or get the cameraman to fiddle the scene. In a novel, I can put a convenient end to some wicked malefactor by having a pack of rabid rottweilers tear him literally to pieces, and even describe the process. On TV, life is still regarded as a little more precious.

The big advantage of TV, of course, is that the viewer can *see* what's happening and where it's happening. A very simple example would be the fabric of the city of Oxford. Whilst I may indulge myself for a couple of paragraphs on describing the effect of sunlight on the cinnamon-colored stone of an Oxford college, TV can do it in a few seconds—and do it *better*. It is the combination of such camera work with the accompanying dialogue that is, and that has to be, the modus operandi of television, this being the only obvious means available of carrying forward the development of any drama. Why? Because it is not at all easy to *think* on TV. What is the point of any actor's face filling the screen for twenty seconds or so, hand to face like Rodin's *Thinker,* saying nothing at all but looking—well, looking *thoughtful,* just above the subtitle "Do not adjust your set"? Unless . . . unless one has a quite remarkable actor (and John Thaw was such a one) who can communicate by silence, by the slightest movement of his facial features, and most particularly by his eyes. In a novel, if he so purposes, a writer may indulge in "thinking" all the time on every page, never veering from some "stream of consciousness" flow, even to get up for a cup of tea.

Television's compensatory benefit is the use it may so readily make of music. None of us expects (or wants) to find an occasional CD stuck onto the pages of a novel. But music has been a wonderfully appropriate accompaniment to many TV programs—as it was to *Inspector Morse.*

How important was music in the TV programs?

Early on in the series, one critic wrote that for him, watching *Morse* was becoming a bit of a routine: bedroom slippers on, wine bottle(s) opened, phone off the hook—all rather like anticipating an evening with Schubert. Well, we'll come to Schubert in a while, but let us start at the beginning.

Barrington Pheloung's introductory theme music was a splendid opening, with its fusion of a fine melody with the "da-ditty-da" rhythm of the Morse code. (Incidentally, it was later put to words and appeared on the pop charts.) It was not, as some have supposed, a clever, surely *too* clever, means of tapping out the letters of the crook's name. It was, quite simply, a poignant, haunting motif that set exactly the right tone and mood for the series. After the individual episodes developed, music became integral to the moods, actions, and meanings of the scenes being portrayed. Let me give some illustrations of how it all worked, for which we owe everything to Barrington.

My own musical loves have centered predominantly on the latter half of the nineteenth century, especially Wagner (of course!), Bruckner, Mahler, and (later) Richard Strauss. Fairly obviously, the musical tastes of Morse mirrored my own. And, being mentioned frequently in the novels, they had some influence on many of the musical extracts used by Barrington, as did the favorites of Kenny McBain, particularly in the latter case Mozart's clarinet compositions. Which illustrations do I particularly remember? Vivaldi's *Gloria* at the beginning of the first TV program, "The Dead of Jericho"; Callas singing *Tosca* in "The Ghost in the Machine"; Ella Fitzgerald's voice in "Driven to Distraction"; Mozart's *The Magic Flute* (passim) in "Masonic Mysteries"; the Schubert Quintet in C in "Dead on Time"; the Immolation Scene from Wagner's *Götterdämmerung* in "Twilight of the Gods"; and the prelude to Wagner's *Parsifal* in "The Remorseful Day." I could go on and on. . . . And I will do a little, since I should not forget Barrington's catchy composition "Truckin' till I'm Dead" in "The Promised Land"; nor his original rave music in "Cherubim and Seraphim."

If, as is often claimed, music is more able than other arts to give expression and form to our innermost feelings, let me single out the two examples I found most memorable of all. First, the ethereal extract from the finale of Richard Strauss's *Der Rosenkavalier* in "Promised Land," when Morse mounts the steps of the Sydney Opera House. Does opera ever rise above such glorious heights? Second, the extraordinarily moving "In Paradisum" from Fauré's *Requiem* in "The Remorseful Day," which includes the wonderful words *"et cum Lazaro, quondam paupere, aeternam habeas requiem"* ("and with Lazarus, once a poor man, you may have eternal rest"). Inspector Morse would have opted for it at his funeral, as I shall at mine.

Did you have any discipline about the times you set aside for writing?
No.

Why did you kill off Morse?
I didn't. He died of natural causes—a virtually inevitable consequence of a lifetime spent with "cigarettes and whiskey," though not with "wild, wild women." The cigarettes were always a problem, and Morse gave them up on innumerable occasions—usually every day. Alcohol, however, was a different matter, with real ale and single-malt scotch his favored tipples. Frequently, with Lewis, he sought to perpetuate the claim that he needed to drink in order to think, and indeed there was clearly some justification for such a claim. Whiskey, if drunk copiously, may have at least three possible effects: the legs may buckle, the speech become blurred, the brain befuddled. But Morse had no trouble with this last effect. His brain was sharper than ever, his imagination bolder, even his deep pessimism concerning the future of the planet a fraction modified. A longer-term effect was that his health grew worse, and he knew the score as well as any of the medical consultants whom he steadfastly refused to visit.

But there were, if I am honest, several other reasons why I decided to end the Morse era. First, it is my opinion that few crime writers manage to sustain their previously high level of output as they get older, and I had neither the ambition nor the need to try to join that select few. Second, my health was not robust, and it becomes progressively worse now. Third, I felt that I had said enough about the relationship between Morse and Lewis, and I realized that the repeated exemplifications of Morse's character traits were becoming somewhat cliché ridden, with a good deal of the original freshness lost. Finally, I realized that I hadn't many (any?) further plots left in my head to construct and develop. All right, we could have had a gentle ending, with Morse at last realizing his dreams of fair women, getting wed, and living happily ever after. But even my great hero Chandler made a sad mistake, in *Playback,* in my opinion, when providing a regular nuptial bed and a beautiful lady for Philip Marlowe.

You wrote only thirteen full-length Morse novels. How come there were thirty-three television episodes?
The Morse short stories I had written were too insubstantial for any two-hour treatment. After the novels were exhausted, I was asked by Kenny McBain if I could come up with four new plot outlines for the subsequent year's quartet. I should have said no, since I was still a greenhorn in this TV business and had little idea what such a task would entail.

I wrote two excessively lengthy "outlines," for "The Ghost in the Machine" and "Deceived by Flight," both over sixty pages, as I recall. I then struggled through a third—and gave up on the fourth, realizing at last that my brain was quite unable to cope with such an assignment. From that point, screenplay writers were invited not just to adapt something I had written, but to produce original scripts. There were two dangers in this.

First, that new writers might not be fully aware of the firm characterization already established for both Morse and Lewis. Second, that perhaps some writers might think it appropriate, knowing the two characters well, to develop them according to their own lights and likings. For one or the other of these reasons, several promising stories could not be accepted. And since the copyright for Morse (and indeed for Lewis) remains and will remain with me, my role developed into that of an amateur consultant, occasionally with the directors but usually with the producers, especially Chris Burt. I hope and believe that such consultations and suggested revisions were of value.

What notice do you take of the critics?

One or two novelists I know would have no hesitation in answering, "No notice whatsoever, since I never read them." I respect their independence of spirit, but I am not among them. When in the early days I got a mention anywhere, I eagerly sought out the review, and I felt deep satisfaction if it was even mildly commendatory, begging Macmillan to send me photocopies of similar mentions in their files. My style, I soon learned, was "mandarin" and "labyrinthine," and although not quite sure of the significance of either epithet, I rather enjoyed them both. "Alas, the style . . ." were the first three words of a shortish review once in *The Times,* and I read no more. I had a mixed bag of reviews from the pens of some distinguished critics, including A. N. Wilson, a writer I (once!) admired, who told his readers that he just could not read my pages. I was tempted to get my own back at him by never reading any more of *his* pages. On the other hand, I well remember treasuring (forgive me!) the judgment of Marcel Berlins, UK's most respected crime critic, who wrote that Morse was now "a giant among fictional detectives."

I wrote to only two reviewers. One was a local woman, herself an embryonic crime writer, I believe, who accused me (or was it

Morse?) of being a "breast fetishist" in *The Way Through the Woods*. Although I could see little reason for being ashamed of such an interest in the female form, I did look quickly through the novel, finding only ". . . and Morse glanced appreciatively at the décolletage of her black dress as she bent forward with the wine list."

The second was Christopher Wordsworth, a fine and perceptive critic, who (inadvertently, I'm sure) had given a red-hot hint about the identity of the murderer. Such lapses are most irritating and, I'm relieved to say, are considerably less common in the UK than in the US, where fuller reviews and detailed blurbs are not infrequently mines of information. Why on earth not allow readers to discover for themselves exactly what is going to happen? Yet I should be grateful that today reviews are taken more seriously than they were a few decades ago, when only two or three carefully crafted sentences would usually suffice—sometimes brilliantly so.

I well recall a film critic giving his judgment on the latest blockbusting biblical epic from Hollywood in four words: "God at his best."

———

Let me add one final sentence. I never allowed anyone, not even my wife, Dorothy, to read my novels before they were dispatched to my publisher. It was only then that I was ready for any criticism. All writers of course will sometimes wince silently at some of their earlier offerings and wish to amend them. I remember, for example, once having Morse enjoying "a pint of the amber fluid" instead of "a pint of bitter." The only changes I always made, when checking copy for omnibuses, etc., involved crossing out *Lancia* and substituting *Jaguar*, because ITV were unable to come up with an ancient Lancia and instead purchased, for some ridiculously giveaway price, a maroon-colored Jaguar Mark II, 1962, which, fully and luxuriously refurbished, recently changed hands for £150,000.

What really makes Morse tick?

Earlier I gave my own three greatest joys in life as crosswords, Wagner, and the poets, and vicariously I tried to exemplify these interests/hobbies/passions, both in the novels and in the TV programs.

Crosswords? Well, Morse could almost invariably finish *The Times* crossword at breakneck speed (he was considerably quicker than I am), and in his vainer moments he would claim that solving that newspaper's puzzle was the veritable benchmark of mental acumen and flexibility. Sometimes, however, he could cheat just a little. In *The Wench Is Dead,* for example, we read that Morse "bought *The Times* at the bookstall, got a seat at the rear of the train and had solved the puzzle in ten minutes before reaching Didcot. Except for one clue . . . He quickly wrote in a couple of bogus letters in case any fellow passengers were waiting to be impressed." He did try once to interest Lewis in the delights of the cryptic crossword, but in vain.

Wagner? I attempted perhaps rather laboriously to explain Morse's passion for music. It would have been very difficult for him to explain such a passion to Lewis, just as it is for me here to put these things into words. Much better, surely, for both of us to *feel* them? Once, in a car, Morse betrayed an impatient arrogance when Lewis mistook an aria from *Tosca* sung by Maria Callas for a lively tune from *Cats*. But, then, Morse was a musical snob who would have had no sympathy whatsoever with a woman I knew who had seen *The Sound of Music* on fifteen occasions. Such contempt was not Morse's most attractive trait, was it? But perhaps we should forgive him.

The poets? Certainly Morse spent much time reading poetry with deep and abiding love, both the English and the classical poets. Occasionally read them aloud, too, as in *The Remorseful Day,* when, seated one summer evening in the Victoria Arms with a pint of beer on the table in front of him, he gazed westward toward a miraculous sunset and recited part of a poem by Housman—a poet who, like Morse, failed to get a degree from St. John's College, Oxford.

Ensanguining the skies
How heavily it dies
  Into the west away;
Past touch and sight and sound,
Not further to be found,
How hopeless under ground
  Falls the remorseful day.

(More Poems, XVI)

Unusually for the melancholy Housman, this poem has an almost playful touch. The remorse here is for unfulfilled intention, an emotion experienced by most of us every day. But not by John Thaw, perhaps, whose life afforded a fulfillment of his ambitions and a manifestation of his extraordinary talents.

Did John Thaw ever say anything to you that you particularly remember?

Let me be honest. No one has ever asked me that question, but I would like to answer it. He told me that he enjoyed playing Inspector Morse more than any other role, and for me that was an unforgettable compliment. I can just about understand why that great actor thought so. For me John Thaw *was* Inspector Morse. And in my will I have specifically stated that for as long as the copyright on the character remains with me, I shall permit no other actor to follow him. No other actor *could* follow him.

JOHN HARVEY

John Harvey was born in London in 1938. After studying at Gold-smiths College, University of London, and at Hatfield Polytechnic, he took his master's degree in American Studies at the University of Nottingham, where he taught film and literature as a part-time lecturer between 1980 and 1986.

Harvey taught English and drama in secondary schools for twelve years. Since then, he has lived primarily by his writing, and has more than one hundred published books to his credit. After what he calls his apprentice years, writing paperback fiction for both adults and teenagers, he is now principally known as a writer of crime fiction, with the first of the Charlie Resnick novels, *Lonely Hearts,* being named by *The Times* (London) as one of the 100 most notable crime novels of the last century. *Flesh and Blood,* the first of three novels featuring Frank Elder, was awarded both the British Crime Writers' Association Silver Dagger and the US Barry Award in 2004. His books have won two major prizes in France, the Grand Prix du Roman Noir Etranger for *Cold Light* in 2000 and the Prix du Polar Européen for *Ash & Bone* in 2007. In 2007, he was the recipient of the CWA Cartier Diamond Dagger for sustained excellence in crime writing.

Harvey has written many scripts for television and radio, spe-cializing in adapting his and others' work. His radio work includes dramatizations of two Graham Greene novels, *The End of the Affair* and *The Heart of the Matter,* as well as *The Frederica Quartet* by A. S. Byatt and (with Shelly Silas) *The Raj Quartet* by Paul Scott.

After living in Nottingham for many years, Harvey now lives in north London with his partner and their young daughter.

CHARLIE RESNICK

BY JOHN HARVEY

To the memory of two fine professionals, Laurence James and Dulan Barber, without whom it is doubtful Charlie Resnick would ever have existed—and for Marian Wood, who, as my US editor at Henry Holt, was responsible for keeping Charlie, and me, more or less in line for a good—a very good—ten years. Thanks, Marian.

That I became a writer at all—and that Charlie Resnick, therefore, was brought into existence—was largely due to a series of convenient accidents. You see, I had never harbored any ambitions to be a writer, at least not a fiction writer, and until the time that my first book (*Avenging Angel,* New English Library, 1975, under the pen name Thom Ryder) was published, I had made no attempts in that direction: no early masterpieces stored beneath the bed or in an adoring parent's drawer, no prize-winning contributions to some children's short-story competition. I had, it's true, both at secondary school and then again at college, edited a couple of student newspapers, gracing them with the occasional review or what I saw as a scathing muckraking exposé, but this was journalism, nothing more or less, and although, looking back, I'm somewhat bemused to understand why, it never occurred to me that it might be my profession. No. I was destined to be a teacher, an inspirational—well, I *was* still young—teacher of English and drama to whatever hapless eleven through eighteen year olds found themselves seated before me.

The twelfth year of this career found me in Stevenage, a "new town" an hour's drive north of London, and I was beginning to feel more than a tad restless. And here, as chance would have it, I resumed close acquaintance with a former college friend, Laurence James, who, sadly, was to die all too early, in the year 2000, when not yet sixty. Laurence had been assiduously working his way up in the book trade—first as a bookseller, then as an editor, and finally as an author. He was living not far from Stevenage, close enough for me to make frequent visits, during which I complained about the nature of my present lot and observed with no little envy the comparatively pleasant life of a full-time writer. Laurence, it seemed—I later learned the truth to be both more arduous and demanding—would rise in his own good time and, after a leisurely breakfast, make his way into his office, where he would sit behind his desk for an hour or so before pausing for the first of several coffee breaks that would occur throughout the day. And at the end of each of those days, two or three thousand words of manuscript would have been created with apparent ease. No bells sounding at forty-minute intervals to announce a new class and a change of lesson, no recalcitrant or obstreperous youths to chivvy along or bully into submission: just your own quiet room with a stereo and coffee machine close to hand and, in Laurence's case, an intelligent and lovely wife, who, having shipped the kids off to school, was most likely working on a novel in a room of her own.

My envy must have been evident for all to see, and now, providentially, more good fortune came to my aid. Laurence had been writing a series of rollicking biker books under the name of Mick Norman, and his publishers wanted another; Laurence, however, was committed elsewhere. "You want to write something," he said. "Here's your chance." Except, of course, I hadn't really wanted to write anything at all: what I wanted was what I saw as the writer's life—the cottage in the country, the Volvo, the ability to organize one's own days. Faced with actually producing anything somebody else might want to read, never mind publish, I gibbered and blanched.

But Laurence was persuasive: he gave me the Mick Norman books to read, helped me to assemble a story line and then a synopsis, and sat patiently—well, mostly patiently—alongside me while I rewrote my sample first chapter more than a dozen times. The whole package went to his editor with a strong letter of recommendation, and a month or so later (things moved speedily in those far-off days), I was in possession of a contract. All I had to do was provide a manuscript of fifty thousand words, and the grand sum of two hundred fifty pounds would be mine in return.

Back in Stevenage, still teaching, I worked at the kitchen table of my small flat—holidays, evenings, weekends—and somehow my deadline was met and the finished manuscript shipped off.

Glancing back, it was a strange book, as much about the iniquities of the education system as the roar of marauding Harley-Davidsons, but, to my delight and no little surprise, it was accepted and, graced with the near-obligatory jacket photograph of a young blond woman in an unbuttoned denim jacket astride a motorcycle, *Avenging Angel* was duly published—and I was offered a contract for a second book at fifty pounds more. I was on my way.

One thing that aided my swift elevation to the ranks of published writers was the happy fact that the mid-'70s were a boom time for British publishing, new paperback imprints springing up seemingly overnight and all greedy for product. And because I had entered the world of writing in the way I had—because to me it was first and foremost an alternative way of earning a living rather than a sign of any higher literary ambition—I was only too happy to oblige. War books, movie tie-ins, apocalyptic adventure stories, teen romances—during the years of my apprenticeship, all was grist for my mill.

Then there was the day an editor from Transworld phoned me and said, "We're looking for someone to write a Western series. I wondered if you'd be interested?"

One of the publishing phenomena of the period was the success of a Western series called *Edge,* written by Terry Harknett under the pen name George G. Gilman. In his role as commissioning editor at New English Library, Laurence James—yes, him again—had suggested that Harknett, up to that point the author of middlingly successful thrillers, try his hand at a new kind of pulp Western, violent and sexy, based to a large degree on the Sergio Leone–Clint Eastwood spaghetti shoot-'em-ups such as *The Good, the Bad and the Ugly* and *For a Few Dollars More*. A brilliant idea, which Harknett fleshed out in spades. After a cautious start, sales of each new book in the series were nudging the 100,000 mark, and, not surprisingly, other publishers wanted a piece of that pie.

Soon there was a small group of British writers—hacks, as we delighted in calling ourselves—Laurence, of course, Terry Harknett, Ken Bulmer, Fred Nolan, Angus Wells, and me—laboring away at the Western cliff face, more often than not sharing pen names. Between us, while the boom lasted, our titles must have gone well into the hundreds; before shifting tastes and the changing economic climate caused me to hang up my spurs, I had myself written between forty and fifty books in different series.

That I was suited to this was to no small extent due to my father, who had been a great Western fan (Zane Grey's *Riders of the Purple Sage* was one of the three books forever at his bedside), and while I was growing up, he had taken me to see every Western movie that played in our part of north London. Under his influence, in my early teens I read and reread many of the Hopalong Cassidy novels of Clarence E. Mulford—what is it about Western authors and that middle initial?—and the *Buffalo Bill Annual* was virtually my bible. With considerable regularity—how did I get away with it so often?—I would skip school and take the Tube into the center of London, the lunch money I had saved bulking out my pockets, and alight at Marble Arch, where, immediately outside the station, a news vendor sold imported American comics: *Superman,* of course, and *Captain Marvel;* but also, more interesting for me, the adventures of minor Western movie stars: Rod Cameron, Allan "Rocky" Lane, and Lash La Rue.

So when it came to it, the frontier background—mythic and heavily romantic rather than realistic—was well in place for me. As an example, look at the opening chapter of *Cherokee Outlet* (Pan, 1980), the first of ten *Hart the Regulator* books, the only Westerns to have my own name, plus the near-obligatory middle initial, on the cover—John B. Harvey, no less.

He was a tall, dark shape coming out of the sun. Shrouded in his own shadow. A man who rode alone.

Like an orange medallion, the sun hung behind him in the afternoon sky. Its light caught the surfaces of misshapen rock scattered on the hill to the north, making them glow red and silver; it shone on the creek water where a whitetail doe drank nervously; it spread the shadow, long and deep, as horse and rider moved slowly to the east.

Wes Hart rode easily, reins resting across the palm of the left hand, the thumb of the right hooked round the pommel of his saddle. The fingers of his hand were spread wide, touching the leather, never far from the pistol that sat snug in its cutaway holster. A Colt Peacemaker .45, the mother-of-pearl grip carved with the Mexican emblem of an eagle holding a snake it its mouth and between its claws.

He was an inch over six foot, wiry under his light brown wool shirt, seeming lighter than the hundred and seventy pounds that had been his weight for thirteen years. His face was lean and stubbled, the high cheekbones strong against his tanned skin. Above them, Hart's eyes were a faded blue.

Romantic, certainly; one could see Gary Cooper in that saddle, perhaps, or Robert Taylor, Joel McCrea. But the majority of our heroes, men like Jedediah Herne in the *Herne the Hunter* series I wrote with Laurence James, were darker, closer to extreme violence and despair. Carved from the same unforgiving granite rock as John Wayne's vengeful character in *The Searchers* and the Eastwood of the spaghetti Westerns, this hero was no longer young, a loner with a tragic and troubled past that had left him imbued with a fierce but melancholic anger and a concern for few lives other than his own. He was, perhaps above all, a man not out of place, but out of time. In some respects he was not dissimilar to the Charlie Resnick to come—you see, I have not forgotten my principal theme and subject—yet in others he was cast from quite a different metal.

I got to thinking about much of the above quite recently, sitting one Sunday afternoon in one of the few London cinemas to maintain a repertory program, watching for the umpteenth time Sam Peckinpah's *Pat Garrett and Billy the Kid*—a movie about men out of time if ever there was one.

There's a moment early on when Billy turns to Garrett, his former running mate, now the lawman who has told him to move on, and says, "We had some times, didn't we?" And this made me think of all the pleasure, the sheer fun the bunch of us hacks had during our years spent churning out cowboy yarns, and also of how important films like *Pat Garrett and Billy the Kid* and *The Wild Bunch* were in forming the vision of the West we had.

Sometimes this was present in the detail—in *Cherokee Outlet,* for instance, Wes Hart recalls his first meeting with Billy the Kid, at which the Kid shot the heads off several chickens, which is a direct reference to the opening of the Peckinpah movie—but more often in the tone and the predicament of the protagonists, who time and again find themselves shut out of a society they know and recognize but that increasingly fails to recognize and accept them.

Inside and yet outside.

Belonging and yet not belonging.

When I began thinking of a central character for the book that was to become the first of the Resnick novels, *Lonely Hearts,* there were only two things fairly clear in my mind: he would be a policeman rather than a private detective, and—somehow—he would belong to the community he was policing and yet be outside it. What I needed, and finally found in the groups of shiny-suited men of an indeterminate age who spent their days hanging around the entrance to Nottingham's Victoria Centre market, was a way of signifying this "difference." (Yes, sorry, I'd been dabbling in structuralist theory while working for my master's degree in American Studies and it had rubbed off.)

The men were Polish, part of a large community that had settled in the area around the time of the Second World War; in Nottingham there were two flourishing Polish clubs and a large and well-attended Polish Catholic church. If, I thought, that was the close-knit community to which my character's family belonged, then it was not too fanciful to imagine him being brought up in a home where Polish was still spoken, but going to local schools where English with a pronounced Notts accent was the common currency, and with one set of customs and expectations vying with the other.

And his name? What about his name?

A friend in New York of Polish origin had the name Resnick; foreign and yet not too difficult for the average insular Brit to pronounce and understand. And then, suddenly, "Charlie" leaped out at me and seemed perfect. Quintessentially English, friendly, unthreatening, approachable, almost—as far as it is possible in England—untainted by class.

Charlie Resnick.

Insider and outsider both.

I remember several long sessions talking about him with the late Dulan Barber, who wrote crime fiction as David Fletcher and supernatural thrillers as Owen Brookes, and was both a generous and an unyielding mentor.

Pretty much following the stereotype, I'd decided early on that Resnick would be living alone and that in his past there would be a failed marriage that would be the source, from time to time, of a certain amount of anguish and regret. Anger too.

"What else," Dulan asked, "do we know about this man?"

His age, his weight, his taste in music, food, clothes?

In a glib moment, I once described Resnick as being akin to Jim Rockford but dressed like Columbo. As shorthand perhaps it works, though the visual equivalent I had most clearly in mind was Sergeant Valnikov, the police detective in Harold Becker's fine film of Joseph Wambaugh's *The Black Marble*. As played by Robert Foxworth, Valnikov is a fairly hopeless alcoholic of Russian origin, prone to nostalgia and self-pity and more often than not dressed in a shabby raincoat, tie askew, hair akimbo. Skip the alcohol, switch Russian to Polish, and the picture that remains is close to the one that was forming at the back of my mind.

I don't know if it was Dulan or myself who first came up with the idea of the sandwiches. But, we thought, a man living on his own and who leads a busy professional life would not have a great deal of time to set aside for serious cooking—though there are instances when he performs near-miracles with a few eggs and whatever leftovers the fridge provides. Sandwiches, though, seemed perfect, especially if the ingredients were mostly bought at one or another of the Polish delicatessen stalls to be found in the market, and at which he could conveniently stop on his way back from the coffee stall where he enjoyed his morning espresso.

It was my decision to make him a lover of jazz. (Dulan's tastes leaned toward high opera and the songs of Richard Strauss, with a strange but understandable penchant for Dusty Springfield.) A long-term listener to jazz myself—and, for a short period, a less than moderate practitioner—I wanted the opportunity to write about the music I knew, to try and give the reader, as far as it can be achieved in words, a sense of what Resnick is hearing when he listens, be it to Billie Holiday or Charlie Parker or whoever, and to describe as accurately as possible the actual sounds. More than that, I hoped I could make Resnick's sympathy and enthusiasm for the music say something about the man himself; it might suggest—as, in another way, I suppose, do his culinary appetites—an imaginative richness not otherwise apparent. I also wanted, if I could, to draw a connection between Resnick's appreciation of that listening experience and his understanding of people and their emotions, the things they feel and do.

Writing in the *Chicago Sun-Times* some years ago, the critic Lloyd Sachs was kind enough to state, "One of the things Resnick draws from the music is the ability to sense deeper possibilities in people, criminals as well as victims of crime. Just as he is aware of Lester Young's hard life producing this beautiful music, he sees people leading difficult lives being able to produce something of worth too. Maybe even something beautiful."

I fear I was less successful with the cats. I had, it's true, owned cats at different times in my life, but I also harbored, since childhood, a recurring fear of them—see the opening of the first Frank Elder novel, *Flesh & Blood* (2004). But it was Dulan who was the real cat lover, and it was probably at his instigation that Resnick's caring nature is revealed through his treatment of no less than four cats, named after jazz musicians, who function as substitutes for the children his marriage failed to provide. In retrospect, I think they are in danger of being cute and little more and too frequently get under the writer's feet in their need for attention. From correspondence, however, I know there are readers—mostly female and mostly, it appears, living in the United States—who will vehemently disagree.

All of the above, however, means that Resnick's basic characteristics were pretty much in place before I sat down to write *Lonely Hearts,* as I think is clear from the beginning of chapter four.

The sandwich was tuna fish and egg mayonnaise with some small slices of pickled gherkin and a crumbling of blue cheese; the mayonnaise kept dripping over the edges of the bread and down onto his fingers so that Dizzy twisted and stretched from his lap in order to lick it off. Billie Holiday and Lester Young were doing it through the headphones, making love to music without ever holding hands. Resnick could not stop thinking about the fact that he had lied to Skelton, wondering why.

His marriage had neither been so bad that he had stricken it from the record of his memory, nor so lacking in incident that he would have truly forgotten. Something over five years and she had walked in while he was painting the woodwork in the spare room and announced that she wanted a divorce. Each year of their marriage he had redecorated that small room at the back of their own bedroom in the hope that one day she might walk in with a glow in her eyes and announce that she was pregnant. Why else did he use alphabet wallpaper in primary colours? Why else the paintwork in bright reds and greens?

Or, as one of the characters observes of him earlier on,

He was an overweight man in his early forties, whose narrow eyes were bagged and tired, and who couldn't find the time to drop his tie off at the cleaners.

This last observation was made by the social worker Rachel Chaplin, with whom Resnick becomes involved professionally and personally. It was my intention, I think, that there would be some kind of romantic interest for Resnick in most of the books, each more or less doomed to end badly. Meantime, a relationship of a different kind was slowly building up between Resnick and the junior member of his team, Lynn Kellogg. *Cold Light* (1994), the sixth in the series, ends (as, in my head, it began) with Resnick thinking of her as "the daughter he had never had, the lover she would never be."

Shows how little I knew.

———

Hand in hand with my decision that my hero would be a serving policeman was the assumption that, as such, he would be one—the central one—of a group of fellow officers, a team. In this I was influenced both by police procedurals I had read—Ed McBain, Joseph Wambaugh, et al.—and those I had seen on TV, early British series like *Z Cars* and later American ones like *Hill Street Blues*. In respect to the latter, Resnick would be the middle-management figure holding it all together—Frank Furillo but with a different tailor.

One great advantage, it seemed, of this kind of structure was that it would enable me to employ a multistrand narrative and shift the focus of the story away from Resnick to other members of the team. In so doing, not only could I introduce characters of differing age and gender and sexual orientation, I could also vary the pace and cover more narrative ground. For every chapter showing Resnick listening thoughtfully to, say, Thelonious Monk at home, I could have another in which one of his young DCs chases an armed villain across the rooftops.

The move from writing Westerns to crime fiction was not an instant one; in between I wrote quite a bit of television drama—from BBC Classic serials such as the dramatization of Arnold Bennett's *Anna of the Five Towns* to episodes of popular crime series like *Spender*. Indeed, the last project I worked on before turning to *Lonely Hearts* was a six-part series I had originated about the probation service, called *Hard Cases*. This was written about and largely filmed on location in Nottingham, where I was then living, and followed, as far as we were able, the *Hill Street Blues* pattern to a T. (I sat down with a stopwatch and timed the sequences of that program exactly before planning my first scene-by-scene outline.)

Scriptwriting not only sharpened my use of dialogue and ability to cut between incidents and characters, it made clear both the importance of place and the possibility—I'm tempted to say necessity—of presenting people and their actions within a social context.

I've already mentioned *Z Cars,* a groundbreaking police series that locked into the strong documentary tradition of British cinema with its use of believable working-class characters, regional accents, and location filming. No wonder this was where such filmmakers and writers as Ken Loach, Alan Plater, and Troy Kennedy Martin did a lot of their early work.

I have always remembered an especially harrowing episode of *Softly, Softly,* the series that grew out of *Z Cars,* in which the police are investigating serious instances of child abuse instigated within the family. In one of the final scenes, after the abusers have been arrested and taken away, a detective is talking to one of the abused children, making sure the child is all right, and in gratitude the child offers to perform a sexual act—it is the only way that child knows to show thanks and gain approval.

The look on the detective's face—expressing in a moment revulsion, understanding, compassion, and deep, deep sorrow—has lived with me and, I'm sure, informed some of Resnick's responses in those parts of *Lonely Hearts* that deal with a similar theme. Beyond that, it convinced me that the crime story, whether in fiction or on film, at its best can—and should—deal with the same themes and situations that provide the subject matter for more supposedly serious work.

The importance of Nottingham to the Resnick books should not be underestimated. In the simplest of terms, I chose it as the setting for the novels as, certain areas of London aside, it was the city I knew best. I had lived there for quite long stretches of time, initially as a teacher, then as a student, and latterly as a writer. Situated in the less-than-fashionable East Midlands and some 120 miles north of London, it is only medium size as British cities go (the current population is just in excess of a quarter of a million) and so representative in its mix of income, class, and race that it is often chosen by market researchers as one of the key places to try out their wares. That very mix, with low-rent and high-income residences often cheek by jowl, makes it also a good test ground for a writer. All human life, as a popular British newspaper used to boast of its pages, is here.

When I first moved to Nottingham in the mid-'60s, the area was still a center for industry—coal mining, textiles and hosiery, Raleigh bicycles, Players cigarettes. Now most of that industry has either disappeared or downsized to unrecognizable proportions, and it is unclear what, if anything, has taken its place. Nevertheless, in the midst of some severe poverty, poor living conditions, and a struggling education system, pockets of wealth and creativity survive and prosper.

Writers have generally portrayed the city as a rumbustious, lively place with a good kicking about as close as the nearest pint of Shippo's, and the area as a whole has nurtured a reputation for roughness and violence. Think of Alan Sillitoe's Arthur Seaton in *Saturday Night and Sunday Morning*, or, further back, the early short stories of D. H. Lawrence, set in the small mining communities to the west of the city (where I began my teaching), in which it was normal for the wives and children to hide under the kitchen tables when the colliers were on their way home from the pub after getting paid.

More recently, Nottingham has acquired an unwanted and to some degree unwarranted reputation as the murder capital of Britain, thanks to a number of high-profile murders occurring within a short period, overstretching the resources of the local constabulary, and too many well-publicized instances of gun crime fueled both by the drug trade and by rivalries between young residents of various inner-city housing estates.

Rightly or wrongly, I felt that in writing about Nottingham, I was giving the Resnick novels a setting that I could portray with a degree of knowledge and conviction and that Resnick himself could be seen to know and understand. And love. Warts, as they say, and all.

————

There's one last question about Resnick I have to address, one I'm often asked: how much, if any, of him is me?

If we acknowledge the fact that, like each of my characters, he comes from some mixture, peculiar to me, of observation and imagination, then the answer is very little. In simple terms, I don't live off sandwiches or have four cats; I am not childless and rarely spill food down my tie. Not that, Detection Club dinners aside, I ever even wear a tie.

But his Nottingham is, or has been, mine. For years I walked across the city center, midmorning, to take my place at the same coffee stall.

My first real experience of listening to Billie Holiday came when shuffling through a pile of old vinyl 78s belonging to a school friend's uncle—"I Cried for You" by Teddy Wilson and his Orchestra, with Billie Holiday, vocal refrain. There among the Earl Bostic and early Duke Ellington and Louis Jordan and his Tympany Five. For Resnick, in *Cutting Edge* (1991), this became an occasion when, as a boy, he visited the house of an uncle who worked as a tailor—*with thumbs like sheet metal and fingers like silk*—who had visited

America and returned with a bundle of recordings that the young Resnick pored over and listened to with wonder.

Resnick had sat in hushed silence with black tea and dry cake while his uncle hand-sewed buttonholes and hems and his cousin swayed her legs softly to the Ink Spots, the Mills Brothers, four voices and a guitar. After a while, his uncle would tap his thimble on the table and wink at Resnick and then they would listen to Mildred Bailey, Billie Holiday, Luis Russell's "Call of the Freaks," Fats Waller and his Rhythm, "The Joint Is Jumpin'."

What helped to make Resnick was a patchwork of things, memories that, as will happen, came back to me in the course of writing and that, where suitable, became in some altered state a part of his past. Other incidents, like the one described below, also from *Cutting Edge,* although slight, could be dovetailed into the story to give a sense of the kind of man Resnick is and the world he inhabits.

It was raining again: a fine, sweeping drizzle that seeped, finally, into the bones, chilling you as only English rain could. On a makeshift stage at the center of the Old Market Square, the Burton Youth Band were playing a selection from the shows to a scattering of casual listeners and a few sodden relatives who had made the journey over on the band coach. Off to one side of the stage, in a row of their own, a boy and a girl, eleven or twelve and not in uniform like the rest, sat behind a single music stand, mouths moving as they counted the bars. Resnick watched them—the lad with spectacles and cow-licked hair, the girl thin-faced and skimpily dressed, legs purple-patched from rain and wind—nervously fingering the valves of their cornets as they waited to come in.

It was close to where Resnick was standing that Paul Groves had sat, staring off, and talked about his friendship with Karl Dougherty.

"I touched him one time and you'd have thought I'd stuck a knife right in his back." Once, while he and Elaine were still sharing the same house, truth spilling like stains everywhere between them, they had passed close together near the foot of the stairs and Resnick, unthinking, had reached to touch the soft skin inside her arm. He could picture now the hostility that had fired her eyes: the already instinctive recoiling.

The band hit the last note of "Some Enchanted Evening" more or less together and Resnick clapped, startling a few dazed pigeons. An elderly lady wheeling her shopping trolley across in front of the stage dropped a coin into the bass drum case that was collecting puddles and contributions towards the band's winter tour of Germany and the conductor announced the final number. Time to go, Resnick thought, but he stayed on as the two beginners lifted their instruments towards their lips. The conductor waved a hand encouragingly in their direction, the wind lifted their sheet music from its stand and their chance was lost. Without hesitation, the boy retrieved it and Resnick watched the girl's pinched serious face as, biting the inside of her mouth, she struggled to find her place in time for the next chorus. Only when they had played their sixteen bars and sat back, did Resnick turn away, tears, daft sod, pricking at his eyes.

STEPHEN HUNTER

Stephen Hunter was born in Kansas City, Missouri, in 1946, and graduated from Northwestern University in 1968. He worked for the *Baltimore Sun* starting in 1971 as a copy reader, feature writer, and book review editor, and eventually became its movie critic, a position he held until 1996, when he assumed the same role for the *Washington Post*. His film criticism was nominated for a Pulitzer Prize on several occasions, and he was a finalist in 1995 and again in 1996; he won the coveted award in 2003. Two volumes of his criticism have been published: *Violent Screen: A Critic's 13 Years on the Front Lines of Movie Mayhem* (1995) and *Now Playing at the Valencia: Pulitzer Prize–Winning Essays on Movies* (2005).

His first novel was *The Master Sniper* (1980), which was followed by *The Second Saladin* (1982), *The Spanish Gambit* (1985), and *The Day Before Midnight* (1989). *Point of Impact* (1993) introduced Bob Lee Swagger, also known as the Nailer. This was followed by *Dirty White Boys* (1994). Bob Lee's father, Earl, starred in three novels: *Hot Springs* (2000), *Pale Horse Coming* (2001), and *Havana* (2003).

Point of Impact was filmed as *Shooter* in 2007, starring Mark Wahlberg as Bob Lee Swagger. Directed by Antoine Fuqua, with a screenplay by Jonathan Lemkin, it also starred Kate Mara and Danny Glover.

Hunter is married and lives in Baltimore.

BOB LEE SWAGGER

BY STEPHEN HUNTER

ob Lee Swagger first dropped in on me sometime in 1990, possibly '91. I was sitting, as I reconstruct it, at the kitchen table, playing with plot ideas, of which I had exactly two, only one of which was technically mine. I had the second book due on a two-book contract for Bantam, and—all writers will know what I am talking about—there wasn't a lot of fuel in the tank.

It was night; the young family (I think I was young also) was asleep. Bob's arrival wasn't abrupt. I heard no voice, I saw no face, I read no body language. It's just that both plots involved somebody who knew a little something about shooting a rifle and watching someone drop.

The first plot was stolen—coldly and treacherously—from a book called *Death of a Thin-Skinned Animal,* which I never read, because if I did, I knew I'd steal more than the premise. Some Britisher wrote it and no other book, and the premise was brilliant—contained, resonant, full of fun things like retribution and righteous violence. A British army sniper is given a mission in Africa to take out a particularly nasty, obnoxious dictator. After he is dispatched and unrecallable, Whitehall affects a rapprochement with the nasty politician. Since nothing can be done to retrieve the sniper, he is betrayed. He is captured and disappears into the cruelty of the small dictatorship's prison system, for presumably appalling treatment unto execution. So it goes in the realpolitik of the world.

Five years later, the dictator, now a proud British ally, arrives for a state visit in London. One night at British Intelligence HQ, a message arrives in code five years old. Deciphered, it appears to be from the betrayed sniper. I will complete my mission, he advises. Complications ensue.

I would move the story to America, to Washington, with an old 'Nam sniper, USMC to the hilt, as the fall guy. I saw it exactly: a reluctant colleague has to hunt him down, but at every turn the old guy is smarter, faster, more creative. In fact, it's so good I may yet do it, though this time the older Bob will be the pursuer, not the shooter, and the shooter will be some young man out of three tours in Iraq, two with the Marines and another with private contractors. Only this time, I hope to have the moral strength to offer to pay royalties on the stolen bit of genius.

The other plot I was thinking about was vaguer, but at least it was my own. It was inspired by a story that had appeared in the *Baltimore Sun* magazine, by an old-boy reporter named Ralph Reppert, on a new theory of the Kennedy assassination. Like many—in fact like all—such theories, it was wrong, but the article had an arresting image. A rifleman stands on a platform in desolate, empty country (as had happened to Rep's subject at the H. B. White Ballistics Laboratory in Maryland). Before him, on a certain angle at a certain distance, is a convertible automobile, traveling at a precise speed. In the backseat are four dummies in a certain arrangement, signifying human targets. He must fire three shots in 6.3 seconds and hit the target in the rear right of the head. Rep's subject knew of course that he was replicating the behavior of Lee Harvey Oswald, but my imagination took off from the idea that the shooter had been conned into the tower and only by recognizing the angles and the speed and the nature of the shooting problem that confronted him did he realize he had been cast in the Oswald role and that the whole thing was meant to gull him into certain predictable behaviors.

In the end, I chose that, if only because it was mine, and began without much more of an idea. I just started typing and whenever I reached a stalling point, I invented a gunfight or a new major character. I had no idea I was changing my life forever, and for the next few years it seemed like the biggest mistake I ever made.

Point of Impact was a bitch to write—so many cuckoos to hide, and they had to pop out at just the right time. The book just got worse and worse. I wrote a two-hundred-page sequence set in the bayous of Louisiana and realized it had nothing to do with anything. I junked it. Ugh. Since I am congenitally lazy, seeing all that work disappear was a particularly crushing experience. I don't know where Nick Memphis came from; he was on no outline or note-to-self before the moment he appeared in the book. I don't even know where the name came from, and I have no idea what the derivation of "Memphis" would be. Is he an Egyptian or a Tennessean? I have no idea. He just showed up on a particularly desperate evening and kicked his way into the book and wouldn't leave. A good thing too.

The book's editor, a brilliant pro at Bantam named Ann Harris, later confided to me that she'd been really unimpressed with the first hundred or so pages of manuscript, until Nick arrived. Then, she observed, it picked up considerably, became more pointed, more incisive, more vigorous in its writing. Everywhere Nick appeared, the book worked; everywhere he didn't, ZZZZZZ.

And I know why ZZZZZZ was the appropriate response. It was all Bob Lee Swagger's fault.

Bob Lee, of course, drifted in from Charles Henderson's *Marine Sniper*, which told the story of the great Marine sniper Carlos Hathcock. Henderson's book is well written and gripping, of course, but it is more than that: it somehow communicates the psychological weight—you might even say spiritual weight—that a sniper carries everywhere. He is, after all, not the designated marksman but the designated killer. He is the one who sees through a 10-power magnifier the impact of 168 grains of metal going at 2,000 feet per second, the tiny hole it drills as it enters, the dam it breaks as it exits, followed by the slow, graceless tumble to earth. I was fascinated by that act, and I was horrified by it, but most of all I was horrified by my fascination with that act.

The facts on Carlos Hathcock were straightforward: career Marine NCO from Arkansas, two tours in 'Nam, the first as an MP. It was during the second, after he had won the Wimbledon Cup (that is, the national thousand-yard shooting match), that he became a sniper and achieved ninety-three kills. He became known as the leading sniper in Vietnam (it turned out, much later, that he wasn't); he also, at least according to Henderson, pulled off some special-ops missions, such as taking out a VC general and, on one occasion, ambushing a VC platoon and killing everyone in it, both brilliant feats of arms. But he suffered two grievous wounds during his year of hunting men. The first was psychological: he lost one of his most gifted spotters, a young man named Johnny Burke. Then he himself was burned seriously when a vehicle he was in detonated a mine. Heroically, he helped get men out of the wrecked and blazing thing even though he was hurt. Later—and why later? another story—he was granted a Silver Star for the effort.

So there was Bob Lee: from Arkansas, professional Marine NCO, a supremely brave and efficient sniper with a couple of spectacular feats of arms that became legendary, then seriously wounded in mind—his lost spotter—and body—the burns. I saw him in a bitter exile, alone and aloof, a recovered drunk, and I knew the emotional trajectory of the book would be his eventual reentry into society, his discovery of love, his engagement, his realization that there were still things worth fighting for. All that was in the first aimless, tortured draft.

And it was awful.

Bob was not alive.

The problem, I realized eventually, had to do with what artists call the "living line" as opposed to the "dead line." A "dead line" is a tracing. It renders a reasonable facsimile of the shape of a thing, but it represents no engagement of the imagination of the artist. It is not spontaneous, surprising, independent. It's just dumbly there; that's all. And that's what I had, this crude tracing of Carlos Hathcock laboriously inserted into an unruly thousand pages of manuscript. (I am sparing you the tales of my technical tribulations and the disk I managed to embalm in jelly as I struggled through my first book written on computer, so there is some mercy in the world.) Bob Lee had all of the Carlos benchmarks, but he was as cold and dull as a stone.

People say to me: "Bob Lee Swagger? Carlos Hathcock, right?" Well, yes and no. The key to Bob Lee Swagger turned out to be not all the places he intersected with Carlos Hathcock, but all the places he deviated from him. It was in the act of breaking away from Carlos Hathcock that he became a freestanding portrait of a complex man, worthy and capable of sustaining an elaborate narrative.

As I reimagined him, I came up with a figure that I suspect the actual Carlos Hathcock wouldn't recognize. I saw him as a kind of Faustian intellectual of war. He had seen things and done things and learned things that no man before ever had. But it was at great cost: his self-removal from society, his self-inflected deadness of soul. I gave him outward manifestations of these turmoils: he became an ex-drunk, and his drunkenness (I know a little about this) had not been the merry, charming kind full of bon mots and toasts and scintillating wit; no, it was dark, surly, violent, self-lacerating, maybe even killing. And thus his greatest victory hadn't been over the North Vietnamese (I gave him a score of 87, because I wanted it clear to people who knew these things that I wasn't offering him as "better" than Carlos), but over himself, in putting that behind him.

I also wanted him to have processesed what had happened to him, to have thought rigorously about it, to have tried to make some sense of it. So I had him essentially reinvent himself through vigorous reading. Up in his trailer in the Ouachitas, he started reading about Vietnam and from that he expanded to reading about war in general and took himself through Homer's *Iliad* and Thucydides' *History of the Peloponnesian War,* all the way to Hemingway, Mailer, and the writers of our time. He was hungry for context, and he saved himself from the self-destructive impulses of the darkest parts of his soul by putting the thoughts and experiences of other warriors between him and those black dogs of depression, self-doubt, anger, and loneliness.

Then there was Arkansas. I knew nothing about it, absolutely nothing, except that as I was writing, some politician from down there was trying to become president. I had never heard of him, hardly heard of it.

I originally sited Swagger in and around Berryville, in northeastern Arkansas, not far from Branson in Missouri and the Ozarks. I chose Berryville because the only thing I knew about Arkansas was that a gunsmith-visionary named Bill Wilson had founded a customized .45 automatic shop there, so in some ways Berryville was a kind of capital of gun culture. So I took a trip down there, and no man has ever traveled to Arkansas more full of romantic possibility and hope. But when I arrived, I have to say, I was disappointed. Berryville was fine, but it was set in the middle of something far worse than nowhere: somewhere. The somewhere was called country musicville. It was all twangy and cornpone; the Arkansas I encountered had been trivialized and sentimentalized and, worst of all, made quaint and cute. I just couldn't see it as a warrior's birthplace.

Dejected, I drove down 71. My destination was Dallas, where I meant to do some JFK research, as at that point, the JFK assassination was part of the book. I suddenly came upon, totally unexpected and unanticipated, the Ouachitas, a magnificent splurge of mountains roaming east and west across Polk County and Oklahoma. I didn't know it was in those mountains that Charles Portis had set his magnificent *True Grit,* but here at last was landscape to match my man. Once I'd found that, I knew I'd found something.

Two other elements I should mention here.

As discreetly as possible, I should point out that on this trip I was not alone. I was with a woman who would later become my wife, and the theme of a man being drawn out of disappointment and solitude and despair by the love of a good woman was something I truly felt and that filled me with hope and joy and pleasures I never thought I'd have. I tried to get that into the book too, in the relationship between Bob and his savior, Julie.

Now, embarrassed, I leave that paragraph to stand alone and move on to another love: rifles. I wanted this to be a rifle book. I was—and always have been, as readers surely all know by now—a gun crank. Gun nut? Is that what you want to call it? Gun buff, gun guy, gunnie, gunner, shooter, Mr. Saturday Night Special, something or other. Well, call it what you wish, but the truth is, the firearm has always, always been a reliable provocateur of my imagination. I even remember when it started. I think it was 1954; I was staying up late, illegally, watching *Dragnet.* My father was out doing something stupid and ugly and drunken, no doubt. My mother was fretting and feeling sorry for herself, and I was watching Joe Friday and Ben Smith hunt down some kind of killer in the San Fernando Valley. Or maybe it wasn't the valley; I don't know: some tract house in a dreary far-flung LA burg. But I do remember when Joe and Ben located the suspect, and under Joe's instructions, Ben called it in to HQ. Joe told Ben, "And tell 'em to bring plenty of .45s for the machine guns. It looks like he wants to go all the way."

He did want to go all the way. He came out of the house pistols blazing, there to run into Sergeant Friday, that icon of '50s righteousness, with his Thompson submachine gun, and Joe spoke for civilization when he blew the guy out of his socks. In any event, the next day I sat down with a piece of paper and a pencil and applied myself and in an hour had drawn a respectable silhouette of a "Fifty Caliber Thompson Submachinegun," as I labeled it, making it, at .50, bigger than Joe's! At that point, firearms entered my imagination formally, and I began to read about them, to notice them on TV and in movies, to dream about them—and to draw them. All my schoolbooks were inscribed with detailed side views, copiously labeled: "Thompson submachine gun M-1928, .45 caliber" or "M-1 Carbine" or ".45 automatic." I conspicuously sought out cap guns that were accurate in their representation, and if I found a cap gun that seemed accurate but whose typology I did not recognize, I tracked it down. In 1956, at the age of ten, I became a subscriber to *Guns* magazine and drank up every word.

Of course today such behavior would get me a daily Ritalin cocktail (or stronger), a permanent appointment with a shrink, and entry onto the school district's watch list, but nobody then thought it was particularly weird, and I must say this: it was fun. God, it was a pleasure to lose myself among the sweeps and curves and struts and screws of the various creations, to puzzle over the subtlety of line. It was so strange. In time I became a passingly good draftsman of the firearm from the 90-degree perspective, and even occasionally tilted them to 45 degrees, to suggest weight and solidity. I could draw anything except—true to this day—a Colt Peacemaker. For some reason, Colonel Colt's genius eluded me: I could never capture the nuance of the curves, the subtle orchestration of the variation between the grip curve, the receiver curve, and the trigger guard curve.

Regardless, that love of guns stayed with me, except for a brief, delusional period in the early '70s when I called myself a liberal and held myself superior to gun culture. But it always beckoned and I always knew it was my true faith, and one of the things that let me progress from wanting to write to writing was acknowledgment of guns' deep import to me and their power to stir my imagination to its most expressive. Still, I really had never shot much and hadn't actually bought a gun until just a few years previous, when I was working on *The Day Before Midnight,* a gun-rich commando novel.

I knew that to make a sniper real I had to make the rifle real, and to make the rifle real I had to shoot it, clean it, take it apart, carry it, make it a part of my life. So I bought as near as I could get to a Marine sniper rifle. It was a Remington 700 in .308, the police model with a heavy bull barrel, plain-Jane it its bluntness and simplicity, with no aspirations toward style or beauty. (This was also a part of my conspicuous separation from Carlos Hathcock, as he'd done all his shooting in Vietnam with a Winchester Model 70.) I mounted a Leupold 10X scope on it, as had the Marines in Vietnam (though theirs were Redfields, but still 10Xs). And I went out to the Marriottsville Road shooting range about five miles north of my house in Columbia, and I shot . . . and I shot . . . and I shot. I learned immediately that everything I'd seen in the movies was fake. I learned, first of all, how hard it was. I learned how subtle it was, how you had to find the strength and yet the suppleness to turn your body to structure, to be tight in some places and loose in others, and you had to take command of your breathing. You had to master your heart and mind, in other words, and if you couldn't, you'd never be any good at it.

I was never any good at it, though in time I became close to adequate. However, the excitement of learning somehow alchemized my writing into something truer. I was aware that the process had never been accurately portrayed in a book, and I thought if I could get that right, I'd have something different, at least.

Finally, there was courage. Bob, I knew, would be brave. He would be one of those rare men (wholly, wildly unlike me, I hasten to add) who could face enemy fire stoically, figure it out as a problem in higher calculus, and work swiftly and efficiently to counter it. It wasn't that he wasn't afraid; it was that he had learned to deal with his fear, or that he had a motive so overpowering that it vanquished his fear. And what would that motive be?

I studied the biographies of war heroes to determine what made them so brave. In the case of officers (that is, leaders), it was a belief in cause and system, a fear of not letting others down, a sense of responsibility. But that's not what would drive a sniper. He's alone, on his own, out there in Indian country. No one knows if he's brave or not; he really answers only to himself. What drives him? I had to find out, because I was determined to create the whole man, and I didn't want to just declare him brave and let it go at that, as happens routinely in B movies and novels.

Ultimately, I hit upon another creature of tremendous will and attainment, who was nevertheless thorny, difficult, even repulsive. I hit upon Tyrus Raymond Cobb. It's part of my attraction to difficult men that I like Ty Cobb. Yes, I know: racist, sexist, violent, outsider to the end, vicious, vengeful, tough as brass bushings, relentless, unpleasant, ultimately spurned by everyone. But his backstory is very interesting. When he was nineteen years old and had just signed his first professional-baseball contract, his mother murdered his father in her bedroom with a shotgun. Her lover was in bed with her. Ty Cobb loved his father, a prominent Georgia lawyer, seen by all as a fair, kind, brilliant, just man. He felt immensely cheated by the fact that his father never saw him play ball professionally, and he was shattered at the squalid circumstances of his father's death, so small in comparison to the attainments of the man himself. Nevertheless, he paid for his mother's defense and saw her get off as not guilty, pleading that she thought it was an intruder at the window.

I decided to give Bob a similar dynamic—a brilliant father,

snatched from him early in squalid circumstances that were no match for the accomplishments of the man, so that the haunted son would miss his father greatly and spend his life trying to live up to the man's brilliance. He would be a man who idealized his father, never having learned that his father was just a man, with his own foibles and flaws.

I remember one night, sitting in the Columbia house, just typing out a paragraph without a lot of thought. I have no idea where it came from. I wrote of—hmm, what's a good Southern-sounding name?—oh yeah, Earl, yeah, that's it, Earl. Let's make Earl a Marine too, and, oh, I know, this'll be cool, let's have him win the Medal of Honor on Iwo Jima; in fact, let's have him fight his way across the Pacific, island to bloody island, killer, hero, Marine, a man of legend. Oh, then he comes back and becomes a state policeman. Now let's have him killed ten years later in a squalid cornfield by two white-trash skanks with those dog-of-the-South names, I know, we'll call them Jimmy and Bub Pye; there you go. Achilles slain by two Yocums, or Snopeses. Yeah.

I typed it up and forgot all about it.

And yet, when I was finished—years later, it seemed—that's what stayed with me. Achilles felled in the corn, two worthless punks crowing. It was so sad; I just had to know more, and the only way to learn it was to write it. And that's what I did. As for Bob Lee and *Point of Impact,* there's not much more to tell. Once I had him, I had the book. Everything else more or less happened in the time it should have happened. There was a last, desperate rewrite, where I solved another narrative problem by breaking a single villain into two, one Colonel Ray Shreck, ex–Green Beret, and the other Hugh Meachum, CIA executive and espionage entrepreneur extraordinaire. (Somehow they became Danny Glover and Ned Beatty in the movie. Go figure!)

Yet, when it was done, published to good reviews but disappointing sales, I found that Bob and his father, Earl, would not go away. I tried to banish them, for until then I had taken craftsman's pride in not repeating myself. But they wouldn't go away, and I had to write another book. And then another. And then . . . My life's work had arrived, and I was the last to know it.

FAYE KELLERMAN

Born in 1952 in Saint Louis, Missouri, Faye Kellerman graduated from UCLA with a bachelor of arts degree in theoretical mathematics in 1974. Four years later, she received her doctorate of dental surgery, although she has never practiced dentistry. She is an Orthodox Jew, as is her husband, bestselling mystery novelist Jonathan Kellerman. The Kellermans are the only husband and wife writers ever to appear on the bestseller list of the *New York Times* simultaneously for two separate books. Jewish themes and characters are frequent and important elements of most of her novels.

In addition to the much-loved novels about Peter Decker and Rina Lazarus, she has written two nonseries mysteries—*The Quality of Mercy* (1989), a historical thriller, and *Moon Music* (1998), a serial-killer novel set in Las Vegas—the short-story collection *The Garden of Eden and Other Criminal Delights,* and two books with her husband, *Double Homicide* (2004) and *Capital Crimes* (2006). *Stalker* (2000) and *Street Dreams* (2003) feature police officer Cindy Decker.

The Kellermans live in Beverly Hills and have four children, one of whom, Jesse, is also a successful mystery writer.

PETER DECKER AND RINA LAZARUS

BY FAYE KELLERMAN

O ne of the most frequently asked questions that I have fielded over my twenty-two years as a published crime fiction writer is: how much of me is in my characters? More specifically, how much am I like the female protagonist of my series, Rina Lazarus? I've answered this question hundreds of times, and usually I respond with the following: I am not Rina Lazarus. Rina Lazarus is a fictional entity that I've created. She is not based on a single representation but a composite of my experiences and my imagination. Then I add: all of my characters have Faye Kellerman in them. How it could be otherwise? They all come from my unique and sometimes subconscious process of blending fact and fiction, real and imaginary.

But the response does beg the question: how much of me is Rina Lazarus? I find it amusing and not unpredictable that people rarely ask: how much am I like my male series character, Peter Decker? More often than not, Peter takes the starring role in my novels, so if there is any character who is a manifestation of me, why wouldn't it be Decker?

To answer the question honestly and completely, I'd like to go back to the origins of Peter and Rina. Where did they come from?

Who were they before they appeared in fiction and how have they evolved?

To best respond, I need to reconsider my first *published* novel, *The Ritual Bath,* where Peter and Rina made their debuts. I've italicized the word *published* because at the time, I didn't know that *The Ritual Bath* was going to be my first novel. I had made a few attempts at writing and was now trying to pen a story that would be interesting, entertaining, and, most important, would capture the eye of some farsighted editor. But the characters didn't come from thin air. To help you understand the biographies of Peter and Rina, I'm going to give you a little background about the author.

As a young child, I had a vivid imagination. Most kids do, but mine seemed to last a little longer and to be just a tad more florid than those of most children. I not only had imaginary friends, I had them in many different locales and diverse centuries. My friends were Greek goddesses of mythology, dames from medieval Europe, turn-of-the-century Boston blueblood girls in boarding schools, barefoot Okies from the dustbowl, and prisoners in concentration camps. Anything I heard or saw was re-created, enhanced, and then acted out in private. My "friends" and I went through a slew of adventures, and all before I reached school age.

School.

Nothing quite kills a fertile imagination like rote learning. No one is saying that times tables aren't important, but how could such humdrum triviality compete with all my terrific escapades? Nonetheless, school is a necessary evil, and at the age of six I started first grade. And that's when I discovered that although I had an elaborate imagination, I was saddled with a brain that had a hard time integrating letters with phonetics. Reading was difficult because I couldn't sound out words. I learned how to read English the same way I learned how to read music—by sight-reading. In actuality, I learned how to read music before I learned how to read words. And, as I did with the notes on a scale, I had to memorize words in order to get my brain to properly translate what my eye saw. To do this, I resorted to a number of memorization and mnemonic tricks. I recall that I could easily identify the word *look* because of the two O's that in my six-year-old mind resembled two wide eyes. My dyslexia stalled my reading for a while, but luckily I was compensated with a facility with numbers. I always say in my talks that I could work with *X, Y,* and *Z* as long as the letters weren't strung together to make words. I did not like English. I did not like writing papers and essays. I did like creative writing, but so little of that is done in school that my preference didn't matter much. As far as learning, I took the path of least resistance and was a math major in high school and college, graduating from UCLA with a BA in theoretical mathematics in 1974.

My next incarnation was in dental medicine. I attended UCLA Dental School and graduated in 1978 fully intending to practice dentistry, but fate had other plans. Jesse Oren Kellerman was delivered about two and a half months after I graduated. I don't know what I was thinking when I thought I'd be up on my feet a week after birth. I must have been on another planet when I thought I could easily integrate career and children. I had to learn on my own that babies are a lot of work. This was a revelation to me. For the first six months of my son's life, I couldn't figure out why I couldn't get anything done other than to take care of the little rascal. It helped to know people in the same situation, but as I had always been a competent person and prided myself on being organized to the point of compulsive, I felt I should be doing better.

By the time I finally reached some kind of equilibrium, Jess was around six months old. I was able to brush my teeth, shower, and get dressed all before noon. I was learning how to become a functional person at the same time my son was becoming a person. He was a lot of work, but with that work was the joy of seeing a human being develop. He was a happy little guy—amusing and engaging—and we had a really good time together. As he grew older, he was very responsive and made my life easier by being an early talker. I decided to put off my illustrious career in dentistry in favor of motherhood and I kept telling myself that I'd soldier on with dentistry just as soon as Jesse was in school.

But then I got pregnant again. By the time Rachel came around, I had come to grips with the fact that I was not just postponing dentistry, I was shelving it. It was an easy decision in some ways, but a very hard one in others. I felt I was wasting years of education and letting my profession down. But at the time, dentistry wasn't calling my name, and honestly, no one from the ADA has ever phoned me and asked, "Where the heck are you?" It seems that dentistry has gotten along just fine without me.

So I went about the business of raising a family. Now, anyone who has ever spent long periods with a child knows that there's a lot of down time—pushing a swing, taking a walk, watching your child play at the park.

The mind abhors a vacuum.

Presented with blocks of time without speaking, my brain began to spark and fill in the blanks. In my head, I listed chores that needed to be done. I planned dinner menus. I considered baby gyms and music classes. I was expected to be thinking about all those things. What I didn't expect was to be making up stories again.

My imaginary friends awoke from the dormancy caused by twenty years of education. They began to make their big-screen comebacks in my head, only this time they materialized in adult form. I began to invent new adventures, more daring quests, more racy and passionate love stories, darker fables, and elusive murder mysteries. Once again, the chief protagonist in all my stories was some kind of Faye Kellerman facsimile, but at twenty-six, I knew better than to act out the stories aloud as I had done as a kid. They put adults away for those kinds of things. I kept all my buddies inside because I felt that there was something a little off with me: making up stories when you're a wife, a mother, and supposedly a sane person. I firmly believe that I would have left my tales deep inside my gray matter *if* I had been married to anyone other than Jonathan Kellerman.

Unlike me, Jonathan was a natural-born writer. I think he emerged from his mother's womb with pen in hand. When I met Jon, I was eighteen. We married a year and a half later, both of us still wet-behind-the-ears kids and very much unformed. Jonathan not only saw me through college and dental school, but elected to go to graduate school in Los Angeles because I didn't want to move from there. Jonathan graduated with a PhD in clinical psychology from USC at the tender age of twenty-four. My husband was a true Renaissance man, with many interests and hobbies, and one of his extracurricular passions was writing. If he saw me through college, I saw him through nine novels, all of them eventually relegated to boxes in storage. His attempts taught him a lot. They taught me what it meant to persevere and how much fun it was to write. Yes, he cared that his novels weren't getting published, but it didn't deter him a whit from writing. It was almost as if writing were an addiction.

Then one day it suddenly dawned on me what he was doing. He was taking his imaginary friends and putting them down on paper and calling himself a writer. If he was brave enough to do that and strong enough to suffer through one rejection after another, what in the world did I have to lose by putting my imaginary friends on paper too? And the timing was perfect. He was on the brink of breaking through into the publishing business. Had he been the monster bestseller that he is today, I would have been much too intimidated to try to write.

Another husband might have been outright discouraging. Another husband might have been encouraging in a discouraging way. Jonathan, bless him, was only encouraging. As the premier author in the family, he was helpful and straightforward, straddling the difficult lines between tutor, critic, and husband. The nights weren't always easy, but the conversation was always honest.

As with a lot of neophyte writers, my first attempts were competently written but went nowhere. The stories dragged, the characters didn't develop, the sense of place was wanting. It was good that my initial forays into fiction never saw the light of day, but all those hours of writing bad stories weren't for nothing. I considered the four-to-five-year experience a protracted course in writing fiction. I had Jonathan's input, but I still had to act as my own student, teacher, editor, and critic.

The main thing was that I discovered my love for writing. It was cathartic, it was an outlet for my zany imagination, and it gave me something to do. I wrote notebooks full of novels, stories, and plays, but deep inside, I knew I was spinning my wheels. It's certainly okay to indulge in creative outbursts, but if I had any hopes of getting published—of having my works out there to be read and critiqued—I had to be a little more thoughtful about what I put down on paper.

I began to think about what I was doing right and what I was doing wrong. Equally significant, I began to wonder what I wanted to write about. That meant structure.

I needed a plot.

In the '70s and '80s, to have a strong story line was somewhat anathema and was eschewed in modern literature. Plot was for chumps, a crutch used in genre writing. But since I wasn't an English major in college and since I didn't follow the vagaries of the literary world, I didn't know that. Plot just appealed to my sensibilities as a mathematician. Well-crafted stories had beginnings, middles, and ends, and propelled the reader forward from the first page to the last. I considered plot to be a good thing. This revelation dovetailed nicely with the kinds of books I liked to read—mystery and suspense novels.

Jonathan had introduced me to Ross Macdonald. He had found *The Zebra-Striped Hearse* in a used-book store near work, and we began to systematically devour many of the best "hard-boiled" writers—Ross Macdonald, Raymond Chandler, John D. MacDonald, James M. Cain, Dashiell Hammett . . . the list was long and impressive.

My choice was clear. I decided to write crime novels, and my timing couldn't have been better. There was a growing renaissance of mystery writing in the '70s and '80s. Joseph Wambaugh and Evan Hunter writing as Ed McBain were pumping out some of the best police procedurals in the business. Elmore Leonard and Donald Westlake had switched over from Westerns to capers and mysteries. There were others: Arthur Lyons, Lawrence Block, Sue Grafton, Sara Paretsky, Linda Grant, Stephen Greenleaf, all of them giving the murder mystery their unique spin.

To me that was the key: to make the murder mystery genre my own, I needed to give my book a *voice.* I needed a narration that told the reader that this was a different kind of suspense novel from a new author named Faye Kellerman. I felt that I could put my imprimatur on my story only if I wrote from a point of expertise, i.e., if I wrote what I knew. The problem was, at thirty-two, I didn't know all that much. I had gotten married at nineteen and had spent most of my adult life being a wife, a mother, a daughter, and a student. I could probably figure out a good plot, but who would my characters be? What could I take from myself that would give my novel an exclusive punch? Who was I and what could I do to set myself apart?

———

Knowing that I wanted to write a mystery novel was a good first step, but I still had to figure out who would people my deliciously intricate plot. I had to start thinking about who I was so I could develop a flesh-and-blood protagonist.

First, I considered the fact that I was female. That was more relevant than you might think, because in the early '80s, women PIs were coming into their own. I thought about writing from the perspective of a woman PI—I certainly admired Sue Grafton and Sara Paretsky—but I had been married for a very long time. As a wife and mother, I didn't see myself as chasing down bad guys and wielding a gun, so the idea of writing a character like that really didn't strike a chord.

Second, I was a dentist. Now, there had been lots of dentists in film and literature, but I struggled to remember the name of any dentist portrayed as a hero. My recollection was that the characterization of fictional dentists usually revolved around their being sadists, louts, or geeks. Although I was sure I could imbue my dentist with sterling qualities, I thought the profession lacked the sexy image that might be needed to interest an editor.

I vetoed a dental protagonist.

Last, I was a Jew.

My Judaism has always been important to me, and I have always loved the rites and traditions of my religion. I was raised in a Conservative home, but we bordered on traditional Orthodoxy. The term used today for my kind of observance is Conservadox. We always kept a kosher home, and we were somewhat Sabbath observant. We didn't cook, sew, or clean on Saturday, nor did we wash clothing or turn on a vacuum. But we did turn on lights and watch TV. My father had come from an Orthodox home and was a native Yiddish speaker. He added a little of the Old Country to our lives. I loved watching my mother light Shabbos candles. I loved going to synagogue on Friday nights and eating stale sponge cake and drinking flat soda in the social hall. I loved cleaning the house for Passover with my mother and buying boxes of matzo—bread dough that has been baked for no longer than eighteen minutes to prevent it from rising. (My mother used to call it hemstitched cardboard.) I didn't even mind fasting for Yom Kippur. I fasted earlier than was religiously required because I wanted to prove to myself that I could do it.

Judaism was such an integral part of my being that I had no real sense of self without it. This affiliation was only fortified when I met Jonathan, who was an observant Jew. For me, the change from Conservadox to Orthodoxy was more like a small step than a giant leap. I liked praying in an Orthodox synagogue—it was what I was used to—and it didn't bother me not to watch TV on Saturday. As I got older, the prohibition against using electricity became a boon rather than a burden.

As I thought about my Judaism and how much it had made me who I was, I began to wonder if I shouldn't make my characters Jewish. If I wanted to write about what I knew, it was a good start for my books to have Jewish content, and what better way than to have my protagonist be an Orthodox Jewish woman? But how would that play in Peoria? Would it be too limiting for the average reader?

I thought about that for a while. Since I enjoyed reading novels that took me into other worlds, I figured that there had to be readers out there who would enjoy learning about religious Jews. There had been some precedent for Jews starring in novels. For me, Chaim Potok was a tremendous source of inspiration. *The Chosen* had been one of the most successful novels of its day because it provided a peek into an ultra-religious life.

But Potok wasn't a crime fiction writer.

Harry Kemelman had penned a very successful mystery series centered on a crime-solving rabbi. The books were informative, but they were also as much about temple politics as they were about murder. The series was far from the crime novels that I had found so compelling.

I narrowed down my definitions. I wanted to write about a Jewish woman in a religious enclave but somehow integrate this into the style of an LA crime novel. That meant darker, deeper suspense fiction. Would it make sense for my religious Jewish woman to run around exposing herself to danger and mayhem to solve a crime? Would it be too artificial to have her chasing clues and outsmarting the police? Might it be better if she was involved in the crime in some way but left the actual nuts and bolts of *solving* the crime to someone else?

Enter the professional.

To do the grunt work, I needed a police detective or a private eye. I chose the former because it was easier and faster to get a police detective involved in a capital crime. Private eyes have to be solicited, whereas the police are the first line of attack when trying to solve a homicide. I could have included a female detective, but I chose a male for contrast. And as long as I had a man and woman, well, what can I say? I'm a sucker for romance. (Which is why Peter was divorced and Rina was a widow.) You have to remember that I had no idea that this was going to be the first novel in a series. I was trying to throw in as much as I could to maybe attract an editor.

This is how Peter Decker and Rina Lazarus first made their public appearance. But to truly understand them, let's look into their backgrounds.

———

My characters talk, and I transcribe what they say. I actually hear dialogue as conversation in my head. When I don't get the words down correctly, my characters correct me. They repeat their conversation to make sure I heard it right. It's as if I have a tape recording of what they say, and when I make a mistake, I put the tape recorder on rewind and listen again.

"I would never say that," Decker tells me more often than not. "You're translating my words like a woman. Understand that I am a six-foot-four, 220-pound man. Write it over."

"You're swearing," Rina tells me all the time. "I don't swear, and even on the rare occasions that I might use foul language, I wouldn't use *those* words in *that* situation."

I met Rina before Peter because we had the most in common, specifically our Judaism. By way of introduction, she said to me, "I am Rina Lazarus and I know you very well. Probably a lot better than you know me."

I told her to go on.

She said, "I know you like reading novels that introduce you to all sorts of people and places. For those two or three hours, you like to be whisked away into an alternate universe involving people of different religions and ethnicities—Catholic priests, American Indians—on the racetracks, in the heart of the Deep South. I bet there are people out there who might enjoy reading and learning about our customs and religion as much as you like reading and learning about other customs and religions. Although we're not exactly alike, we have much in common. Why don't you write a story that includes me?"

"Who are you?" I asked her.

"Write me into a story and I'll let you know."

I agreed. When Rina first started talking to me, I felt that although she was smart and pretty, she was overly analytical and a little bossy. But that was before I got to know her well. So I decided that it wasn't enough for Rina to tell me who she was going to be in my story, she also had to let me know who she was before I met her.

Rina Miriam Elias, born Regina Elias, is a child of Holocaust survivors. Her parents, Magda Laslow and Stefan Elias, were born in Budapest, Hungary, and were transported to Birkenau-Auschwitz in 1943, roughly a year and a half before the end of the war in Europe. They knew each other very briefly before the war, and they met again in the camps. Magda worked in the kitchen and helped her husband-to-be survive by stealing food and sneaking it to him. It was a very big risk. Had she had been caught, she would have been put to death immediately.

After the war, Magda and Stefan were sent to a DP camp in Cyprus. They married there and emigrated to the United States two years later, sponsored by Magda's uncle. Eventually, they settled in Southern California and went about the business of making a living and raising a family. Stefan went into the "schmata" business, manufacturing clothing for Sears, Penney's, and later for Target. He did very well, allowing him to send his three children to private religious school. Rina's older brother, David, is an ophthalmologist and lives back east with his wife and their children. Her middle brother, née Scott now Shlomo, lives in a religious area of Tel Aviv, Israel, and he and his wife have seven children.

Rina was the youngest child and only daughter, a beautiful little girl with thick black hair and bright blue eyes, just like her mother. She was a daddy's girl with an impish sense of humor, but she was always a bit on the serious side. She grew up in a Conservative home, she was a spiritual girl, and was greatly influenced by her religious day school training. When she was only eighteen, she married, even though her parents were very disapproving at her taking such a permanent step at such a young age.

But at least they liked the boy.

Yitzchak Lazarus was smart, handsome, and very idealistic. Within a year of their marriage and at Rina's urging, the couple packed up their belongings and moved to a religious outpost in Kiryat Arba in the Judean and Samarian area of Israel. Within two years, they had two sons, Shmuel and Yaakov. Life was not only hard on an outpost of civilization, it was dangerous. The area was surrounded by enemies. To prevent the infiltration of suicide bombers, the vast acreage was enclosed with barbed wire, and when the men of the community weren't learning Talmud, they were doing guard duty. Just a simple trip into Jerusalem to buy food and supplies was a perilous trek. The rigors of life finally began to take a toll, and a few years later, Yitzchak and Rina moved back to the States.

Yitzchak and Rina were still committed to an ultra-religious Jewish life. Since Yitzchak was from New York, they debated moving to the East Coast, where he could study at any one of the many fine established yeshivot, or seminaries. But then Yitzchak heard of a new yeshiva called Ohavei Torah in the North San Fernando Valley in California. It was headed by Rabbi Aaron Schulman, who was not only a renowned scholar but also a dynamic human being. The community was built in the middle of a large area of undeveloped land and bordered by mountains. The rural setting appealed to Yitzchak. He had grown up in Brooklyn and after two years in the wilderness of Israel, he wasn't anxious to go back to city living. He was also very considerate of his young wife. He thought it might help her if she was a little closer to her parents.

About a year into his studies, Yitzchak began to get headaches. Rina pressed him to go to a doctor, and when he did, the news was devastating. He had an inoperable brain tumor. Within a few years he passed on, and at the age of twenty-four, Rina was a widow with two young sons to care for.

There is no role or place for a single woman in the community of a yeshiva, which is essentially a men's college of Torah learning. Rina had made friends with some of the married women, but now that she was single, she was the odd one out. Although couples continued to be polite, most social interaction revolved around Rina inviting people to her home for one of the two main Sabbath meals or someone inviting her to eat with them. She had a few girlfriends, but without Yitzchak, she felt awkward and alone. She knew she didn't belong, but with no college education and no real skills, she had nowhere else to go—except back home with her parents. It was a move she considered until Rabbi Schulman insisted that she stay at the yeshiva in order to regain her equilibrium.

The kindly rabbi, or rav, told her to remain in her house on the premises for as long as she wanted. This way, while she was formulating a life plan, her children could continue to go to school at the yeshiva. In exchange for room and board, Rina would help with day care of the younger children and she could also run the yeshiva's ritual bath, or mikvah.

For the next two years, she settled down into a bland, monotonous, loveless life. Though many couples tried to set her up with other religious men, nothing clicked. After a year of shidduch dating—matchmaking—she gave up altogether and went about the business of raising her sons without a father.

Then one night while Rina was working in the mikvah, the unthinkable happened. A woman walking back to her house was abducted into the thick brush surrounding the yeshiva and raped. The unfortunate woman, Libba Sarah, was traumatized but managed to escape with her life. When Rina found her, she was dazed. Rina took her back into the mikvah and immediately called her husband, Zvi, who wasn't home. The second call Rina made was to Rabbi Schulman, who was teaching a class. The third call was to the police.

Enter Detective Peter Decker.

An oldest child in every sense of the word, Decker was a natural leader. With his can-do, take-charge attitude combined with his obsessive nature, he could have been a CEO for any major corporation. He could have been a high-priced attorney raking in the big bucks. Instead he went into police work.

Adopted in infancy by Lyle and Ida Decker, salt-of-the-earth Baptists, Decker grew up in Gainesville, Florida, a university town near a lot of wide open space. When the boy turned four, the Deckers adopted a second son named Randall. The two boys were close and had a typical sibling relationship. The elder bossed around the younger, and the younger idolized the elder.

The Deckers had their roots in Kentucky and Tennessee, and

Peter's upbringing was decidedly homespun and miles away from the glittering Miami coastline. He was a tall and muscular kid with an easy personality that garnered him many friends—boys and girls. But he was also book smart and quick witted, and that made him a favorite with his teachers. He played football, he souped up engines on cars and raced them, he rode horses at his uncle's ranch, and he excelled at shop classes. He probably would have gone to a local community college if it hadn't been for the Vietnam War. It was never in Decker's plans to volunteer for the war, but when he was called up—saddled with a low lottery number—it never occurred to him to try to get out of military duty.

Two years in Southeast Asia, working as a medic on the front lines, changed him markedly. He grew from a lanky, carefree teen to a troubled man who had witnessed the worst of humanity. Two years later, at the end of his tour and at the age of twenty, he came back to civilization without a clue as to where he was going.

He could have gone back to college—he certainly wasn't much older than the average college freshman—but academics no longer interested him. Studies seemed sterile and pointless. Plus, the average student held little sympathy for veterans, calling them a variety of nasty epithets. He wasn't exactly a flag waver, but he had grown up with a sense of duty and loyalty and he couldn't understand why students were so angry with army vets even when they personally didn't believe in the war. It was a case of shooting the messenger.

Within weeks, Decker grew restless with people, and he suspected why this was so. Having lived through two years of horror and panic, he had gotten used to the adrenaline rush. After experiencing years of crises and stress, his heartbeat had gotten used to an accelerated pace. If an event didn't cause a rise in his blood pressure, it wasn't worth anything.

He thought about flight school. He had keen vision and good coordination, but flight school cost money, and there were loads of trained pilots coming out of the military. He considered racing cars, but the job market for professional drivers was very small. For lack of anything more attractive, he signed up with the police academy. It was a paramilitary organization—he was used to that—and at times, it was exciting. He had a keen sense of justice, so he figured why not put bad people behind bars? Six months later, he was a uniformed officer for the Gainesville Police Department.

The decision pleased his father but didn't sit too well with his mother, who felt her elder son had the capability to achieve much more, especially in the way of education. But that was Decker's decision, and he was not about to be swayed. As a concession to his mother, he agreed to take night classes at the local college and pursue an Associate of Arts degree.

The police in Gainesville had a full-time job on their hands. Although the university wasn't a hotbed of protest, in the late '60s and early '70s all universities had their elements of agitating students. One warm day near the start of the spring session, a particular sit-in became a raucous event that bordered on a riot. Arrests were made, including a California girl named Jan Cohen. She was outspoken and fiery in temperament and she told Peter Decker, her arresting officer, just what she thought of him and the Gainesville Police Department: the words were X-rated. Her lawyer father, Jack, quickly posted her bail and told her it was time for her to come back home to Los Angeles, wanting to keep an eye on his headstrong daughter.

Eventually Jan did return home, but not as her parents had envisioned. She brought with her a husband and a newborn who was the living embodiment of the statement that opposites attract, although the magnetism was all physical.

Jan and Peter had crossed paths in a local bar a few weeks after her arrest, but this time Decker was wearing civilian clothing. Both quickly decided that there were no hard feelings between them, and they struck up a conversation. Decker thought she was cute, and Jan was surprised that Decker wasn't a cretin. Neither thought that the relationship would ever progress beyond a couple of quick romps, but God had other plans. Jan became pregnant. Though distressed and conflicted, she opted for abortion. She made an appointment unbeknownst to anyone. This was her problem and she'd take care of it by herself.

A few days before the procedure, she ran into Decker by chance. To this day, she still can't recall why, but she told him about her plans. Jan expected Decker to support her, to be relieved that this was her decision. After all, they were both kids and they had very little in common. But Decker was raised in a pro-life household and though he didn't have a problem with abortion in general, he had a big problem with abortion of his child. He implored her not to act rashly, and immediately offered to marry her.

She refused, but at least agreed to think about it for another week . . . which turned into two weeks. She knew she was on the fence with her own feelings, and his passionate pleas gave her pause. By the time she started her second trimester, Jan couldn't bring herself to get rid of something with a beating heart. She finished out her term at Gainesville, had her baby six months later, and then the trio moved to Los Angeles.

They had no money, but Decker did have job experience. Since the times were turbulent and the police were considered the enemy, the LAPD was not inundated with applications. Decker quickly got a job in the North Valley, and he and Jan lived just a half hour away from Jan's parents. His mother-in-law was nice but reserved, and Decker's father-in-law turned out to be a terrific guy. The two of them hit it off immediately. Jack Cohen recognized Decker's innate intelligence and suggested that he go to college and law school at night to further his economic potential. When he offered to pick up the tab, Decker couldn't refuse. Jan and her mother seconded the motion. Being a lawyer's wife was much more appealing to Jan than being a cop's wife. Coming from a white-collar home, Jan was quick to remind Decker of everything they could have *if* he made more money.

Decker enrolled in Cal State Northridge and went on to take courses at a very expensive and non-accredited law school. It was then that Jan realized you should be careful what you wish for.

As a full-time police officer and a part-time student, Decker was always busy. With hours alone, Jan embraced motherhood and went about raising their daughter, Cynthia, an alert and active baby with a wide smile. In this way, Jan was able to stave off loneliness. And it worked until two years later, when Decker was upgraded to detective. Jan didn't think it was possible, but her husband's hours became even longer.

The two never saw each other. It seemed to Jan that Decker cared a lot more about police work than about being a lawyer, but she pushed those thoughts from her mind. Jan kept quiet and accepted her lot because she was waiting for the light at the end of the tunnel: the time that Decker would graduate law school, pass the bar, and become a lawyer. It was lucky for Jan that Decker was a good test taker. He passed the bar, albeit on his second try, and finally the couple celebrated with a champagne dinner—paid for by Jack Cohen. Of course it was decided that Decker would work in Jack's firm, doing estates and trusts. The work was clean and it had regular hours.

For Jan, her husband's new job was a blessing. Decker was actually able to make it home before Cindy went to bed, and for the first time, they could enjoy things as a family. His increase in salary allowed them to buy a house—Jack helping with the down payment—and the family quickly settled into life in suburbia.

Jan was happy, but Decker was not. Being a lawyer—especially an estate lawyer—bored him to tears. He toughed it out for a year or so, then abruptly announced that he was quitting the firm. He had decided to look for a job in the district attorney's office. Jan was not happy with the decision, but it was tolerable. Yes, there would be a decrease in salary, but an ambitious deputy DA could go on to become a private defense attorney. Some of those wound up printing money. Plus, Decker's experience as a cop would probably give him a leg up in understanding what went on in criminal justice.

There were no immediate spots available in the downtown division of the DA's office. Jan thought that Decker would work with her father until a spot opened up. Instead, he did the unthinkable.

He rejoined the LAPD.

Decker was lucky enough to find an opening as a Juvenile and Sex Crimes detective in his old stomping ground in the North Valley. When a position for a downtown DA opened, Decker conveniently forgot to apply until the deadline had passed. His unilateral decision permanently ruptured their marriage, although they slugged it out for another six years or so, with Decker turning a blind eye to the slow death of their union. When Jan found love in the arms of another man, Decker was forced to concede defeat. They divorced when Cindy was nine, Jan keeping the house and Decker moving into a small apartment that could barely contain his six-foot-four frame. After several years of scrimping and saving, he bought a horse ranch with acreage that led into public trails near the mountains. The best part was that it was only about twenty minutes from his work.

The house and the stalls were in serious disrepair, but Decker had nothing but time on his hands. It took him about two years to get the house and the stalls in decent condition. By the time he was done, he had three bedrooms—one for himself, one for Cindy, now thirteen, and one for an office—three baths, and a six-stall horse stable. He built a corral, planted some citrus groves, got himself a couple of horses, and began his new life as a gentleman rancher.

For the first time in his life, Decker experienced the delicious taste of freedom. When he didn't have Cindy every other Wednesday and on weekends, his nights were his own, and he felt like a kid again. He went out with his colleagues after work, going to bars and drinking too much. He dated lots of women and spent too much money. He worked extra hours and smoked too much. It's not that his newly found lifestyle wasn't fun for the next couple of years, but as he reached his midthirties, it began to wear a little thin. There were too many hangovers, too many cigarettes, and too many strange women in his life. He was in a rut. The problem was he didn't know how to get out of it until happenstance put him in line to catch the next sex crime call. The incident was a rape at Ohavei Torah.

———

Rina's telephoning the police became an immediate source of controversy and tension at the yeshiva. Almost everyone agreed that she should have waited to hear from Rabbi Schulman before she contacted the outside world. Rina never for a moment assumed that the yeshiva would want to handle it in-house only and without the police being involved. A terrible crime had been committed, and there was a rapist on the loose. Of course the police had to be brought in. And once the call was made, there was nothing anyone could do to put things in reverse. The crime became a police matter, and that was that.

Decker and his partner, Marge Dunn, arrived on the scene and began to divide up labor. Decker would interview the witnesses while Marge would talk to the victim. Both of them knew that the yeshiva was an isolated and provincial enclave, but neither was prepared for the closing of ranks that followed. It seemed that only the mikvah lady, Rina Lazarus, was willing to talk to the cops. Decker flattered himself that he was the reason that she took him into her confidence and helped him navigate the yeshiva world.

In truth, there was an initial physical attraction between the two of them, but Rina knew that having a relationship with someone not religious and probably not even Jewish was out of the question. But there was no denying kismet: the two were destined for each other. They talked and people whispered. The two of them danced around the issue of religion for a couple of years—and a couple of books— until finally they made a commitment to each other. Peter promised that he would try to live as a practicing Jew, and Rina promised that she would accept Peter as he was—an obsessive police detective who worked long and odd hours.

The two of them married between the novels *Milk and Honey* and *Day of Atonement*—off camera, so to speak. They decided on a quiet wedding because it was the second time around for both of them and there were children involved. After the wedding, Rina and her boys moved to Decker's ranch and started a new life there. The boys got along well with their stepfather, although he was very different from Yitzchak Lazarus. Rina got along with her stepdaughter, Cindy, by frequently playing the second girl in Decker's life. It was a blended family, not without its issues, but it functioned pretty well.

Having been a widow for years, Rina was used to having time alone and was self-sustaining. She didn't relish long nights by herself, but she could cope. She kept busy by raising her two sons. When she found she was pregnant, she was ecstatic.

Peter, on the other hand, had a much tougher time. His integration into Orthodoxy was a long and tough journey. Rabbi Schulman was kind enough to help him with classes and tutoring, but still there were many times when Peter felt he was backsliding, at least psychologically. Many times he was unhappy being part of a community with so many rituals and rules. And the fact that his parents disapproved of the union and of Peter's adoption of a new religion only made things worse. But even if he had been inclined to back out, Decker wouldn't have made the move. He was loyal, a man of his word, and he genuinely loved Rina and her boys. As soon as their daughter, Hannah Rose, was born, with Rina almost dying in the process, he knew he was in for the long run. He had made a promise and he'd fulfill it to the best of his capabilities.

The breakthrough in their relationship came when Peter sold the ranch and he and Rina bought a home together. It signified a new start that didn't carry any baggage from previous relationships. The house they purchased was set up for a family. The boys would continue to share a large bedroom, and little Hannah could have her own space. In their new place, they could start fresh and build their life together.

Both felt comfortable with a traditional marriage arrangement. For the first twelve years of their marriage, Peter worked full-time and Rina took care of the children. She loved being home with her baby. She loved to cook, she loved to garden, she loved to sew, and she loved to potchke—or tinker—around the house.

When Hannah grew to school age, Rina decided to do something other than homemaking. She began to take community college courses in teaching and education. Eventually, she was solicited to teach Hebrew at the local Jewish day school. Because the institution was Orthodox, she never had to worry about making it home on time for Shabbos or being absent from work because of the numerous Jewish holidays. Her summers were her own, and although she didn't make much money, she loved what she did and she loved the kids. Rina continues to teach, but several parents have suggested that she should consider being the school principal. She hasn't decided yet. Although she has been with the school almost since its inception, she knows that the added responsibility may be beyond what she's willing to take on. So far, she's resisted, but who knows what will happen in the future?

During the years of his marriage to Rina, Decker has been assigned to some of his most difficult cases. He has worked steadily and hard, taken necessary exams, and has gotten several promotions.

Currently, he's a detective lieutenant, and although his job includes a lot more paperwork and politics, he is still out in the field if the case is unusual and needs his attention. He still enjoys the feeling of getting his hands dirty and his heart racing, but he doesn't mind the desk work as much as he might have sixteen years ago.

———

For the living, the march of time is inexorable. Fictional characters have a lot more leeway. Some of them never age, fixed in the year of their appearance. Some age but not in real time. Peter and Rina have certainly aged, and their children are firsthand accounts of how old they are.

Decker started the series in his thirties; he is now in his fifties. His once bright red hair is streaked with silver, and his joints ache every once in a while. But he's kept off the extra pounds and is still strong and vibrant. He continues to wear a thick mustache even though it's no longer in style.

Rina, being much younger than her husband, is still in her early forties. She's dynamic and full of energy, especially because her children are older and require less attention, although she keeps in daily contact with all of them, including Cindy.

For Decker, having worked twenty-plus years with the LAPD, retirement is an option, although it isn't imminent. Once Hannah leaves home for college, both Rina and Decker would like to do a little traveling. They have never been together for extended periods of time without a child in tow and they look forward to taking a long-overdue honeymoon.

They can afford to do so. First of all, they have savings. Second, if Decker lasts a few more years—and all indications say this will happen—he will retire with a pension equal to his salary. Third, Rina inherited some valuable paintings from an acquaintance. It wasn't until later that they realized that some of the artists were well-known and that their paintings were valuable. They've already sold a few at Christie's Auction House, and the money helped defray the tremendous burden of private education for Rina's sons and their daughter. Decker had help when sending Cindy to college. Jack Cohen picked up the lion's share of the tuition, God bless him.

Cindy is now a GTA detective in Hollywood and aspires to homicide detail. She is married to Yaakov "Koby" Kutiel, who works as a neonatal nurse at Children's Hospital. Recently Decker helped the two of them expand their tiny house and hopes the remodel was done in order to eventually welcome a new addition to the family. At last, all that shop class instruction paid off.

Sammy Lazarus is now in Einstein Medical School in New York. He is engaged to his longtime girlfriend, Rachel, who is also at Einstein but a year behind her fiancé. They both want to finish school before they marry. Jacob Lazarus is studying molecular biology at Johns Hopkins in Baltimore. He also has a steady girlfriend, named Ilana. Hannah Decker is sixteen. Driver's license in hand, she prides herself on being completely independent except when she needs money. She adores her parents even though she sometimes considers them a little wacky. But unlike a lot of her friends, she still talks to her parents, confiding intimate details of her life that sometimes Decker feels he'd be better off not knowing. She has many male admirers, although at the moment she is without a boyfriend. This pleases her father immensely.

Where the future will take them is anyone's guess, including my own. I don't schedule their lives; I don't formulate their adventures. Peter and Rina live like any other married couple with children, one day at a time. I'm grateful that from time to time they decide to include me in their plans.

JONATHAN KELLERMAN

Born in New York City in 1949, Jonathan Kellerman grew up in Los Angeles, receiving a BA in psychology from UCLA and a PhD in psychology from the University of Southern California. He worked his way through school as an editorial cartoonist, a columnist, an editor, and a musician. He went on to become a clinical professor of pediatrics at the Keck School of Medicine. His first two books were about medicine: *Psychological Aspects of Childhood Cancer* (1980) and *Helping the Fearful Child* (1981).

His first mystery, *When the Bough Breaks* (1985), introduced Alex Delaware and won the Edgar Allan Poe Award from the Mystery Writers of America. It also won the Anthony Award at the World Mystery Convention (Bouchercon) and became a *New York Times* bestseller as well as a television movie.

In addition to the perennially bestselling Delaware series, he has written four novels about a beautiful Los Angeles homicide detective with a complicated past, Petra Connor: *Survival of the Fittest* (1997), *Billy Straight* (1998), *Twisted* (2004), and *Obsession* (2007); two stand-alone bestsellers with his wife, Faye Kellerman (also a bestselling author and the creator of the Peter Decker and Rina Lazarus series): *The Butcher's Theater* (1988), *The Conspiracy Club* (2003), and *Capital Crimes* (2007); and two children's books: *Daddy, Daddy, Can*

You Touch the Sky? (1994) and *Jonathan Kellerman's ABC of Weird Creatures* (1995).

The Kellermans have four children, one of whom, Jesse Kellerman, is also a professional writer of crime fiction. They live in Southern California.

ALEX DELAWARE

BY JONATHAN KELLERMAN

Back when I practiced child clinical psychology, if you visited my private office in Sherman Oaks, California; or my hospital digs at Childrens Hospital of LA, in east Hollywood; or the suite I shared with two pediatricians in Glendale, you'd find few clues about my personal life.

No photos of the wife or the kids propped on the desk, no shots of me driving fast cars or playing guitar or posed with Faye in Hawaii or Paris or Santa Fe or Jerusalem. Nothing but a few framed diplomas.

The successful—and ethical—practice of psychotherapy depends upon a thorough ego vacuuming: putting your own needs, desires, conceits, and fantasies into cold storage during the forty-five minutes you spend facing another human being in emotional crisis. Realizing it's all about that person and *not* about you.

According to some schools of psychotherapeutic thought, an occasional smidgeon of "self-disclosure"—dribbling out judicious bits of autobiography in the name of empathy—can benefit the patient. But even proponents of that open approach are clear that the only shrinks qualified to risk exploiting their private lives as therapeutic tools need to be experienced, rigorously self-appraising, and acutely aware of psychological boundaries—the precise spots where they end and the patient begins.

One cardinal trait of an effective psychotherapist is the ability to "actively listen," a talent that transcends gimmicky phrases such as "I hear what you're saying" and depends on a sincere suspension of the judgmental self as well as a genuine interest in the emotional life of the patient. After a few years, learning to listen on twelve cylinders can carry over to the so-called real world. You start to do it outside the office.

During my years as a psychologist, I prided myself on not playing shrink with my loved ones; when I left work, I was intent on being just another husband-dad. Sure, I'd try to be patient and sensitive, but I also needed to be free to occasionally lose my temper, pass judgment, and, yeah, even discipline the kids if they needed it. One of the nicest things my acclaimed novelist son, Jesse, ever told me was "Dad, you never treated me like a patient." (Jesse's a great guy and a terrific son, but I'm sure there were many less charitable appraisals by him and his three sisters when I blew my stack or otherwise indulged a sometimes bellicose nature.)

Despite all that, there were times when I'd like to think my training helped me as a father. I understood the developmental stages that affected children's thoughts and feelings. I got that while kids weren't miniature adults, they deserved to be treated with respect. Perhaps most important, I realized that quality time wasn't sufficient; you needed quantity time. I spent a lot of time with my kids, and when I wrote fiction in my home office—which was, and still is, festooned with personal stuff—the door was always open, literally and figuratively.

When I wasn't the cause of my kid's problems, I tried to be part of the solution by actively listening.

I haven't treated patients in a decade and a half, but there are occasions when I still slip into listening mode. That's because I'm an extremely, perhaps pathologically, curious guy, genuinely interested in other people and the stories they tell. That has led to what my kids describe as "Uh-oh, Dad made a new friend."

Hence, the guy in the Southwest Airlines departure barn at Albuquerque Airport who started schmoozing with me during a two-hour delay getting back to LA after a family vacation in Santa Fe. He was an interesting fellow who fixed mammoth oil rigs for a living, often under storm conditions. He had a lot to say about the challenges of his job and his life, and I listened. I learned a lot about heavy equipment and life on the Texas gulf.

Then there was the leather-clad former corporate CEO I ran into at a Malibu restaurant who now filled his spare time with cross-country jaunts on his Harley.

The woman who planned high-level parties in Washington, DC, and had met quite a few . . . interesting people.

The kidney transplant surgeon who used to own a country music station and now bought insurance companies, aiming for one purchase a year.

The former child actress who sold real estate. The septuagenarian great-grandfather who washed cars for a living and spent his free time Rollerblading.

Et cetera.

People talk to me; I listen.

Nothing bores me more than my own story. I want to hear about other people's lives, and the only way to do that is to Stay Out of the Picture.

I mention all this because it goes a long way toward explaining Alex Delaware and the structure of the novels that feature him.

People talk to him; he does his best to keep the focus on them.

———

When I was twenty-one, I won a literary prize and thought I was hot stuff.

Unfortunately, no one in American book publishing agreed.

Thirteen years of late-night typing in my unfinished garage earned me enough rejection slips to paper a hedge fund honcho's Xanadu. Finally, I got good enough to publish my first novel, *When the Bough Breaks*. But even that was no quickie; I wrote the book in 1981; it was accepted in 1983 but held until 1985 because the editor who bought the book left and the corporate drones at my publisher couldn't figure out what to do with a story featuring a psychologist, a gay cop, and a story line that ventured into the then-uncharted territory of child sexual abuse.

My advance was six grand, which amounted to about three bucks an hour, meaning *Bough* was bought as what's charitably termed a "small book" in the publishing biz.

This means it was predestined to disappear and that would be the end of my literary career.

Being totally naive about the business of publishing, I had no idea that I was being set up to fail, and was, in fact, as happy as a pig in swill. Because I'd been vindicated: no longer was I a pathetic, self-deluded mope with a good day job.

I was a *novelist!*

To my publisher's amazement, *Bough* earned a hefty (by 1985 standards) paperback sale and garnered rave reviews, including a gracious showcase by the eminent British-born critic John Gross (whose departure from the *New York Times* has rendered that tedious periodical sorely lacking in sparkling critical talent).

Mr. Gross featured my book in a *Times* daily review along with write-ups of new novels by Dick Francis and John D. MacDonald. Which is kind of like opening for the Beatles.

Dick and John and I all got good reviews, and people went out looking for *When the Bough Breaks*. Some people even managed to find it. Reorders poured in. The book became a word-of-mouth bestseller.

The rest, as they say, is history. But by no means linear history. It took two more bestsellers, including one that stayed on the *New York Times* list for three months, and switching to a new publisher to get me working with people who understood what I was about.

None of this is intended as a gripe-fest. I didn't deserve to get published one second sooner than I did, because until then I simply wasn't good enough. And one vital component of getting good enough was embracing an old saw: *Write what you know.*

Yeah, in retrospect that's a great big *duh.* But prior to 1981, I simply wasn't ready for self-revelation—for what sportscaster Red Smith described as "sitting down every morning at your typewriter and opening a vein." (I paraphrase, but you get the gist.) Nor had I experienced quite enough of life's dark side to have something important to say.

In 1981, my thick skull finally cracked open just wide enough to absorb the obvious epiphany: It was time to create a protagonist who shared my background as a child clinical psychologist.

———

Like me, Alex Delaware earned a PhD in psychology at age twenty-four.

Like me, he'd worked in a pediatric hospital, including long hours on the cancer ward, and had burned out.

Like me, he'd treated kids who'd experienced severe trauma, including as crime victims. Like me, he'd learned more than he believed possible about the darkest side of life.

Like me, he had dark hair and blue eyes, though his locks were curly and mine are wavy.

He's right-handed; I'm a southpaw. He's Midwestern to the core (more on that later), and I was born in New York City and raised in LA.

He sees twenty-twenty; I'm myopic.

He's taller and thinner than I am. And, of course, he's younger, because one of the nicest things about writing fiction is playing God, and the benevolent deity that I pretend to be has chosen not to age his characters in real time.

Overall, I think of Alex as a down-to-earth yet dashing fellow. Energetic, confidently masculine, analytical, insightful, hopelessly compassionate, and, most important, addicted to the truth. In a perfect world, these are all virtues I'd choose for myself.

Right from the beginning, I set out to create a true hero, not an antihero, because in 1981, the antihero was the default cliché.

Unlike me, Alex lives in an idiosyncratic house up in the hills of Bel Air and is single. That last detail is most important, because a married guy with kids wouldn't—shouldn't—get into the kind of fixes Alex finds himself in. I, on the other hand, have been married since the age of twenty-two, and I am the father of four and, to date, the grandfather of one.

Truth be told, I am a thoroughly domestic guy who has suppressed a natural tendency toward recklessness and risk taking in order to let my loved ones maintain a sense of security. Exceptions do arise: a few years ago I was zipping around the Laguna Seca racetrack at 130 mph in a Formula 1 car. I've owned an Alfa Romeo, an Aston Martin, and a supercharged Porsche, so you can see where my heart lies, automotively. And sure, there have been dark moments. Years ago, I was nearly stabbed to death in San Francisco. I've played guitar for a room full of homicidal maniacs at a state hospital for the criminally insane. Have been the only Jew on a bus full of Arabs during a jaunt to the West Bank town of Hebron. Walked the old city of Jerusalem at three a.m. Survived cancer. But no more motorcycles, no flying lessons, no bungee jumping, no carving tools or power saws because, enough scars.

The most dangerous tool I wield nowadays is a '65 Fender Stratocaster.

Delaware, on the other hand, throws caution to the Santa Anas. Therefore, he will forever remain single and just a bit alienated from the loyalties and routines of domestic life.

For some reason, there is a cadre of readers that really want him to get hitched. Sometimes they write me requesting nuptials in an upcoming book. I appreciate their loyalty, but my response is consistent: when wedding bells chime for Alex, you can be sure the series is over. Unlike a police officer, whose involvement in crime is part of his routine, Dr. D's entrée to murder necessitates a deft suspension of caution. He simply *must* be maritally untrammeled in order to take the kinds of risks that contribute to a gripping story.

When, after thirteen years of failure, I began writing *When the Bough Breaks,* I believed the process to be my final attempt at breaking in as a novelist. Maybe it would've been. Who knows? Thank God that hypothesis was never put to the test. The point is, because I saw the book as my final audition, I obsessed about coming up with something fresh and different. If I wasn't able to come up with something new, I didn't *deserve* to break in. As part of that scheme, I set out consciously to sidestep as many of the conventions of the hard-boiled-detective novel as I could while preserving the guts and soul of the genre.

Write what you know meant there was no other kind of book I could've written.

My day job as a psychologist was nothing but sleuthing—hour by hour (forty-five-minute segment by forty-five-minute segment) I conducted investigations that traversed the back alleys of the unconscious. Every time a new patient arrived in my office, the process unfolded: solving a psychosocial whodunit in order to ameliorate suffering. A lot of nasty stuff got unearthed along the way.

What I was attempting to achieve as a psychologist were daily triumphs of psychic archaeology: digging up long-buried shards of experience in an attempt to build a coherent picture of a troubled human being, in order to help that human being. If that's not detective work, I don't know what is. I'm anything but a Freudian, but I do believe that we ignore the past at our peril. That belief has informed every novel I've written.

Still, detective story or not, *When the Bough Breaks* might very well have turned out as the gravestone marking the death of my literary aspirations. This was do or die, dude; clichés needed to be *shunned.*

Hence, a troubled psychologist in a nice home office, instead of a wisecracking PI with a seedy inner-city office, a chronic drinking problem, and a buxom secretary whose barely secret love for the boss inexplicably evades the boss's notice.

Hence, a detailed, accurate, compelling investigation that didn't test the limits of reality more than it had to.

Most important: my book would feature no effete amateur prancing about as he shows up the pros. Because I detest books that treat murder like a parlor game. You know the type: plummy-voiced, tuxedoed twits with all the character depth of a sandwich sign huff-huffing in the parlor as a body molders yards away.

What could be more dehumanizing than viewing homicide as just another fatuous riddle, easily solved by applying the flimsiest approximation of logic?

Having witnessed the effects of violence as a psychologist and court consultant, I was determined to communicate the nightmare that is homicide and its repercussions. That proved easy, because Alex Delaware, like me, turned out to be a driven perfectionist whose persistence often draws him into some rather extreme territory. (Several years ago, I delivered the keynote address at the national convention of the American Psychological Association. Facing an audience of a couple thousand shrinks, I felt like the ultimate clinical demonstration. Maybe that's why I began my speech, "I stand before you as living proof of the positive aspects of the obsessive-compulsive personality.")

Driven, yes. Able to leap tall buildings by himself, no.

My hero would eschew a tortured relationship with the cops. Not only was that the most hackneyed of plot devices, but experiences working with the courts and the criminal-justice system had taught me that detectives from the private and public sectors often meshed quite well and that experts were well received.

This was going to be a crime novel. I needed a cop.

The problem was, yet another gruff, world-weary homicide dick was the woolliest cliché of all.

On the other hand, a gruff, world-weary *gay* homicide detective . . . interesting.

Enter Milo Sturgis.

————

One of the questions I'm asked most frequently is what led me to make Milo homosexual. The answer is simple: the quest for something new and interesting and original. And what could be more compelling than a man, newly open about his sexuality, whose very *presence* in the Los Angeles Police Department would engender tension.

The timing was right. Long gone were the days when LA cops routinely busted gay bars—and gay heads. (Though I was able to plumb that brutal territory for flashback scenes in *The Murder Book*—a novel about which I will have more to say.) Which doesn't mean that the Los Angeles Police Department during the early eighties was in any way gay friendly. Quite the contrary. Even nowadays, when a handful of gay cops have gone public, I'm doubtful that homosexuality will ever be totally accepted in the paramilitary organization that is the LAPD.

In 1981, there were . . . ahem . . . no gay cops in the LAPD. If you believed the official account. I knew from my contacts that there were several gay cops in the LAPD. And that, for the most part, they went about their jobs without much fuss—neither running from nor flaunting their sexuality.

Just cops, like any others, doing the job.

In 1981, "gay but so what" seemed to me a revolutionary concept.

The more I thought about it, the fresher and more innovative became the notion of a homosexual homicide detective operating within a homophobic organization that tolerated him, barely, because he did the job better than anyone else.

But Milo couldn't be *gay*—the feather boa, lisping, limp-wristed gay of camp theater and episodic TV and West Hollywood Halloween parades. Because, apart from being the worst sort of cliché, a guy like that wouldn't survive a single shift in the LAPD. No matter how high his solve rate.

No, the cop I conceptualized would be different: tough, grumpy, sloppy, and also altogether professional and highly intelligent. A homicide veteran with a precarious foothold in the world of law enforcement based on nothing other than raw talent.

Milo's homosexuality is right out in the open in *When the Bough Breaks,* as he announces it to Alex because he doesn't want Alex to find out some other way and freak out. Alex reacts with surprise, then acceptance. The two of them become friends.

After the book was published, I received a ton of nice mail from gay people along the lines of "I've always loved mystery novels, but they're so homophobic. Thanks so much for Milo."

Bear in mind that in 1985, gay characters in mainstream fiction were just about nonexistent. No *Will & Grace,* no *Brokeback Mountain.* No *Project Runway.*

Was I out to create a social revolution? Hell, no. With thirteen years of abject failure behind me, I never even expected to publish the darn thing, let alone write a series or build the foundation of a durable career. Looking back, I realize that low expectations fed my courage: with nothing to lose, I had the fortitude to create a novel that, at first glance, had absolutely no commercial potential.

Shrink, gay cop. Scores of molested kids.

Once my editor left, the drones at my publisher opined that the book was weird, hard to characterize, and, y'know, kind of yucky.

The reading public thought otherwise, which is why I answer all my fan mail. But for the graciousness of ordinary folk who took the time to traipse to the bookstore and plunk down their hard-earned dough for that first novel—and all the novels that have followed—I wouldn't be able to avoid honest labor and work the greatest job in the world.

———

But back to Milo and the reception he's received from the reading public over a two-decade tenure.

Straight people rarely complain; in fact, I've only received a handful of letters complaining about the "gay agenda" and such. Apparently, most individuals—at least those who read my novels—are tolerant. They buy into "gay but so what" because they understand that whom we sleep with has nothing to do with how effective we are in doing our jobs.

Americans—and people all around the world—believe in live and let live. How nice.

More interesting—and, to me, more amusing—has been the evolution of the response from gay readers.

Shortly after its publication, *When the Bough Breaks* received an award from an advocacy group aimed at promoting positive images of gay people.

But as gay people gradually began receiving greater focus in books, in films, and on TV, I occasionally became the recipient of snarkiness in the gay press. E.g., "How can Kellerman, as a straight man, presume to write about the gay experience?"

Which is not only narrow-minded and stupid, it betrays an utter lack of understanding about what writing fiction is all about. If I had to limit myself to the confines of my own direct experience, I could never write about women, anyone older than I am, anyone from a different ethnic or religious background. Yes, that sounds obvious, but you'd be amazed at the limited thinking of those who choose to incarcerate themselves in sociopolitical cell blocks.

The apex of reverse discrimination arrived several years ago, in the form of a review in a British gay magazine opining that if Alex Delaware were really a great shrink, he'd realize he was in love with Milo.

I laughed. What else can you do?

Since I consider writing fiction a profoundly narcissistic exercise— I shut out the world and aim at pleasing myself—I pay no heed to any of that blather and continue to engage in the same routine that has been part of my life for decades: entering a quiet room, sitting down, typing until fatigue rules. And over the two decades since they first dropped in and introduced themselves to me, Dr. D and Lieutenant S have continued to explore the darker side of the human experience as friends and cocompulsives.

———

One point of commonality between Alex and Milo is their Midwestern origin. Milo hails from Indiana, and Alex, like my wife, is Missouri born. This is no accident; to me, the Midwest represents much of what is praiseworthy about America, with its emphasis on humility, hard work, and loyalty, rather than the LA–New York ethos, with its emphasis on cosmetics, self-invention, and spin masquerading as truth.

But LA's so much fun to write *about*. And what better eye to cast upon the city formed by Hollyweird than that of a Midwestern boy who drove cross-country at age sixteen. In order to . . . well, Alex really wasn't sure about his goals, but he did know it was time to escape his alcoholic father and his chronically depressed mother and the older sister who never stuck up for him.

And Milo . . . gay, Catholic, one of a gaggle of six macho brothers. Need I say more?

Like so many other loners, both men migrated to California in order to escape their personal histories, but they will never be able shed those early, formative years in the flatlands of the Midwest. Though they've never really discussed their childhoods with each other, surprisingly similar backgrounds have imbued both of them with a burning desire to learn the truth. To obsessively churn forward until the truth shows its sometimes ugly little face.

These are not guys who have any patience for situational ethics. In the world that Alex and Milo inhabit, the distinction between good and evil is clear. That is not to say they are simpleminded, naive, or blithely unaware of life's nuances. Quite the contrary; they are complex, intelligent, *thinking* men who, precisely because they weigh the moral consequences of every situation, are guided by a firm sense of right and wrong.

Alex and Milo are unabashed good guys who are out to get the unabashed bad guys, and they will always be that way because I've created them and hell if I don't think that's the right way to be.

Alex and Milo admire the same people I admire and they despise the chumps who bring my blood to a boil and who seem to populate the Third World nation that is Los Angeles: smarmy psychopaths, petty politicians, backbiting weenies, faceless bureaucrats, citizen-fascists pretending they can't smell the stink of the concentration camp a block away. Not to mention pig-headed bigots, manic poseurs, downright frauds, smooth and not-so-smooth cons, ass kissers, buck passers, small-minded wimps, shiftless shirkers. And just plain mopes who evade responsibility.

Working as a psychologist is all about refraining from imposing one's values on others.

Writing fiction is such a *lovely* vacation from that. I judge. Oh, boy, do I judge.

I like real heroes. And, unlike the television network executive cretin who opined that Alex Delaware would be more appealing if he had a limp or some other physical defect, I have no problem working with a good-looking, good-thinking good guy.

You want antiheroes who are just as unredeemable as their quarry, go somewhere else. But close the door lightly and don't wake me up. *Nothing* is more yawn inducing to me than the conspicuously flawed antihero.

None of that should imply that either Alex or Milo is devoid of problems. In *When the Bough Breaks,* Alex debuts as a tormented, disillusioned, insomniac burnout unable to maintain a steady relationship or to function professionally. And one recurrent motif of the Delaware novels is the therapist getting through the rough spots of his own life by putting them aside and concentrating on solving the problems of others.

Then there's Milo. Slovenly, constitutionally grouchy, compulsively stuffing his face, ever a malcontent. He is certainly no poster boy for Perfect Adjustment. But unless his foibles are germane to the story, they are handled lightly. Yes, he's got issues. No, they won't stop him from getting to the bottom of horrible murders.

Alex is a hero, but he is also a real person who lives in my head and tells me great stories. And real people evolve and develop and go through rough patches.

In *When the Bough Breaks,* Dr. D's past involvement with a group of abused children ends up connecting, quite terribly, to other, similarly mistreated kids, as well as to multiple murder. Alex becomes an integral part of the story. But in the next two novels, *Blood Test* and *Over the Edge,* he steps back, is allowed to accrue some objectivity as he assumes the role of behavioral scientist and ad hoc detective.

The success of those books, particularly *Over the Edge,* which remained on the bestseller list for months, led me to realize that I was going to write a series, and that I needed to acquaint myself more fully with my recurring protagonist. The result was a vacation from Alex, so that I could attain perspective and understand him more fully. During that time, I wrote a stand-alone novel, *The Butcher's Theater*, a massive, disturbing account of serial killings (before they became known as such) in the holiest of cities, Jerusalem. The following book, the fourth featuring Delaware, *Silent Partner*, falls squarely in the noir tradition but also edges into surrealism and horror. Because one of the driving forces of that book was for me to solidify my understanding of Alex, he reverts to the role of primary player, as a supposedly chance encounter with a former lover—a beautiful, troubled, enigmatic graduate student named Sharon Ransom—draws him into a nightmare world of betrayal and corruption.

Confident that I'd buttoned down enough about my hero to continue the series with authority and verisimilitude, I next penned *Time Bomb*, a book that allowed Dr. D to fade back into the role of expert. Though his love life did take some interesting turns.

That approach continued for the following three novels, until, once again, I felt Alex needed some shaking up in order to enlarge his character. The result was *Bad Love*, in which a vindictive patient from Alex's past threatens his very survival. Then back to Dr. D as expert for eight more novels.

Nine years after *Silent Partner*, I decided it was time to learn more about Milo. The result was *The Murder Book*, in which we delve into the inimitable Detective Sturgis's days as a rookie homicide cop, a period when homosexuality, per se, was automatic disqualification for employment in the LAPD. A period during which secrets ruled Milo's life and affected his ability to solve a particularly brutal homicide. It is only when a newly integrated Sturgis—by which I mean a Sturgis caught up with his own psyche—reexamines the file that what has become a brain-itching cold case can finally be solved.

The Murder Book also marked a stylistic departure for a Delaware novel in that exclusive first-person narrative—a form I believe has the potential to increase a sense of intimacy between reader and character—was abandoned. Instead, I alternated first person with the third-person flashbacks necessary for excavating Milo's initial days as a novice detective. The book could only have been written at that particular time, as it took me that long to build up the courage to deviate from the form.

I decided to break free after reading my brilliant wife's superb novel *Justice,* in which Faye initiated that same point-of-view flexibility for her series. I'd be remiss if I didn't note that being married to Faye has proved an enormous confidence builder in general; she has taught me, always by example, never pedantically, that one needn't be locked into a stylistic straitjacket in order to maintain thematic and artistic consistency across a series.

Faye's unintentional mentoring has extended to another area: Anyone who knows my wife knows she is All Girl. Despite that, she displays an almost freakishly masterful ability to write from a male perspective. (Many writers have commented on her brilliance in that regard. The Edgar®-winning author Brian Garfield has opined that no one does it better than Faye.) Faye's exceptional gift made me wonder if I could pull off a female chief protagonist. The result was Petra Connor, hero of *Billy Straight* and *Twisted* and an all-around great gal who surfaces as a collaborator in the Delaware novels when her talents are needed by Alex and Milo.

Milo, Milo, Milo.

He, as opposed to Alex, is described in great physical detail in every single Delaware novel, because we view him, as we view the world, through Alex's eyes. Despite that, I have received several inquiries from readers wanting to know if he's white or black. At first, I was puzzled by the puzzlement of those loyal fans, since allusions to Milo's pallid complexion, straight black hair, and bright green eyes seemed to preclude anything but Caucasian. Then I realized that I'd described him several times as "Black Irish," a tag that refers to a subset of Emerald Isle Celts with dark hair—probably the result of long-ago genetic contribution from Roman invaders. A common term during my youth but one that has, apparently, lost currency. I may need to be less subtle.

I have also fielded countless questions about *Alex's* ethnicity, including one rather rambunctious reader who insisted that, let's face it, Alex is Jewish.

Let's face it; he's not.

I am Jewish; Alex is a self-described "mutt," and that was a deliberate choice. One of the many things that working as a psychologist taught me was that once we get over what I call the hurdle of ethnicity, we're all pretty darned similar, intra-psychically. For that reason, and because I see myself as an inclusive man, I yearned to create a universal character—to write universally appealing books that avoided the ethnic tunnel vision that would be distracting and detract from meta-themes.

There may be some Semitic protein floating around in Dr. Delaware's ribonucleic acid. I couldn't tell you, as I've never seen the results of any lab test. There's probably American Indian, German, English, French, and Lord knows what else in there too. But Alex is nothing if not ethnically ambiguous—a distinctly American persona cobbled together from what is best about the greatest nation in history, a truth seeker undeterred by Orwellian notions of "diversity" or by base, creativity-murdering political correctness.

All fiction is to some extent autobiographical, but it is also a particularly entertaining variant of the Rorschach test—a series of deliberately hazy images upon which the reader projects his or her own fears, affections, and drives. Vegans want Alex to eschew meat. Liberals, conservatives, libertarians, all shudder at the possibility that he might not agree with every single opinion they possess on any given topic.

Sorry, he's his own guy.

Nearly thirty years ago, when Alex Delaware popped into my head, I had no idea he'd ever stay alive long enough to serve as the springboard for exploring my own existential questions, let alone those of tens of millions of other people.

The fact that he continues to do his obsessive, heroic thing without adhering to—or even touching upon—any particular orthodoxy brings me tremendous joy as I continue to tell the stories to which Dr. Delaware directs me.

I love my job.

JOHN LESCROART

Born in 1948 in Houston, Texas, John Lescroart (it's pronounced Les-kwah) had a varied career background before becoming a successful author who is a regular on the *New York Times* bestseller list in both hardcover and paperback. After graduating from the University of California at Berkeley in 1970 with a BA in English with honors, he worked as a computer programmer, advertising director, moving man, housepainter, legal secretary, fund-raiser, management consultant, bartender, and musician. He wrote about five hundred songs and performed for more than two years with Johnny Capo and the Real Good Band (he was Capo). Although the band was somewhat successful, he retired to write full-time. His affection for music never disappeared, though, and he has recently founded his own recording label, CrowArt Records.

His first book, *Sunburn* (1981), a non-mystery paperback original, was followed by *Son of Holmes* (1986) and *Rasputin's Revenge* (1987), both of which featured Auguste Lupa, the son of Sherlock Holmes (a character reminiscent of Nero Wolfe).

Many of the Dismas Hardy novels also feature Abe Glitsky, a somewhat acerbic and disillusioned San Francisco policeman. Lescroart has recently created yet another popular character, Wyatt Hunt, a private detective who starred in *The Hunt Club* (2005) and *The Suspect* (2007).

Lescroart lives with his wife and children in Davis, California.

DISMAS HARDY

BY JOHN LESCROART

I wrote my first book in college.

It was what would now be called a legal thriller, based on the idea that capital punishment was cruel and unusual because the condemned person knew that the execution was coming. I developed the conceit that the death penalty would be more humane if the condemned didn't know about the sentence, if one day he merely went to the prison doctor for a routine injection or vaccination, and instead the "medication" was a fatal one. No doubt it's for the best that this book remains unpublished, but in it, I named the condemned man Dismas Hardy. He appeared for about one page, was dispatched, and disappeared.

But the name struck me as particularly memorable, in the mold of, say, Travis McGee or Sherlock Holmes. (It was probably the single best thing in the book.) In any event, I resolved that if I ever did get to writing a mystery series, my hero would be called Dismas Hardy. I knew that Dismas was the name of the good thief on Calvary, who was crucified next to Jesus, and it was always good to have a biblical antecedent to help provide kind of an instant sense of gravitas in a hero. As for the surname Hardy, I had grown up with the Hardy Boys—Frank and Joe—and it seemed to me that there really couldn't be a better all-American, highly-pedigreed last name for a detective. So that was settled; my hero would be called Dismas Hardy.

Of course, I wasn't planning on becoming a mystery writer in those days. After all, I was studying the continental novel in translation at UC Berkeley—Stendahl, Camus, Tolstoy, etc. I was *serious*. But I was a confident cuss, and a part of me thought that I could probably write a Nobel-quality literary work every few years and pay the bills by whipping out a steady stream of entertaining mystery fiction (under a pseudonym, of course) at the rate of about a book a year. And in that case, it was good to have a ready-made name for my protagonist.

But meanwhile, I had to get working on the craft of novel writing. I had already finished the aforementioned legal thriller, which I knew to be literarily dubious in qualitative terms. It lacked certain elements that seemed to be a feature of other books I wanted to emulate, both "literary" and not, such as humor, irony, verisimilitude, and—most strikingly—plot. Seeking to correct these deficiencies, I sat down and wrote a book-length Sherlock Holmes–Nero Wolfe pastiche that I entitled *Recipe for Murder*. It was, granted, a mystery, and so would be outside the main thrust of my *serious* work—in fact, I wrote it under the pen name Dan Sherb. I never really thought that this novel would be published either. In fact, after I'd finished it, I showed it to one or two readers, who were universally enthusiastic (parents tend to be!). Then I put the manuscript in my sock drawer and forgot about it.

For the next seven years, I worked as a musician. My creative life mostly revolved around the songs I was writing. After my first two attempts at novel writing—one faintly literary and one a derivative mystery—I had realized that I needed to garner a little life experience before embarking on the serious phase of my art.

I had to see the world.

And I did, traveling all over the United States and overseas in

Europe and Africa. Returning to the United States in 1976, I gave the whole singer-songwriter thing a good effort, forming a band— Johnny Capo (me!) and His Real Good Band—that performed regularly for about two years in the San Francisco Bay Area. In fact, we weren't too bad, and we worked consistently.

Gradually, though, the old familiar but long-suppressed urge to write fiction began to nudge out music's prominence in my creative life. I started to write short scenes, to experiment with form, to sketch characters, to play with voice and point of view. No plot yet, but still.

Over the course of seven years, I'd written hundreds of songs, and I had become proficient at the craft. Ironically, though, the songs often left me creatively unfulfilled and frustrated. The expression that called to me more and more was fiction. I didn't even know what I would write about, but I sensed that I was getting close to the point where I might have something important, something serious, to say. I'd almost died in Africa, I'd been cheated out of half a summer's pay in Spain, I'd had friends die (and even commit suicide). Beyond that, I was married and thought I was getting some understanding of the complexities of adult relationships, of commitment and responsibility.

Hell, I was almost thirty!

Time was running out.

It was time to get serious about my art and my life. If I couldn't start writing my literary books now, maybe I never would.

On my thirtieth birthday, I bit the bullet and told my band I was quitting to write books. Over about the next two months, I threw everything I had into my first "real" book. Based loosely on some of my experiences in Spain (for that old Hemingway feel), *Sunburn* fell rather neatly into the classic "first novel" matrix—sensitive young man sees the real world for the first time and comes of age while tragedy and political turmoil rage around him.

In *Sunburn,* I took the opportunity to write in all three persons. I experimented. I was daring, pushing the fictional envelope. It was heady and wonderful and literary and above all *serious*—this was clearly what I was meant to be doing with my life and my art. To top it all off, *Sunburn* went on to win the San Francisco Foundation's Joseph Henry Jackson Award for best novel by a California author, beating out *Interview with a Vampire,* among 280 other entries.

Next stop, Sweden. I began working on my Nobel acceptance speech. They'd never chosen a thirty-year-old before, but . . .

So I'd written the first of my literary works, the start of my oeuvre. While I waited for the publishing world to discover *Sunburn,* I wanted to keep the creative flame burning, so I quit my daytime job (always a bad idea) at *Guitar Player* magazine and immediately began another novel, *Liner Notes,* about some of my experiences in the music and performing world.

Flush with confidence, enamored of my own first-person writer's voice, I produced this six-hundred-plus-page tome in four or five months and started sending it out to the same literary agents who, much to my surprise, had been turning down *Sunburn* with a frustrating regularity. My prizewinning literary book, they said, was not "commercial."

And neither, by the way, was *Liner Notes.*

Well, what did they know? Great writers have always had to suffer for their art. This would be yet another life experience that would only enrich my later work. My critics would be sorry. I piss in the milk of these commercial cretins.

When *Sunburn* eventually found a paperback publisher, I realized that the $2,000 advance would not go very far toward giving me the time to write another comparable masterpiece. In the meanwhile, I had to make a living, and I decided that it was time to move to Plan B—to whip out a quick mystery under a pseudonym.

I began working on a novel about San Francisco's famous Zodiac

Killer. Entitled *Imperfect Knowledge,* this book imagined that the Zodiac, who to this day has not been caught, simply retired from his first spate of killings and emerged from retirement a decade later, only to be pursued and apprehended finally by . . . private investigator Dismas Hardy.

"But wait!" you say. "Hardy is not a private investigator. He's an ex-cop, yes. An ex-Marine, a father and husband and attorney."

Yes, he is, all of those. But he wasn't then. It wasn't yet time for him to be born.

———

When I had finished the first draft of my Plan B non-literary mystery, featuring Dismas Hardy, I sent it out first to the publisher that had taken *Sunburn,* certain that my award-winning writing skills would carry the day and that *Imperfect Knowledge,* though nothing like *Sunburn,* would be snapped up as a matter of course. I would then take the money and live on that while I wrote my next literary offering, my next "real" book.

This was not to be.

My publisher passed on *Imperfect Knowledge.* After about ten more rejections, I went back and reworked the manuscript from beginning to end, cutting about two hundred pages, working mostly on plot and pacing issues that agents and editors had suggested.

Among the things I did *not* consider changing was Dismas Hardy, who happened to be the linchpin of the book. He was a private eye, very much out of the gumshoe mold, the kind of guy I didn't want readers to have to think much about. He did what other PIs had done, in pretty much the way they had done it. My vision of mysteries in those days was that there was a kind of generic private-eye template, and if one followed it religiously, the hero would "work," the book would get published, everybody would be happy. In this benighted view, originality wasn't really part of the equation, and so I created a Dismas Hardy who, though he wasn't an out-and-out cliché, failed to sustain interest.

I must have thought it was somehow "mysterious" that he was such a loner and had no history and, really, no life. No love interest. No pets, no kids, no friends. I was saving all that good human stuff for my serious work. And so I sent out another round of submissions with a completely revised manuscript (essentially a new book) and probably shouldn't have been so surprised with the by now predictable results.

Although, of course, I was.

Devastated was more like it. I had tried to make a career in music and failed, and now I had written at least four complete manuscripts, only one of which had been published, and published as a paperback original at that. The heady confidence that characterized my attitude toward writing up until then was beginning to erode. Could it be that I wasn't, after all, a genius?

———

But there seemed to be no other interpretation.

Sunburn had certainly failed to attract a readership. The other manuscripts—even the two drafts of my Plan B mystery—weren't exciting anyone in the publishing business either. I started to consider the possibility that I wasn't meant to be any kind of a writer after all. Even more portentously, I didn't have any more ideas of what I wanted to write about, literary or otherwise.

Three years passed. I remarried well. I took a lucrative day job writing technical papers and put my literary aspirations aside. I was going to be an adult and wear a suit to work every day and not think about my earlier foolish ambitions.

But I knew it was a lie, and my wife knew it too. "You want to write," she said. "You want to be a writer. You *are* a writer."

"But I don't even have anything to submit," I told her. "Everything's been rejected many times over."

"Not everything," she said. "You've never even submitted your first book." This was *Recipe for Murder,* the Sherlock Holmes–Nero Wolfe pastiche I'd written fourteen years before.

"Of course I haven't sent that out," I said. "That's a mystery. I don't do mystery. I'm a literary writer. And I didn't even write *Recipe for Murder* as a book. That was just an exercise to see if I could sustain a plot and characters over a book-length work."

"I thought it was good," Lisa said. "I thought it was a book."

She was right. I scanned the old brittle typed pages into a computer, reprinted them with a new copyright date, and sent them off to New York. Six weeks later, Donald I. Fine bought the book and published it in hardcover under the title *Son of Holmes*. Better yet, he asked for a sequel, which he'd release as *Rasputin's Revenge* the next year.

At last, somebody was paying me to write novels. True, they were mystery stories prominently featuring characters—Sherlock Holmes and Nero Wolfe—that had been created by someone else. Plus, they were both set during World War I in Europe. As entertainments, they could not have been more non-*serious*. But after my earlier disappointments with publishing, I was glad to be on the boards at last, glad to be getting the chance to write regularly.

Donald I. Fine asked me for another book, and I told him I wanted to change directions and write a story set in the present day, and in the United States, with a modern protagonist. I didn't envision it as a mystery, but as a story of one lost man's redemption after his world is suddenly shattered by . . . what? What literary conceit could drive a plot, or shatter a world?

The idea—startling in its clarity, profound in its implications—hit me like a thunderbolt.

A crime!

In fact, a murder.

And a murder turned my *serious* "literary" idea into a mystery.

Suddenly the inherent and irreconcilable dichotomy I had always perceived—maybe *projected* is a better word—between serious literature and the mystery genre vanished. I could tell an important story, perhaps even one containing a universal truth or two, and at the same time provide the kind of narrative drive that a strong plot could guarantee, or at least facilitate. I could talk about moral and social and character issues—surely the province of serious literature—and write a fast-moving and entertaining story at the same time. This was an enormous revelation—I didn't need to pursue a Plan A for my *serious* work and a Plan B for stuff people might enjoy reading. They could be the same thing!

And Dismas Hardy, waiting in the wings all this time, began to reveal himself to me not just as a (snooty literary word) protagonist, but as a *hero*.

At this point, fate stepped in. I had begun subscribing to the Mystery Writers of America's newsletter, *The Third Degree*. Sometime in the late 1980s, the writer and critic Dick Lochte wrote a cover story for that periodical, urging writers to stop writing about "private eyes." The world didn't need any more private eyes, he said. They had been done, and done to death. He pleaded for originality, new voices, a new approach to the mystery novel.

He couldn't have hit me (and Dismas Hardy) at a better time.

Suddenly, Dismas Hardy the San Francisco private eye had to become what he in his wisdom always knew he was meant to become—a full-fledged human being. He wasn't a private eye. He'd never been a private eye. No wonder those agents and editors hadn't bought him back in the day. He hadn't been original or authentic. He'd been a hackneyed literary conceit in those earlier manuscripts, little more than a cartoon. Now, if I wanted to write about him, first I had to find out who he was, why he was important, and how he was worthy to carry the moral weight with which I was about to burden him.

Dismas Hardy was not going to be my Plan B character. Dismas

Hardy was going to be no less than my Everyman. He would carry the hopes and dreams of every man, suffer the losses, savor the triumphs. He would have a family, friends, and enemies. He would get sick, make mistakes, drink too much, work too hard, fail to understand. But mostly he would hunger and thirst for what we all ultimately desire—justice.

All writers have heard the admonition to "write what you know." My confidence had taken a big enough hit during the rejection years that I no longer felt like any kind of a genius. If I wanted to create a memorable character, and I did, I'd take whatever advice was out there. And I decided that if he was to be authentic, Hardy had to be full of stuff I knew, and knew intimately. That was the main thing. I had to know him.

So he was my age, thirty-eight.

He'd gone to a Catholic all-male high school, quite possibly my own Serra High in San Mateo, California.

He lived on Thirty-fourth Avenue at Clement in San Francisco.

He was a bartender at the Little Shamrock, as I had been.

He was divorced.

Though not an alcoholic, he tended to kill his pain with drink.

The arc of this book was to be Hardy's resurrection and redemption—two good Catholic themes about which I knew plenty. I also knew that Hardy's life and career had been shattered, but I didn't know why.

(Except that it wasn't because he'd failed as a writer. I wanted to identify with his failure, though I knew it wasn't going to be the same as mine. He was to be the appealing Everyman, not the effete artist type his creator had once and no longer fancied himself.)

Did I know enough about Dismas Hardy to begin? I thought so. The great thing about the actual experience of writing is its revelatory character. Though I had no idea how I was going to get a thirty-eight-year-old bartender involved in a crime that would somehow redeem him and restore the equilibrium and happiness to his life, I had written enough to believe that the process would provide the answers.

And *within the first three pages* of *Dead Irish*, these words appeared on the screen in front of me:

"It was the first time Hardy'd had a woman's arms around him in four and a half years. And that time had been just the once, with Frannie née McGuire now Cochran, after a New Year's Eve party."

And then:

"In a way, he thought, it was too bad the plane hadn't crashed. There would have been some symmetry in that—both of his parents had died in a plane crash when he'd been nineteen, a sophomore at Caltech."

And finally:

He just felt he'd lost track of who he was. He knew what he did—he was a damn good bartender, a thrower of darts, a medium worker of wood.

He was also divorced, an ex-marine, ex-cop, ex-attorney. He'd even, for a time, been a father. Thirty-eight and some months and he didn't know who he was.

He tipped up the glass. Yeah, he thought, that wouldn't have been so bad, the plane crashing. Not good, not something to shoot for, but really not the worst tragedy in the world.

He figured he'd already had that one.

That was how long it took—three pages—for Hardy to assert that, for all our similarities, he wasn't me. I, for example, had not been orphaned. I'd never even visited Caltech. I hadn't been a cop or been in the service. I wasn't an attorney. I sucked at darts. I'd never carved a piece of wood in my life.

Where did all this come from?

And, more important, what was the tragedy Hardy was talking about, the worst tragedy in the world, the one he figured he'd already had?

I didn't know.

I wouldn't know until I'd finished the entire first draft of the book and started the second. This is all the more amazing considering that the tragedy—the death of his young son, Michael, in a crib accident—is what caused the breakup of his marriage, the collapse of his legal career, his decade-long hibernation as a bartender in the bar owned by his friend Moses McGuire, whose life Hardy had saved in Vietnam.

See? Even when I hadn't known him, he'd always been a hero.

Other things began to happen. Hardy goes to a Giants baseball game, where a fan plunges to his death from the upper deck, and there at the ballpark he runs into a Jewish mulatto cop named Abe Glitsky, with whom he used to walk a beat in his policeman days. I am blessed with two great brothers and several very close male friends, without whom life wouldn't be nearly as fun or interesting. And suddenly, writing what I knew, I watched as Hardy and Glitsky fell into the patter of a long-standing and deep bond. These were old friends, connected in some nearly spiritual way. I didn't know Abe yet, but I knew the relationship.

And Abe's job gave me a way to connect Hardy to a crime.

Except, apparently, it's not a crime. It's a suicide. The suicide of Eddie Cochran, an idealistic young man who is married to Frannie, the sister of Hardy's boss, Moses McGuire. Frannie has just found out she is pregnant.

Hardy doesn't believe Eddie would have ever killed himself. And there is insurance money for Frannie if someone murdered him. Though it's formally none of his business, Hardy—as Everyman thirsting for justice—must find the answer.

And in searching for that answer, he discovers to his surprise that the active grieving period for his son has somehow come to an end, and that there can be meaning and even joy in reconnecting with life and getting to know the people around him. Hardy is redeemed, reborn, and ready to take up the role in life that he'd planned and prepared for before his personal tragedy derailed him—a man who lives and if necessary fights to see justice done.

Dead Irish reveals Dismas Hardy as the lead character in a novel that happens to have a crime in the center of it. At that time, and unlike many of the young people who come to the profession of writing today, I did not have a game plan for how I would pursue my career. I was not aware enough of the publishing business to even have an agent yet, much less the savvy to decide to write a series for which I would supply the next six plots and maybe a second one featuring cats. For me, when I wrote it, *Dead Irish* was a stand-alone novel, not the first book in a series. Though it meant abandoning the well-loved name Dismas Hardy, I felt sure that I would find another name for a character in my next book that would please me. I'd say good-bye to Diz, thank him for the yeoman efforts, and move on.

Then *Dead Irish* got nominated for the Shamus Award for best novel (which I found highly ironic, Shamus being a synonym for private eye), and Donald Fine asked me to write a true sequel featuring Dismas Hardy.

I didn't know how I was going to do that. I'd already written Hardy's character arc. He was redeemed, he was back together with his first wife, he was happy bartending at the Shamrock, which he now owned a quarter of.

What would be the conflict? How would he grow as a character? I didn't know, and I didn't think that revisiting him in a new setting was a particularly great idea.

But here I was, four published books into my career, and if I wanted to keep getting paid to write, this was a bird in the hand—a bona fide offer from a New York hardcover publisher. It was still not even close to enough money to live on, mind you—just a small step up from *Dead Irish*. But it would give me another chance to see if I could write a commercially successful novel. And I could look at both the Dismas Hardy character and the plot as challenges in pure storytelling.

In the course of writing *The Vig,* I continued to learn a little more about Hardy, and to be surprised by these discoveries. The most surprising element was his love life. Although in *Dead Irish,* he'd reconnected with his first wife, Jane Fowler, *The Vig* wasn't twenty pages old when Hardy found himself drawn to the much younger Frannie Cochran, widow of Eddie from *Dead Irish,* the sister of Moses McGuire. The whole time I was writing this book, I didn't know what would finally transpire in Hardy's choice of his mate. Jane was certainly a worthy person, smart and sensitive. But there was lots of baggage there with Jane. And a certain idealism and freshness in Frannie.

Beyond that, simply in plot terms, I was wrestling with the question of romance. It never hurts the readability of a novel—even a serious literary novel—if one of the plot or subplot elements is romance. Will the boy get the girl or vice versa? My experiences writing both *Rasputin's Revenge* and *Dead Irish* had taught me that this was a powerful, perhaps even essential, device to elicit empathy for main characters and also to create suspense and a level of humanity without which a book might seem dry and lifeless.

Finally, I was still trying to write what I knew, and I was married to a woman who was eleven years younger than I. The issues and decisions that Hardy and Frannie would face and make together might in many ways be similar to those Lisa and I were confronting. Drawing upon our personal experiences might inform the character of Hardy in a way that would simply be impossible if he chose Jane.

And so in this fundamental way, Hardy's character development took another step—albeit a very small one—in *The Vig*. But as I wrote that book, I couldn't escape the feeling that it lacked the depth of its predecessor. I thought it was a good read, with a strong plot and interesting characters, yes, but to me it lacked the inherent gravitas that had characterized *Dead Irish*.

Perhaps this was because I'd approached its writing as an academic exercise, much the same way I'd written *Son of Holmes* right after college. It other words, though I took the craft of it seriously, I treated it almost as a Plan B work that in an earlier incarnation I probably would have written and published under a pseudonym, and with a different more or less generic mystery protagonist, certainly not my Everyman, Dismas Hardy, as its main character. (Despite that, since the book's publication, I've watched with a somewhat bemused eye as *The Vig* continues to attract new readers and remains healthily in print nearly twenty years after its first publication.)

Ironically, this was probably the time that I came closest to giving up on Dismas Hardy, and on what was now at least a fledgling career as an acknowledged mystery author. I was forty-one years old and had published five books—four of them mysteries. I couldn't pretend, and certainly no one in the publishing industry thought, that I was a "literary" author. Why was I kidding myself?

I was making very little money writing, which I did out in my garage in Altadena between 6:00 and 8:00 a.m., five days a week. My other two day jobs included full-time work as the word-processing supervisor at a large Los Angeles law firm, and then piecemeal typing every night at other law firms among the towers that made up the LA skyline. My days began at 5:30 and often ended at 11:30. By now, Lisa and I had two children, and I rarely got to see them except on weekends. And even with all the hours I was working, and the books I was publishing, we were struggling financially. Maybe it was time I got a professional career-track job. Go to law school. Quit writing and recognize it for what it was—a foolish, youthful dream that hadn't quite worked out.

Of course, in the LA area, there was also the ever-present distraction and lure of the screenwriting-movie business. And as a published author, I was able to "take a few meetings." I got paid to write a screenplay for a B-movie producer. I wrote a few synopses for TV pilots. More piecemeal work. Hackwork.

My lofty ideals had atrophied; the *serious* writer I'd once wanted to become was nowhere to be found. I needed to make money so my family could survive, and I probably could have been talked into writing a snuff film if it paid enough. And when I realized that this was what it had gotten to, I decided to stop writing altogether. If it wasn't a noble and beautiful calling, some kind of artistic expression, what was the point? Was it all just the ability to juggle words?

I didn't want that. I started sending out résumés for career-oriented jobs. Donald Fine asked for another sequel, and I told him no. I wasn't going to do another formulaic mystery. I'd learned my lesson. My writing life was over.

———

This was where things stood until one Sunday in August of 1989, when I woke up with a severe earache, bad enough that I couldn't rouse myself to go to a Dodgers game for which we had tickets. By that evening, I had a good fever and an even better headache. At 3:00 a.m., Lisa packed our two infant kids in the backseat and drove me to the emergency room of our local hospital, where the doctor told her that I had spinal meningitis. His prognosis was that I would probably not survive the next two hours.

For the next eleven days, I was mostly unconscious in St. Luke Hospital's intensive-care unit. After they released me, I spent another thirty days at home recuperating, intravenously treating myself with 90 million units of penicillin a day. (For the next year, I smelled like a mushroom.) Finally, when I returned to my day job at the word-processing department of my law firm, I found that the office manager—believing that I would probably die—had hired three full-time, permanent employees to take my place. This left me in an awkward position that realistically could not continue for long. This job—my one constant source of income over the past six years—was going to end soon. None of the résumés I'd sent out had borne fruit.

Lisa and I had to make some decisions.

We felt we'd given LA a good try. I'd worked six years with my law firm, and in that time had published three novels. But living there was expensive and in many ways dispiriting. Our daughter was about a year away from kindergarten, and the public schools in our area of LA were dismal. Last but certainly not least, nobody was breaking down my door with any kind of a job offer. We decided we would move to northern California, where life was much less expensive, and that before I got another full-time day job, I would give full-time writing one last good try. This was really in my heart what I wanted to do; further, it was what I was getting to be good at. I thought that if I could just focus on the right kind of Plan A book—something like *Dead Irish* but with a bigger canvas and wider-ranging themes, I might have a chance of finding an audience.

By now, with the meningitis and recovery, I'd given Dismas Hardy nearly two years off. I knew from *Dead Irish* that he could carry the weight of a big story, and I would no longer sell him short, as I felt I had with *The Vig*. I would plumb the depths of his Everyman persona in this new book.

To do it, of course, I was aware that I had to find those last personal elements that I knew so intimately from my own life. I was a father of two, and now Hardy would be a father of two. I would know his home life, and it would be central to who he was. Since having my own children, I had come to understand something that no one can know until they have the experience—that children and family are the center of life for most people. Though these domestic relationships didn't provide quite the zing of romantic entanglements, and although the role of husband and father certainly wasn't the expected reality for a hard-boiled hero in a mystery, nevertheless it was central in everyday life. In the life of Everyman. As so it would be in that of Dismas Hardy.

Beyond that, I had worked in a business legal environment for six years and knew the basic routines of lawyers' lives, the stresses of the job, the conflicts, the hours, the betrayals, the moral ambiguities. I didn't know much, if anything, about criminal law, but then again, I realized that after ten years away from the law field tending bar, Hardy wouldn't be so hot on the details himself. And, in fact, his interest was never so much in fighting crime and prosecuting criminals as it was in seeking justice.

As I started *Hard Evidence,* featuring no longer a bartender, but a married working attorney named Dismas Hardy walking a shark, trying to keep it alive in the Steinhart Aquarium, I knew that he had finally revealed the last secrets of his nature to me. He was not and could not be a larger-than-life superhero. He was a regular guy, a working-stiff, nonglamorous defense attorney with a closely knit (yet often conflicted) family and a coterie of loyal friends. You'd like him—he might beat you at darts, but he'd buy you a drink afterward. He was the kind of person you'd care about if he showed up in any kind of novel at all, not just a mystery.

And in fact, while I was writing *Hard Evidence,* I discovered to my joy and satisfaction that the distinction in my mind between so-called genre work and "real" novels had somehow all but disappeared. I was writing a Plan A novel now, a serious, grown-up novel about the human condition, and that's what I'd be writing in the future.

And whenever Dismas Hardy came up and told me he was ready to shoulder the load again, he'd be my man.

There is a last chapter, a postscript, to the story of Dismas Hardy.

Hard Evidence was published to a minimum of fanfare with a relatively small print run. Nevertheless, because I believed that Dismas Hardy had become a fully self-actualized character, and because I had what I thought was a terrific plot idea for another book, I started working almost immediately on *The 13th Juror*.

The vagaries of publishing being what they are, there is usually a significant lag between sending a book to a publisher and its actual publication. Likewise, there is often a further hiatus between publication and the sale of any subsidiary rights, such as paperback or foreign deals. I sent *Hard Evidence* to my publisher in about March of 1993, and it was published in 1994, by which time I was nearly finished with *The 13th Juror*. In the summer of 1994, I offered *The 13th Juror* to Donald I. Fine, but the advance he offered was unacceptable—actually less than he'd offered for *Hard Evidence*—so I decided to take *The 13th Juror* to the open market.

It was a depressing experience.

Although twelve publishers had indicated that they would be willing to take part in an auction for the book, on the actual day, none of them made a bid. Eventually, I received more than twenty rejection notices. They were from just about every New York publisher except two, William Morrow and Donald I. Fine. In the end, Fine outbid Morrow, but my decision to accept Fine's offer was a long, drawn-out, and exhausting one.

And reluctantly, with those twenty or so rejections of the best I could do with Dismas Hardy hanging heavily in my heart, I decided that much as I liked him, I would have to let him fade into the background. He was clearly not a commercial character. There was no sign that he'd resonated in any important way with readers or with publishers.

It was time to give another character a shot.

Abe Glitsky—Hardy's long-standing friend from his days as a cop and already a major character in the earlier Hardy novels—couldn't have been more different from Hardy, but he was a pretty fascinating guy in his own right. I decided to explore his life and character first in *A Certain Justice* and then, because I enjoyed being with his cursed and curmudgeonly self so much, in *Guilt*.

But a funny thing happened two years after I'd initially submitted *The 13th Juror,* when I was halfway through the process of writing *Guilt. The 13th Juror* finally came out in paperback and jumped onto the *New York Times* bestseller list, where it stayed and stayed and stayed. By this time, I had changed publishers to Delacorte, and that house's paperback imprint, Dell/Island, had published *The 13th Juror,* which was suddenly a very hot property.

And that made Dismas Hardy commercially viable at last.

Could Hardy, my publishers wondered, ever be coaxed into coming back again? Could he take another big novel with a big theme onto his big shoulders and carry it all—or mostly—by himself?

I allowed as how he could.

And that's what he's been doing ever since.

LAURA LIPPMAN

Laura Lippman was born in Atlanta, Georgia, in 1959. Her family moved to Baltimore, Maryland, in 1965, when her father took a job as an editorial writer for the *Sun*. It was here that she grew up, a couple of doors down from the Monaghan family, which included three boys and two girls. She went to Northwestern University's Medill School of Journalism. Seeking a job as a reporter, she landed a position in Waco, Texas, then another in San Antonio, before moving back to Baltimore, where she was hired by the *Evening Sun*, which soon merged with the morning paper. She was able to write a book a year about Tess Monaghan, the self-described "accidental private eye," while working full-time as a Baltimore newspaper reporter, until she retired from that position in 2001.

Laura Lippman has been nominated for virtually every mystery-writing award that exists and has won most of them; she has arguably had more honors per book than any other mystery writer alive, winning the Edgar®, Anthony, Agatha, Shamus, Nero Wolfe, Gumshoe, and Barry awards. She was also the first genre writer to be recognized by the Maryland Library Association as author of the year. In addition to the Tess Monaghan novels, she has written numerous short stories, edited the anthology *Baltimore Noir*, and produced four stand-alone crime novels: *Every Secret Thing* (2003), *The Power of Three* (2005), *What the Dead Know* (2007), and *Life Sentences* (2009).

TESS MONAGHAN

BY LAURA LIPPMAN

The Accidental Detective
By Laura Lippman
Special to the *Beacon-Light*

BALTIMORE—Tess Monaghan spends a lot of time thinking about what she calls the relief problem. Not relief to foreign hot spots, although she can become quickly heated on almost any political subject you wish to discuss. No, Monaghan, perhaps Baltimore's best-known private investigator, thinks a lot about what we'll call *feminine* relief.

"If you're a guy on surveillance, you have a lot more options," she says, sitting in her Butchers Hill office on a recent fall morning and flipping through one of the catalogs that cater to the special needs of investigators and private-security firms. Much of this high-tech gadgetry holds little interest for Monaghan, who admits to mild Luddite tendencies. That said, she's so paranoid about caller ID that she uses two cell phones—one for outgoing calls, one for incoming.

"Do you know that at the racetracks in Delaware, the ones with slot machines, they find dozens of adult diapers in the trash every day?" she asks suddenly. "Think about it. There are people who are so crazed for slots that they wear Depends, lest they have to give up a 'hot' machine. Do you think Bill Bennett wore Depends?" Monaghan, who assumes that others can follow her often jumpy train of thought, has moved on to the former secretary of education, reported to have had an almost pathological addiction to slot machines, even as he made millions advocating family values.

"No, no, no," she decides, not waiting for answers to the questions she has posed. "That's why he had the machines brought to him in a private room. Slots—what a wussy way to lose money. Give me the track every time. Horse plus human plus variable track conditions equals a highly satisfying form of interactive entertainment. With gambling, that's the only way to stay sane. You have to think of it as going to a Broadway show in which you have a vested interest in the outcome. Set aside how much you're willing to lose, the way you might decide how much you're willing to pay to go to a sporting event. If you go home with a dollar more than you were willing to lose, you've won."

So now that Monaghan has held forth on compulsive gambling, adult diapers, and, by implication, her own relief needs, could she share a few biographical details? The year she was born, for example?

"No," she says with a breezy grin. "You're a reporter, right? Look it up at the department of motor vehicles. If you can't track down something that basic, you're probably not the right woman for the job."

Rumor has it that Monaghan loathes the press.

"Rumor," Monaghan says, "isn't always wrong."

Baltimore Born, Bred, and Buttered

She has been called Baltimore's best-known private detective, Baltimore's hungriest private detective, and, just once, Baltimore's most eligible private detective. (Her father went behind her back and entered her into *Baltimore* magazine's annual feature on the city's "hot" singles.) But although her work and its consequences have often been featured in the news, Monaghan, a former reporter, has been surprisingly successful at keeping information about herself out of the public domain. At least until now. Oh yes, Ms. Monaghan, this reporter knows her way around public documents.

Monaghan was born at St. Agnes Hospital, and while official documents disagree on the year, she's undeniably a member of Generation X or Y, a post-boomer born to an unlikely duo who prove the old adage that opposites attract. Patrick Monaghan, described by his daughter as the world's most taciturn Irishman, was the oldest of seven children. He grew up in a crowded South Baltimore row house and, later, the Charles Village area.

Meanwhile, Judith Weinstein was the youngest of five from a well-to-do Northwest Baltimore family. She was just entering college when her father's eponymous drugstore chain entered a messy and devastating bankruptcy. Monaghan and Weinstein met via local politics, working on Carleton Sickles's failed 1966 bid for the Democratic nomination for governor. The couple remain active in politics; Monaghan remembers riding her tricycle around the old Stonewall Democratic Club as a five-year-old. Her father worked for years as a city liquor inspector, then began running his own club, the Point, which has thrived in an unlikely location on Franklintown Road. Her mother works for the National Security Agency and says she cannot divulge what she does.

"I'm pretty sure she's a secretary," Monaghan says, "but for all I know she's a jet-setting spy who manages to get home by 5:30 every night and put supper on the table."

The family settled in Ten Hills on the city's west side, and Monaghan attended public schools, graduating from Western High School's prestigious A-course and then attending Washington College in Chestertown, where she majored in English. By her testimony, she discovered two lifelong influences on the Eastern Shore— rowing and Whitney Talbot. A member of a very old, very rich, and very connected Valley family, Talbot has a work ethic as fierce as the one instilled in Monaghan by her middle-class parents, and the two have long reveled in their competitive friendship.

Upon graduation, Monaghan joined the *Star* as a general-assignments reporter, while Talbot—who had transferred to Yale and majored in Japanese—landed a job on the *Beacon-Light's* editorial pages. But Monaghan's timing turned out to be less than felicitous—the *Star* folded before she was twenty-six, and the *Beacon-Light* declined to hire her. Cast adrift, she relied on the kindness of family members to help her make ends meet on her meager freelance salary. She lived in a cheap apartment above her aunt's bookstore in Fells Point and depended on her uncle to throw her assignments for various state agencies. It was in Kitty Monaghan's store, Women and Children First, that she met her current boyfriend, Edward "Crow" Ransome. When she was twenty-nine, she fell into PI work; she likes to call herself the "accidental detective," a riff on Anne Tyler's *The Accidental Tourist*.

"Does anyone plan to become a private detective?" Monaghan asks. "It's not a rhetorical question. I suppose somewhere there's a little boy or girl dreaming of life as an investigator, but everyone I know seems to have done some other kind of work first. Lawyer, cop. All I know is I did a favor for a friend, botched it royally, and then tried to help his lawyer get him out of the mess I created. When it was over, the lawyer pressed me to work for him as an investigator, then pushed me out of the nest and all but forced me to open my own agency."

That lawyer, Tyner Gray, would end up marrying Tess's aunt Kitty. Monaghan pretends to be horrified by this development but seems to have genuine affection for the man who has mentored her since she was in her late twenties.

Her agency, Keys Investigation, Inc., is technically co-owned by Edward Keys, a retired Baltimore police detective who seems to spend most of his time on Fenwick Island, Delaware. (Asked to comment for this story, Keys declined repeatedly and would not respond to rumors that he has, in fact, met Monaghan in the flesh only once.) Monaghan appears to be the sole employee on the premises of the onetime dry cleaners that serves as her office, although she jokes that there are two part-time workers "who have agreed to accept their compensation in dog biscuits." Those would be Esskay, a retired racing greyhound named for her love of Baltimore's best-known sausage, and Miata, a docile Doberman with infallible instincts about people. "If she had growled at you, I wouldn't have let you over the threshold," Monaghan says. "I've learned the hard way to trust Miata."

The office is filled with Baltimore-bilia—the old "Time for a Haircut" clock from a Woodlawn barbershop and several Esskay tins. "People give them to me," Monaghan claims. "I'm not prone to collecting things."

Has anyone ever commented on the irony that Monaghan, who sits beneath that "Time for a Haircut" clock, once had a most untimely haircut, when a serial killer sliced off her signature braid? Monaghan shot the man in self-defense, but not before he killed a former transportation cop with whom she was working.

"I don't talk about that," she says. "I understand you have to ask about it. I was a reporter, and I'd have asked about it too. But it's something I never discuss."

Okay, so life and death have been shot down as topics. What would she prefer to talk about?

"Do you think the Orioles are ever going to get it together? One World Series in my lifetime. It's *so* depressing."

A Day in the Life

Monaghan lives in a renovated cottage on a hidden street alongside Stony Run Park in the prestigious Roland Park neighborhood. That's how she puts it, her voice curlicued with sarcasm: "Welcome to the *prestigious* Roland Park neighborhood." The house continues the rather whimsical decorating themes of her office, with a large neon sign that reads "Human Hair." What is it with Monaghan and hair?

"You're a little overanalytical," she counters. "One of the liabilities of modern times is that everyone thinks they're fluent in Freudian theory, and they throw the terms around so casually. I don't have much use for psychiatry."

Has she ever been in therapy?

"Once," she admits promptly. "Court ordered. You know what, though? I'd like to reverse myself. In general, I don't have much use for psychiatry and I thought it was bulls———t when they put me in anger management. But it did help, just not in the way it was intended."

How so?

"It's not important," she says, reaching for her right knee, a strange nervous tic that has popped up before. "Let's just say that it doesn't hurt sometimes to be a little angry."

Monaghan is speaking in low tones, trying not to awaken her boyfriend. Six years her junior, Ransome works for Monaghan's father, scouting the musical acts that appear at his bar. Ransome's workday ended a mere four hours ago, at four a.m., while Monaghan's day began at six a.m. with a workout at the local boathouse.

Monaghan and Ransome have been a couple, on and off, for more than four years. Do they plan to marry?

"You know what? You and my mom should get together. You'd really hit it off. She asks me that every day. Ready to experience the exciting life of a private detective?" She draws out the syllables in *exciting* with the same sarcasm she used for *prestigious*.

What's her destination this morning?

"The most wonderful place on earth—the Clarence Mitchell Jr. Courthouse."

And, truth be told, the courthouse does seem to be a veritable fairyland to Monaghan, who stalks its halls and disappears into various records rooms, greeting many clerks by name. But wouldn't it be more efficient to work from her office? Isn't most of the information online?

"Some," says Monaghan, who also relies on an online network of female investigators from across the country. "Not all. And there's a serendipity to real life that the Internet can't duplicate. Do you use the library? For anything? Well, sometimes you end up picking up the book next to the book you were looking for, and it's that book that changes your life. Google's great, but it's no substitute for getting out and talking to people. Plus, the courthouse is only a block from Cypriana. So whenever I come here, I can reward myself with a celebratory chicken pita with extra feta cheese."

Isn't 11:30 a little early for lunch?

"I've been up since six! Besides, you want to get there before the judges release the various juries for their lunch break."

A Tree Grows in Baltimore

Whitney Talbot strides into Cypriana with the authority of a health inspector on a follow-up visit. Her green eyes cut across the small restaurant with laserlike intensity.

"She's the opposite of Browning's duchess," Monaghan whispers. "Her looks go everywhere, but she *dislikes* whatever she sees."

"I heard that," Talbot says, even as she places her order. "And I like Cypriana just fine. It's the clientele that worries me. I saw the mayor in here just last week. How am I supposed to digest lunch under those circumstances?"

She settles at our table with an enormous Greek salad, which she proceeds to eat leaf by leaf, without dressing. "Whitney's not anorexic," Monaghan assures me. "Her taste buds were simply destroyed by old WASP cooking."

"I prefer to get my calories through gin," Talbot says primly. "Now, what do you want to know about Tess? I know everything— *everything*. I know when she lost her virginity. I know the strange ritualistic way she eats peanut M&M's. I know that she rereads *Marjorie Morningstar* every year—"

"I do not," Monaghan objects, outraged only by the last assertion.

". . . and cries over it too. *I* reread the *Alexandria Quartet* every year."

"Because you're so f——ing pretentious."

"Pretentious suggests pretending, trying to make others believe that you're something you're not. There's not a pretentious bone in my body."

"There's nothing *but* bones in your body, you fatless wench."

Perhaps it would be better if Talbot were interviewed separately, out of Monaghan's hearing?

"Why?" Talbot wonders. "It's not as if I could be any more candid. My first name should have been Cassandra. I'm a truth teller from way back. It saves so much time, always telling the truth—"

"And never worrying about anyone's feelings," Monaghan mutters.

"Tess is still miffed because I'm the one who called her Baltimore's hungriest detective, back when the *Washington Post* did that travel piece on her favorite haunts. She does like a good meal, but she wears her calories well. So, okay, here's the unvarnished truth about Theresa Esther Weinstein Monaghan, aka Tesser, although Testy suits her better."

Talbot leans forward, while Monaghan visibly steels herself.

"She's a good friend, utterly loyal. She lies as if it were her second language, but only when she has to. She's smarter than anyone gives her credit for—including Tess herself. She's brave. You know those tiresome women who don't have any female friends? I'm not one of those. I don't have any friends *period*. I don't like people much. But I make an exception for Tess."

"With friends like these . . ." Monaghan shrugs. In the time it has taken Talbot to eat five lettuce leaves, Monaghan has polished off her chicken pita, but she still seems hungry. "Vaccaro's?" she suggests hopefully. "Berger cookies? Otterbein cookies? Something? Anything? I rowed this morning and I plan to run this afternoon. I'm almost certainly in caloric deficit."

Does she work out for her job? How much physical stamina is required? (And does she know that she won't be able to eat like that forever?)

"There's actually very little physical activity involved in my work, and when there is—look, I'm five foot nine and my percentage of body fat is under twenty. I can run a mile in seven minutes and I could still compete in head races if I was that masochistic. And for all that, there's not an able-bodied guy on the planet I could beat up. So no, it's not for work. It's for peace of mind. Rowing clears my head in a way that nothing else does—alcohol, meditation, pot—"

"Not that Tess has ever broken the drug laws of this country," Talbot puts in.

Monaghan sighs. "With every year, I become more law-abiding. A business, a mortgage. I have things to lose. I want to be one of those people who lives untethered, with no material possessions."

"She talks a good talk," Talbot says. "But you've seen the house, right? It's filled with stuff. She's put down roots—in Roland Park, of all places. You know what Tess is like? The ailanthus, the tree that grew in Brooklyn. Have you ever tried to get rid of one of those things? It's darn near impossible. No one's ever going to be able to yank Tess out of Baltimore soil."

"Now, that's a novel I *do* read every year," Monaghan says. "An American classic, but not everyone agrees. *Because it's about a girl.*"

Talbot yawns daintily, bored. "I vote for Otterbein cookies. They have them at the Royal Farms over on Key Highway."

Family Ties

It is late afternoon at the Point, and Crow Ransome—"No one calls me Ed or Edgar, *ever*," he says, and it's the only time he sounds annoyed—agrees to take a break and walk along Franklintown Road, where the trees are just beginning to turn gold and crimson.

"I love Leakin Park," he says of the vast wooded hills around him. The area is beautiful, but best known as the dumping ground of choice for Baltimore killers back in the day, a fact that Ransome seems unaware of. "I'm not a city kid by nature—I grew up in Charlottesville, Virginia—and I like having a few rural-seeming corners in my life."

Will he stay in Baltimore, then?

"It's the only real condition of being with Tess. 'Love me, love my city.' She can't live anywhere else. Truly, I think she wouldn't be able to stay long in any place that wasn't Baltimore."

What is it about the private eye and her hometown?

Relative to his girlfriend, Ransome is more thoughtful, less impulsive in his comments. "I think it's an extension of her family. You know Tess's family is far from perfect. Her uncle Donald Weinstein was involved in a political scandal. Her grandfather Weinstein—well, the less said about him, the better. Her uncle Spike, the Point's original owner, served time, although I've never been clear on what he did. No one ever speaks of it, but it had to be a felony, because he wasn't allowed to have the liquor license in his own name. Anyway, she loves them all fiercely. Not in spite of what they've done, but because they are who they are; they're family.

"I think she feels the same way about Baltimore. It's imperfect. Boy, is it imperfect. And there are parts of its past that make you wince. It's not all marble steps and waitresses calling you 'hon,' you know. Racial strife in the '60s, the riots during the Civil War. F. Scott Fitzgerald said it was civilized and gay and rotted and polite. The terms are slightly anachronistic now, but I think he was essentially right.

"The bottom line," Ransome says, turning around to head back to the Point, "is that Tess really can't handle change. When I first knew her, she had been eating the same thing for breakfast—at Jimmy's in Fell's Point—for something like two years straight. Oh, she will change, but it's very abrupt and inexplicable, and the new regimen will simply supplant the old one. When she crosses the threshold of our neighborhood coffeehouse, they start fixing her latte before she gets to the cash register. She's that predictable.

"Truthfully, I keep worrying that I'll wake up one morning and *I'll* no longer be one of Tess's ruts."

But Ransome's smile belies his words. He clearly feels no anxiety about his relationship with Monaghan, whatever its ups and downs in the past.

What about marriage or children?

Unlike Monaghan, he doesn't sidestep the question. "If children, then marriage. But if children—could Tess continue to do what she does, the way she does it? The risks she takes, her impulsiveness. All of that would have to change. I don't want her on surveillance with our baby in the car seat, or taking the child on her Dumpster-diving escapades. I'm well suited to be a stay-at-home father, but that doesn't mean I'll give Tess carte blanche to do whatever she wants professionally."

Is he signaling, ever so subtly, an end of Monaghan's involvement in Keys Investigations?

"Everything comes to an end," he says. "When you've had near-death experiences, as Tess and I both have, that's more than a pat saying or a cliché."

Yes—about those near-death experiences—but here Ransome proves as guarded as his girlfriend.

"She doesn't talk about it, and I don't talk about it. But I'll tell you this much—when she reaches for her knee? She's thinking about it. She has a scar there, where she fell on a piece of broken glass the night she was almost killed. Sometimes I think the memory lives in that scar."

Not a Lone Wolf

The private detective has been a sturdy archetype in American pop culture for sixty-plus years, and it's hard not to harbor romantic notions about Monaghan. But she is quick to point out that she has little in common with the characters created by Raymond Chandler and Dashiell Hammett, and not just because Philip Marlowe and Sam Spade are fictional.

"I'm not a loner, far from it. I live with someone; I have friends. I have so much family it's almost embarrassing at times. My father was one of seven, my mother one of five. I was an only child, but I was never a *lonely* one. In fact, most of my clients are referrals from people I know." A rueful smile. "That's made for some interesting times."

A favor for her father, in fact, led to Monaghan's identifying a Jane Doe homicide victim—and unraveling an unseemly web of favors that showed, once again, that Maryland is always in the forefront when it comes to political scandals. Her uncle Donald asked her to find the missing family of furrier Mark Rubin. And it was Talbot who, inadvertently, gave Monaghan the assignment that almost led to her death. Once one pores over Monaghan's case work, it begins to seem as if almost all her jobs have been generated by nepotism.

"Whew," she says. "Strong word. A loaded word, very much a pejorative. How did *you* get your job?" When no answer is forthcoming, she goes on: "How does anyone get anywhere, get anything in this world? I got into Washington College on my own merits, I guess, but otherwise I've needed family and friends. Not to pull me through or cover for me, but to help me here and there. Is that wrong? Does it undercut what I have done?"

Then what's her greatest solo accomplishment? What can she take credit for?

Monaghan waits a long time before answering. We are in the Brass Elephant, her favorite bar, and she is nursing a martini—gin, not vodka, to which she objects on principle. Monaghan is full of such idiosyncratic principles. She won't drink National Bohemian since the brewery pulled up stakes in Baltimore. She says Matthew's serves the best pizza in town, but confesses that her favorite is Al Pacino's. She doesn't like women who walk to work in athletic shoes, or people who let their dogs run off lead as a sneaky way to avoid cleaning up after them. She hates the Mets even though she wasn't alive for the indignity of 1969, and has a hard time rooting for the Ravens because of "bad karma." (Cleveland Browns owner Art Modell brought the team here in the mid-'90s, and although the NFL made sure Cleveland kept its name and records—a concession not made to Baltimore when the Colts decamped for Indianapolis—it still bothers Monaghan.)

"I've managed, more or less, to live according to what I think is right. Not always—I can be unkind. I've indulged in gossip, which should be one of the seven deadly sins. I'm quick to anger, although seldom on my own behalf. Overall, though, I'm not a bad person. I'm a good friend, a decent daughter, and a not-too-infuriating girlfriend."

She slaps her empty glass on the counter and says, "Look at the time. We have to go."

Where?

"Just follow me."

She runs out of the bar, down the Brass Elephant's elegant staircase and into Charles Street, heading south at an impressive clip. In a few blocks, she mounts the steps to the Washington Monument, throwing a few dollars into the honor box at its foot.

"Come on, come on, come on," she exhorts. "It's only 228 steps."

So this is the run that Monaghan planned to take this evening. The narrow, winding stairwell is claustrophobically close and smells strongly of ammonia, not the best fragrance on top of a gin martini, but Monaghan's pace and footing seem unaffected by her cocktail hour. She jogs briskly, insistent that everyone keep up.

At the top, the reason for her rush becomes clear. The sun is just beginning to set, and the western sky is a brilliant rose shade that is kind to the city's more ramshackle neighborhoods, while the eastern sky is an equally flattering inky blue. To the north, Penn Station is a bright white beacon dominated by the monstrous man-woman statue with its glowing purple heart. To the south, lights begin to come on along the waterfront. Monaghan points out the Continental Building on Calvert Street.

"Hammett worked there, as a Pinkerton. And the birds that are used as ornamentation, the falcons? They're gold now, but it's said they were black back in Hammett's day, so we might be looking at the birthplace of the Maltese Falcon. Look to the southwest, toward Hollins Market, and you can see where Mencken lived, and Russell Baker. Anne Tylerville is out of sight, but you were there this morning, when you visited my home. That church, virtually at our feet? It's where Francis Scott Key worshipped, while his descendant F. Scott Fitzgerald liked to drink at the Owl Bar in the Belvedere, only a few blocks to the north."

She inhales deeply, a little raggedly; even Monaghan isn't so fit that the climb has left her unaffected. She seems drunker now than she did at the bottom, giddy with emotion. She throws open her arms as if to embrace the whole city.

"I mean, really," she says. "Why would anyone live anywhere else?"

DAVID MORRELL

David Morrell is the author of *First Blood,* the award-winning novel in which Rambo was created. He holds a PhD in American literature from Pennsylvania State University and taught in the English department at the University of Iowa until he gave up his tenure to devote himself to a full-time writing career. "The mild-mannered professor with the bloody-minded visions," as one reviewer described him, Morrell is a cofounder of the International Thriller Writers organization. His numerous bestselling novels include *The Brotherhood of the Rose* (the basis for a top-rated NBC miniseries), *The Fraternity of the Stone, The Fifth Profession,* and *Extreme Denial* (set in Santa Fe, New Mexico, where he lives). He is also the author of *The Successful Novelist: A Lifetime of Lessons about Writing and Publishing.*

Morrell has been called "the father of the modern action novel." He is a three-time recipient of the distinguished Bram Stoker Award, the latest for his novel *Creepers.* ITW honored him with its prestigious ThrillerMaster Award. To learn the full story of his relationship with Hemingway scholar Philip Young, please read his foreword to *American Fiction, American Myth: Essays by Philip Young,* which Morrell coedited with Sandra Spanier. You can also visit his website at www.davidmorrell.net.

RAMBO

BY DAVID MORRELL

From 1966 to 1970, I lived in a town surrounded by mountains in the middle of Pennsylvania. The town was State College–University Park, the main campus of Pennsylvania State University. I was a graduate student in the English department. More important with regard to the creation of Rambo, I was a Canadian, born and raised in the twin city of Kitchener-Waterloo in southern Ontario.

The path that led me to Penn State was unusual. In high school, I was hardly what you'd call a motivated student. I liked English classes. I enjoyed acting in local plays. Otherwise, I spent eight hours a day watching television. Truly, I didn't go to bed until our local station signed off for the night. My high school principal once summoned me from a trigonometry class (merciful salvation) and told me that I would never amount to much.

As things turned out, television showed me the way. At 8:30 p.m. on the first Friday of October in 1960, I watched the premiere of a new television series, *Route 66,* and my life changed. That series was about two young men in a Corvette convertible, who drove across the United States in search of America and themselves. It was filmed entirely on location. It was brilliantly acted and photographed.

But what I grew to care about was that the majority of the scripts—a blend of intense action and powerful themes—were written by Stirling Silliphant. They so impressed me that at the age of seventeen, I decided that I wanted to be a writer and that Silliphant would be my model. I wrote to Silliphant to tell him so and received a two-page, single-spaced letter that encouraged me to pursue my ambition. Realizing that a writer ought to have an education, I suddenly wanted to get a BA.

St. Jerome's College (now a university) was then an affiliate of the University of Waterloo in southern Ontario. It was so small that the English honors program consisted of six students. Often, in the manner of an Oxford tutorial, one of us was required to teach a class while the professor watched and made comments. I received a wonderful education there, but in the process, I forgot my ambition to be Silliphant. At the start of my fourth year in the BA program, I got married. I planned to become a high school English teacher, but then another writer changed my life.

St. Jerome's had a library the size of a large living room. One afternoon, expecting to be disappointed, I looked for books that analyzed the work of one of my favorite authors, Ernest Hemingway. To my surprise, I found one. Written by Philip Young, this is how it began:

> On the Place Contrescarpe at the summit of the rue
> Cardinal Lemoine, Harry remembered, there was a room
> at the top of a tall hotel, and it was in this room that he
> had written "the start of all he was to do."

If you've ever studied literature in college, you know that scholarly books don't start that way. But Young's book had so much tone and vitality that in parts it had the drama of a novel. His style was spellbinding. He made me feel that he was talking directly to me, and he not only informed me, he made me smile. Indeed, a couple of times, he made me laugh, causing a librarian to give me a disapproving look.

By the end of the afternoon, I was so overwhelmed that I went home and said to my wife, Donna, who was a high school history teacher, "I read this amazing book about Hemingway. It's written by Philip Young, who's a professor at Penn State, and it's so fabulously written that I suddenly have this crazy idea. I'd like to go to graduate school at Penn State. I'd like to study with Young. Would you be willing to quit your teaching job and go there with me?"

Donna, who had just learned that she was pregnant, answered, "Yes."

Thus, in the summer of 1966, shortly after Donna gave birth to our daughter, we packed everything that was important to us into our green Volkswagen Beetle and set off on our odyssey to the United States, where I eventually became Young's graduate assistant and, under his supervision, wrote my master's thesis on Hemingway's style.

This is where Rambo comes in. Penn State paid me to teach freshman composition courses. It also provided reasonably priced apartments at a place called Graduate Circle. Shortly after we moved into one of the units, I met a neighbor, and almost the first thing he said to me was "This damned Vietnam War is getting worse and worse. If it keeps up, the government might stop giving out student deferments."

I had no idea what he was talking about. The only time I'd heard about Vietnam was three years earlier, in a 1963 *Route 66* episode, "Fifty Miles from Home," in which Silliphant had written about a US soldier who returned from Vietnam (wherever *that* was) and had trouble shutting down his war mentality. (The episode illustrates how ahead of its time that series was.) In Canada, I'd never paid attention to any news about the Vietnam War. It simply wasn't on my radar. But at Penn State, typical of universities across the United States, I soon discovered that the war was a constant topic.

Unwilling to admit my ignorance and stand out as a foreigner, I headed for the library, where I discovered that North and South Vietnam were in Southeast Asia. Since 1959, the United States had been involved in a conflict between the two, siding against the Communist regime of the north. In 1964, two American destroyers claimed to have been fired upon by North Vietnamese torpedo boats. An outraged US Congress issued the Gulf of Tonkin Resolution, which gave President Johnson the power to conduct military operations against North Vietnam without declaring war. (Many years later, declassified documents revealed that the torpedo boat attacks did not occur and that members of the Johnson administration knew they hadn't occurred but preferred to use bogus intelligence reports to justify the attacks on North Vietnam.)

I also learned that increasing numbers of young American men were being conscripted and sent to Vietnam. The burden of the draft fell on the unemployed and the uneducated, while college students tended to be given deferments. The pressure to receive scholarships and earn higher-than-average grades was intense, and some students, such as my Graduate Circle neighbor, worried about a time when students would no longer be exempt (this eventually happened in 1971). I didn't share the same concerns because, in addition to being a student, I was also married with a child, and on top of that, I was foreign, but I didn't want to set myself apart by admitting that. Moreover, the documentation that came with the temporary-resident card allowing me to stay in the United States made it clear that as a guest, I should refrain from expressing political opinions, and of course, political activities were out of the question. Failure to meet this requirement could result in deportation.

The result was that I fell into a habit of listening to what my fellow students said about the Vietnam War and of studying news reports about it while keeping my opinions to myself. As the decade continued, demonstrations against the war increased across the country. At Penn State, some student teachers made Norman Mailer's *The Armies of the Night,* about the 1967 antiwar march on the Pentagon, a required reading assignment in freshman courses.

Meanwhile, some returning veterans enrolled at Penn State. A half dozen of them were assigned to one of my composition courses, where they had major problems accepting me as an authority figure. We were the same age, but they'd been risking their lives in a far-off jungle. As far as they were concerned, I was a draft dodger. Their hostility was strong enough that I asked for an after-class meeting. There, I explained my unique circumstances and won their trust enough to persuade them to tell me about themselves. I learned about how they had nightmares and broke out in spontaneous sweats and dove behind cover whenever an unexpected loud noise sounded like a gunshot. I learned about their anger, their frustration, and their fears. These days, we have a term for what they were enduring—post-traumatic stress disorder. But back then, the only description I could think of dated back to World War I: shell shock.

Across the United States, the antiwar protests became more frequent and more extreme. In early 1968, the government's insistence that there was a light at the end of the tunnel lost credibility during Tet, the Vietnamese Lunar New Year celebration, when eighty thousand North Vietnamese guerrilla fighters attacked more than a hundred strategic targets in South Vietnam, including nearly all the provincial capitals and Saigon itself.

But my wife and I didn't need to pay attention to the news to realize that the war wasn't getting better. In those days, Penn State was on a quarterly system. Four times a year, after classes ended, Donna and I packed suitcases, secured our daughter in a car seat, and drove our Volkswagen Beetle north to visit our relatives in Canada. There wasn't a direct route. We often took back roads through small towns suffering hard economic times. During our back-and-forth trips in 1966, we passed cemeteries that had occasional American flags on graves, signifying soldiers who had died in Vietnam. In 1967, there were more flags. In 1968, the percentage had increased so dramatically that we wondered if the casualty reports the government released were understated.

Nineteen sixty-eight: Martin Luther King Jr. was assassinated that year. So was Bobby Kennedy. At Columbia University, student protests escalated to the point that five buildings were occupied and the university was shut down. I watched the *CBS Evening News* and was struck by two back-to-back stories. The first showed American soldiers during a firefight in Vietnam. The second showed American National Guardsmen patrolling a riot-devastated street in a burned-out inner city of America. I can no longer recall which riot it was. There were so many. Within days of the King assassination, for example, there had been 110 of them, including one in Washington, DC, ten blocks from the White House. While these were race riots, they had relevance to Vietnam because, compared to whites, a disproportionate number of blacks from inner cities were being drafted due to their poverty and lack of education. It occurred to me that if the television sound were turned down, the two stories might seem like aspects of a single story. The devastated street might appear to be in Vietnam and the firefight might appear to be in the United States.

Watching another television news broadcast, I was stunned by the violence at the Democratic National Convention in Chicago. War protesters marching toward the convention were greeted by almost twelve thousand Chicago police officers, who waged a riot of their own, assaulting anyone in their path, including reporters. These police rioters were so out of control that they didn't care if their violence was broadcast for hours on network television. It suddenly occurred to me: What if one of those protesters was like those angry veterans I'd encountered in the classes I taught? What if one of those veterans was a man with exceptional combat skills, a former member of a Special Forces team, an escaped POW, and a recipient of the Medal of Honor? What if he'd decided the war was wrong and believed that he'd earned the right to protest it without seeming to be unpatriotic? What if he was furious to begin with, and a police club striking his skull now filled him with an absolutely destructive rage?

In that fashion, the idea for *First Blood* began growing in me. I recalled a newspaper item about a group of hippies who'd been arrested in a southwestern town. Their beards and hair had been forcibly shaved off, after which they'd been driven out of town, left among the sun-baked yucca plants at the side of the road, and told to keep going. What if one of them had been my imaginary Special Forces veteran, whose experiences in Vietnam had so disturbed him that he'd dropped out of society? How would he have reacted to a policeman coming at him with a razor?

The violent polarization of America became so intense that many of my fellow students feared that the country was headed toward a civil war. I wondered if that could be the subject of a novel. I didn't know how to dramatize a countrywide civil war, but perhaps I could invent one in miniature. Or perhaps I could invent a small version of the Vietnam War itself, but this private war would take place in the United States.

The question was, how to tell the story. I started thinking about the person who'd made me want to be a writer in the first place: Stirling Silliphant. After *Route 66* had gone off the air in 1964, he'd become a much-in-demand screenwriter, eventually receiving an Academy Award for his 1967 adaptation of John Ball's novel *In the Heat of the Night*. That story is about a black homicide detective from Philadelphia who travels via train to visit his mother in Mississippi. A change of trains requires him to spend a few hours in a town where a prominent industrialist has just been murdered. The local police seize this black outsider as a likely suspect, only to discover that not only is he innocent but his professional skills can be an asset to them, something the murdered industrialist's widow insists upon. As the black detective and the southern police chief tensely assess each other, it becomes obvious that the movie is actually a civil-rights story masquerading as a murder mystery.

In creative-writing classes, you often hear that there are only five kinds of stories: a human being against another human being, against nature, against him- or herself, against society, or against God. I've never understood how these classifications are helpful, but there they are. Maybe there are only two classifications, however. They're very powerful and consistent with the theories in Joseph Campbell's *The Hero with a Thousand Faces,* a book I was reading in 1968 when I began thinking about *First Blood.* Someone goes on a journey, or else a stranger comes to town.

A stranger comes to town. Eight years after *Route 66* premiered, making me want to be a writer, Silliphant inspired me to write a quite different version of the stranger who comes to town.

His name was Rambo, and he was just some nothing kid for all anybody knew, standing by the pump of a gas station, on the outskirts of Madison, Kentucky. He had a long heavy beard, and his hair was hanging down over his ears to his neck, and he had his hand out, trying to thumb a ride from a car that was stopped at the pump. To see him there, leaning on one hip, a Coke bottle in his hand and a rolled-up sleeping bag near his boots on the tar pavement, you could never have guessed that on Tuesday, a day later, most of the police in Basalt County would be hunting him. Certainly you could not have guessed that by Thursday he would be running from the Kentucky National Guard and the police of six counties and a good many private citizens who liked to shoot. But then, from just seeing him there, ragged and dusty by the pump of the gas station, you could never have figured the kind of kid Rambo was, or what was about to make it all begin.

It took me months of false attempts before I could write that first paragraph. Originally, the plot was a massive, sprawling investigation of a town's hostility toward a stranger whose looks the residents don't care for and their too-late discovery that he's the last man they should anger. But I eventually realized that the story's focus was Rambo and the police chief, Teasle, who confronts him. The result was that I cut every scene in which Rambo or Teasle wasn't a viewpoint character and ended with a lean A-B, A-B structure based on scenes that alternated between them.

As for the manhunt aspects of the story, they are based on an actual incident that occurred in central Pennsylvania a few months before I arrived there in 1966. A man named William Hollenbaugh had kidnapped a seventeen-year-old girl and dragged her into the mountains. For the next eight days, state police, FBI agents, local police officers, tracking dogs, and helicopters searched those mountains in what became the largest manhunt in Pennsylvania history and ended with the girl's rescue and Hollenbaugh's death.

Locals were still talking about that manhunt in 1968, and although there aren't any parallels between Rambo and Hollenbaugh, I used details from what became known as "the Shade Gap incident" to make the hunt for Rambo as realistic as I could. I set the book in Kentucky because I wanted a slight southern flavor and because that state has a wilderness area that some people call the Grand Canyon of the East, a dramatic setting for the manhunt in my novel. But essentially, the book has a central Pennsylvania locale, to the point that Bellefonte, a town near State College, is the model for the town of Madison in *First Blood*.

I hadn't yet decided on a name for my angry Vietnam veteran. I knew that it had to give the impression of a force of nature, but nothing I tried seemed effective until one afternoon my wife made a big difference by coming home from grocery shopping. She had stopped at a roadside stand that sold apples and had been so impressed by the taste that she bought some.

"You've got to try one," Donna said. "They're delicious."

Hunched over my typewriter in search of a name, I was hardly interested in apples, but I figured if I tasted one, I could get back to work, so I took a bite and was so surprisingly impressed that I asked for the apple's name.

"Rambo," she said.

"What?" I was stunned by what I was hearing. I thought she was saying "Rimbaud," the French poet whose *A Season in Hell* had a big influence on me.

"Rambo," Donna repeated, and spelled it.

I suppose my jaw dropped. If ever a name sounded like a force of nature, that was it.

———

At Penn State, one of the texts I was required to teach to freshmen was *The Last Days of Socrates*. In it, Socrates says that no one commits evil intentionally. I'm not sure he's right about that, but he makes a good point. Most of us have a rationale for our behavior. I might be appalled by what someone else does, but that other person will provide all sorts of reasons for what he or she considers a justifiable act.

That was the logic of *First Blood*. Rambo is a radicalized Vietnam War hero who comes into conflict with a police chief who is a war hero from Korea's Chosin Reservoir. In addition, the chief is an Eisenhower Republican who is old enough to be Rambo's father and whose ideas about warfare are based on conventional tactics as opposed to the guerrilla tactics that are Rambo's specialty. They are opposites representing the divisions in American culture that led to the violent protests against the war. Rambo and the police chief are so different that they can't possibly understand each other. In angry frustration, they keep escalating their hostility until they and the town are destroyed.

It's an allegory of sorts. At one point, the police chief decides that "the kid's a better fighter, but I'm a better organizer." He sends for the man who supervised Rambo's training, Colonel Sam Trautman. The "Sam" is important. He's "Uncle Sam." He's the system that created Rambo, and inevitably that system must destroy Rambo. As the private war ends, Rambo kills the police chief, and then Uncle Sam kills Rambo.

It's an anti–Vietnam War novel that's also about bullheaded escalation and the obstinate refusal to see things from someone else's point of view. It's about the anger of student protesters who saw older people, especially those in authority, as the enemy. It's about the arrogance of people in power who won't admit they're wrong or tolerate being disagreed with. But as a Canadian who'd been required to sign a loyalty oath before he received his temporary-resident's card, I couldn't explicitly say any of that without risking exile from a country I now thought of as my home. Vietnam is hardly mentioned. My task became to write about what was happening in and to the United States and yet to present it as a thriller without moralizing and desk pounding.

In 1969, I interrupted the book to write my doctoral dissertation. Meanwhile, the war continued to escalate, spreading to Laos and Cambodia. The demonstrations against it escalated also, and suddenly they were in my backyard—on February 24, four hundred protesting students occupied the Penn State administration building. Fifteen hundred students with quite different attitudes surrounded the building and threatened the radicals inside. With difficulty, a truce was negotiated. The protesters surrendered.

In 1970, I returned to the novel. On April 15, the Penn State administration building was again occupied by demonstrators. Buses brought in seventy-five state policemen. Students stoned them as they evicted the building's occupiers. Eighteen policemen were injured. On May 4, three weeks later, Ohio National Guardsmen opened fire on unarmed student demonstrators at Kent State University. Four students were killed. Nine others were wounded. Many of the victims were bystanders. Across the country, eight million students went on strike, shutting down numerous universities. Again, I wondered what would have happened if my radicalized Vietnam veteran had been one of those students who were shot at, or if the police chief in my novel had been one of those state troopers who were pelted with rocks at Penn State.

Although my status as a guest in the United States prevented me from putting any of this in *First Blood*, I could certainly use my anger, dividing it between Rambo and the police chief, heightening their conflict. I kept thinking of Socrates and never favored one character over the other. I wanted the reader to understand both of them and to be dismayed that the protagonists in the novel weren't capable of doing the same. Their fury guaranteed their mutual destruction.

In August of 1970, Donna and I again packed suitcases, put our daughter in our little green car, and set out on another odyssey, this time to the University of Iowa, where Philip Young had written his PhD dissertation on Hemingway and where I was now employed as an assistant professor. There, one of the first things I heard about was the massive student protest that had shut down the Iowa campus after the Kent State shootings. Accounts of that event stoked my emotions when, between preparing classes and teaching, I found time to continue writing *First Blood*, eventually finishing it in the summer of 1971.

Back at Penn State, a creative-writing professor, Philip Klass (whose pen name is William Tenn), had introduced me to Henry Morrison, a literary agent who accepted me as a client. Until that time, few novels had the amount of action that *First Blood* had. Henry wondered if a hardback publisher would be comfortable with it, but six weeks after the novel was submitted, a hardback house, M. Evans and Co., accepted it. Evans was known for its bestselling nonfiction books *Body Language* and *Open Marriage,* and promoted *First Blood* with the enthusiasm it had brought to those other titles.

Columbia Pictures purchased the movie rights for Richard Brooks to write and direct. High schools and colleges taught the book. Before he was a bestselling author, Stephen King used it as one of his two texts when he taught creative writing at the University of Maine (the other was James M. Cain's *Double Indemnity*).

Columbia, evidently not liking the script that Brooks prepared, sold the film rights to Warner Bros., which hired Sydney Pollack to direct Steve McQueen, only to realize after six months of script development that McQueen, in his mid-forties, was far too old to be a returning Vietnam veteran. In another possible production, Paul Newman was considered. It's interesting that the two protagonists are so balanced in the novel that Newman's role would have been the police chief, whom some book reviewers considered to be the main character.

The project was sold to another studio, and another. Twenty-six scripts were prepared. Finally, ten years after the book's publication, a new company, Carolco, hired Ted Kotcheff to direct Sylvester Stallone, and the resulting 1982 movie was the most successful autumn release in memory.

Some changes were made. The setting was moved to the Pacific Northwest (to get Canadian financial incentives). The character of the police chief was simplified. The degree of action was reduced. Rambo was allowed to live (although in an early version of the film, he did die). Perhaps most important, the character was softened. My Rambo is furious about his war experience. He hates what he was forced to do, and he especially hates that he discovered he had a skill for killing. It's the only thing he knows how to do, but he's a genius at it, and in the novel, when the police chief keeps pushing and pushing, Rambo finally explodes, almost with pride in the destruction he can accomplish.

Not in the movie. Concerned that the character might not be sympathetic, the producers made him a victim. At the start of the film, Rambo walks soulfully to a home near a lake where a black woman hangs washed clothes on a line. Rambo, we discover, is looking for a friend who was in his Special Forces unit, but as the black woman explains, Rambo's friend died from cancer. Agent Orange, a defoliant used by the military in the Vietnam War, killed him.

After pressing these sympathetic emotional buttons, the script arranges for Rambo to walk into town, where the police chief gives him trouble because he doesn't like the look of him. In the novel, this motivation works because Rambo has the long hair and beard of a hippie, an automatic target for police officers when I wrote the book. But by 1982, ten years after the novel's publication, just about all American men had a long-haired hippie appearance. People in the audience murmured to one another, "What's wrong with the way he looks?" But then the plot got down to business, showing Rambo being harassed by the police, and when the razor came toward him, the book and the movie coincided.

I was fascinated to see how the same story could be interpreted in different ways, but I became even more fascinated when, three years later, I saw how the 1985 sequel film, *Rambo (First Blood Part II)*, interpreted the character in yet another way, as a jingoistic superhero who rescued American POWs, long rumored to still be in Vietnam, and single-handedly won a second version of the Vietnam War, which had ended with the North Vietnamese invasion of Saigon in 1975. One often-quoted line from the film was "Sir, do we get to win this time?" The obvious implication was that American politicians, influenced by the antiwar protests, had hampered the military's ability to show its full strength.

President Ronald Reagan made frequent references to Rambo in his press conferences. "I saw a Rambo movie last night. Now I know what to do the next time there's a terrorist hostage crisis." Not surprisingly, the novel was no longer taught in high schools and colleges. The jingoistic Rambo also appeared in 1988's *Rambo III,* in which he fought Soviet forces in Afghanistan, but this time audience emotions weren't as engaged because the day the movie premiered in American theaters, the Soviets pulled out of Afghanistan. Perhaps they'd heard that Rambo was coming. The political controversies struck me as being ironic inasmuch as I'd made so strong an effort to conceal the politics that had prompted me to write the book.

The ironies became stronger. In 2001, now an American citizen, I was on a publicity tour in Poland. So many journalists asked for interviews that I met with them for twelve hours in a row. They all spoke excellent English. A woman in her mid-thirties noted that I seemed surprised by all the journalistic attention I was receiving. She told me that I needed to understand the way Rambo was viewed in her country. During the Solidarity years of the late 1980s, when Polish youth protested against the Soviets, the Rambo movies were not allowed to be shown, but illegal videotapes were smuggled in. She said that protesters would watch the movies to fire up their emotions. They would then put on forehead sweatbands resembling the one Rambo wore and go out to demonstrate. In an indirect way, she said, Rambo was an element in the dissolution of the Soviet Union. Her explanation reminded me that in 1989, when the Berlin Wall fell, demonstrators were filmed painting "Rambo" on the wall before they tore parts of it down.

Rambo's name is in the *Oxford English Dictionary*. In positive and negative ways, it continues to be part of daily vocabulary around the world. The novel has been translated into twenty-six languages. It has never been out of print. But I didn't expect to see a fourth movie about Rambo. Released twenty years after the previous one, the new film, simply titled *Rambo,* took the character into one of the most politically repressive and violent regions in the world, Burma, the official name for which is Myanmar. Yet again, my character was reinterpreted, but now, to my surprise, for the first time he was presented in the way that he had appeared in my novel so many years ago: angry and disillusioned. Sickened by violence but knowing that killing is what he does best, Rambo has fallen into despair. He hunts cobras for a snake farm and is so at home with death that he handles them with indifference, just as they seem to recognize a kindred soul and submit to being handled. He spends a lot of time in the rain, trying to cleanse himself of what he has done. People call him "the Boatman," with all the Greek-myth implications of death and the River Styx. During an anguished scene in which he forges a knife to go into yet another battle, he tells himself: "Admit it. You didn't kill for your country. You killed for yourself. And for that, God won't forgive you."

In a Rambo movie. Absolutely astonishing. After four films and thirty-six years, the character returned to the tone of his origins in my novel. It felt like old times to see him again.

CAROL O'CONNELL

Born in New York in 1947, bred in New England and New Jersey, Carol O'Connell attended the California Institute of the Arts. This was back in the days when it was located not far from LA's MacArthur Park (anarchy heaven of the 1960s). She was a hippie without portfolio (wrong wardrobe, no love beads, no albums of Indian sitar music, and she never bothered to lay out the cash for her own bong). Edging eastward, she completed her studies at Arizona State University, where she earned a bachelor of fine arts degree (the major she had the most credits in when it came time to leave school). O'Connell then moved to Denver, Colorado, regarding it as a largish halfway house between coasts east and west. After a few years as a papergirl for the *Denver Post,* on to Manhattan. During the early New York years, she earned her living as a freelance proofreader, working at mind-sucking graveyard-shift jobs while doing the starving-artist thing. Upon publication of *Mallory's Oracle,* the first of ten novels, she was (in her own words) incredibly overpaid, and this enabled her to quit the rent-money gigs. The author also trashed her alarm clock. Now O'Connell goes to bed when she gets tired and wakes up when she's completely finished sleeping.

She writes every day.

MALLORY

BY CAROL O'CONNELL

In 1994, after my first book was published, I received a fan letter and a great deal of religious material from a woman who wanted to save me from eternal damnation. That was when I realized that I was onto something with my protagonist, who is an officer of the NYPD, a woman, and a sociopath. Call her Detective Mallory or just plain Mallory, neither Miss nor Ms., but never call her Kathy. She likes that chilly distance of the surname.

Aloof? Perhaps. In *Stone Angel,* she is likened to a cat:

The cat hissed and arched its back as Charles's hand moved toward the sugar bowl. Apparently, he had violated some house rule of table manners. Slowly, his hand withdrew from the bowl and came to rest on the table by his cup. The cat lay down, stretching her lean body across the checkered cloth, and the tail ceased to switch and beat the wood. When his hand moved again, she bunched her muscles, set to spring, relaxing only while his hand was still. The cat controlled him.

    Now who did that remind him of?

    The old woman was back at the table. "Don't touch that cat. She doesn't like people—barely tolerates them. She's wild—raised in the woods. When I found her, she was too set in her ways to ever be anybody's idea of tame. She had buckshot all through her pelt and chicken feathers in her mouth. Now that told me, right off, that she was a thief. And she is perversity incarnate. Sometimes she purrs just before she strikes.

Charles nodded while the woman spoke, and he ticked off the familiar character flaws as she listed them. Now he peered into the cat's slanted eyes. Mallory, are you in there?

Miss Trebec bent down to speak to the cat, to explain politely that an animal did not belong on the table when company was calling. The cat seemed to be considering this information, but she left the table in her own time, as though it were her own idea. The tail waved high as she disappeared over the edge.

It was disconcerting that the animal made no sound when she hit the floor. It crossed his mind to look under the table, to reassure himself that the cat did not float there, waiting to catch him in some new breach of etiquette. Instead he peered into his cup as he stirred the sugar in his coffee. When he looked up to ask his hostess a question, the cat was riding the woman's shoulders.

(And, after wading through all of that, here is your punch line: A passage from James Joyce's *Ulysses* inspired Mallory and best defines her in only eleven genius words. Mr. Joyce wrote, "Cruel. Her nature. Curious mice never squeal. Seem to like it.")

However, like a cat, Mallory seems to have no affinity for these animals. In *Dead Famous* she had an encounter with New York City's only attack cat, a pathetic creature with nerve damage. When he's in pain, he lashes out at strangers, and this earned him the name Huggermugger, Mugs for short. He was softly creeping up behind Mallory when a tiny squeak of excitement gave him away. Then he paused as their eyes met, and they mutually agreed that she could kill him any time she liked. Mugs, wise cat, retreated to his basket.

I am nothing like my protagonist. Consequently, I am, in person, a huge disappointment to everyone who expects her and gets me. Mallory is tall, I'm short; she's blond, I'm not; she carries a gun, and I don't. Yet every time I lecture, someone will ask, "Is Mallory autobiographical?" I'm always stunned, but I never harm these people. I say, "No. Mallory is a sociopath, and I'm a *nice* person. . . . I'm a *relatively* nice person." Given that proviso, people generally do not push their luck with the question.

I blame this on the Germans.

When I arrived in Berlin on tour with my first book, I was told that a local journalist had written an article that mistook *Mallory's Oracle* for a rather strange third-person memoir. In every interview, and there were many, I set the reporters straight. Mallory was a work of pure fiction, I said, "Not me. Nothing like me. I'm a wimp." But they preferred the earlier, erroneous version of me, and my correction never appeared in any of their newspaper interviews. To this day, many German people believe that I'm a tall blonde with disturbing defects.

So where did the fleshed-out Mallory come from? Well, in the usual order of things, she began as a *little* sociopath. The detective's introduction to the NYPD came at a tender age.

The haunt of Grand Central Station was a small girl with matted hair and dirty clothes. She appeared only in the commuter hours, morning and evening, when the child believed that she could go invisibly among the throng of travelers in crisscrossing foot traffic, as if that incredible face could go anywhere without attracting stares. Concessionaires reached for their phones to call the number on a policeman's card and say, "She's back."

The girl always stood beneath the great arch, pinning her hopes on a tip from a panhandler: Everyone in the world would pass by—so said the smelly old bum—if she could only wait long enough. The child patiently stared into a thousand faces, waiting for a man she had never met. She was certain to know him by his eyes, the same rare color as her own, and he would recognize Kathy's face as a small copy of her mother's. Her father would be so happy to see her; this belief was unshakable, for she was a little zealot in the faith of the bastard child.

He never came. Months passed by. She never learned.

Toward the close of this day, the child had a tired, hungry look about her. Hands clenched into fists, she raged against the panhandler, whose fairy tale had trapped her here in the long wait.

At the top of the rush hour, she spotted a familiar face, but it was the wrong one. The fat detective was seen in thin slices between the bodies of travelers. Though he was on the far side of the mezzanine, Kathy fancied that she could hear him huffing and wheezing as he ran toward her. And she waited.

Crouching.

One second, two seconds, three.

When he came within grabbing distance, the game was on—all that passed for sport in the life of a homeless child. She ran for the grand staircase, shooting past him and making the fat man spin. Sneakers streaking, slapping stone, the little blond bullet in blue jeans gained the stairs, feet flying, only alighting on every third step.

Laughing, laughing.

At the top of the stairs, she turned around to see that the chase was done—and so early this time. Her pursuer had reached the bottom step and could not climb another. The fat man was in some pain and out of breath. One hand went to his chest, as if he could stop a heart attack that way.

The little girl mouthed the words, Die, *old man.*

They locked eyes. His were pleading, hers were hard. And she gave him her famous Gotcha *smile.*

One day, she would become his prisoner—but not today—and Louis Markowitz would become her foster father. Years later and long after they had learned to care for one another, each time Kathy Mallory gave him this smile, he would check his back pocket to see if his wallet was missing.

So . . . obviously not one of the more charming sociopaths, the detective rarely feels the need to show her badge in order to gain respect—even in a truck stop:

Mallory carried her tray to the most remote table, aware that all the truck drivers were smiling her way. Their conversations had stopped, and now they stripped her naked with their eyes. They were so fearless in their sense of entitlement—as if they were ticket holders to a strolling peep show. Oh, if eyes could only whoop and holler. She set her knapsack on the table, then removed her denim jacket and draped it over the back of a chair.

"Oh, Lord," said a passing waitress.

Sans jacket, Mallory displayed a shoulder holster and a .357 Smith & Wesson revolver. With the tight unison of chorus girls, the men turned their faces downward, as if finding their plates infinitely more fascinating.

Problem solved.

Only the waitress seemed to take the gun in stride, shaking her head, as if the lethal weapon might be some minor violation of a dress code.

This gambit has also proved useful in finding parking spaces anywhere in Manhattan and for upgrading hotel rooms elsewhere.

The denim jacket is not part of her usual wardrobe. Shopping at the Gap is Mallory's idea of going in disguise. On a normal workday, she dresses well beyond the paycheck of a civil servant. In her partner's opinion, she delights in leaving the impression that she might be a cop on the take. (This passes for a sense of humor in Mallory's world.) A well-respected art critic once took notice of her outfit.

Though Mr. Quinn could not see the back pocket of her jeans, he knew a designer's name would be embroidered there. A long black trenchcoat was draped over the shoulders of her blazer, which was cashmere, and her T-shirt was silk. He would have bet his stock portfolio that her curls were styled in a Fifty-seventh Street salon, but not dyed there, for this was that most unusual creature, a natural blonde. In every other aspect of her, a lifetime's experience in stereotyping had failed him. He could not hazard her occupation or her exact status in the world. And then, as she drew closer, he realized that, if it was true that one could read another's soul by the eyes—this young woman didn't have one.

So, she gets on well with truck drivers and art critics, but she is not overly sentimental about children or puppy dogs. And frail little old ladies should never get between Mallory and a case. This is best illustrated with a grand dame of the New York ballet who mistook the young detective for a prospective student of the dance. Madame Burnstien was small and slight, hardly threatening. Her white hair was captured in a bun, and every bit of skin was a crisscross of lines. The only hand visible through the crack of the door was a cluster of arthritic knots wrapped round the cane.

"I'm Mallory. I have an appointment with you."

"You are Rabbi Kaplan's young friend?"

Mallory could not immediately place the woman's accent, but then Anna Kaplan had said that Madame Burnstien hailed from too many countries to call one of them home. In youth, she had danced for the whole earth. Mallory could not believe this crone had ever been young.

"Rabbi Kaplan said you would see me."

"I said I would look *at you, and I have. You're a beautiful child, but too tall. Go away now."*

The door began to close. Mallory shot one running shoe into the space between the door and its frame. The old woman smiled wickedly and showed Mallory her cane, lifting it in the crack-width to display the carved wolf's head and its fangs.

"Move your foot, my dear, or you'll never dance again."

The cane was rising for a strike.

"Madame Burnstien, you only think *I won't deck you."*

The old eyes widened and gleamed. The smile disappeared and her brows rushed together in an angry scowl as the cane lowered slowly. There was exaggerated petulance in her cracking voice. "I like determination, child, but you waste my time. You're still too tall."

"Everybody's a critic." Mallory showed her the gold badge and ID. "I want to talk to you about Aubry Gilette."

"I have many students. Aubry was a thousand dancers ago. What do you expect me to remember about one girl?"

"Oh, I think you remember her better than most. Don't make me show the autopsy photo. You're old. It'd probably kill you."

And she has a grudge against nuns. Well, *one* nun. Mallory takes great pride in her enemies, and she is particularly proud of Sister Ursula. One night, she interrupted a poker game to ask a case-related question on religion. And here Rabbi David Kaplan points out that she has better sources for Roman Catholic dogma:

"Kathy, as I recall, you had four years of a very expensive Catholic school education. Go and ask Father Brenner. He's semi-retired now, but I believe he's filling in the vacation schedule at St. Jude's this week."

"Father Brenner and I aren't exactly on friendly terms. Maybe you could ask him."

"It's been what, maybe ten years now? He's not one to hold a grudge. It's not as if you broke that nun's leg."

After Mallory left the room, the other poker players fixed upon the face of the rabbi in dead silence. He cast his sweet smile on each player in turn, which was easy because he was holding the best cards of the evening. But he never said another word about Kathy Mallory and the nun, not even when they withheld his sandwiches and beer for a time. He would not talk.

Why do people like this character? I don't know. If I had to guess, I'd say it harks back to old high school issues of *making the cut,* and this idea works well on both sides of the gender divide. Let's say that it was possible for you to meet her on the street or in a bar. Would Mallory talk to you? Would you even register as a solid object, or would she look through you? These are trick questions and very Darwinian in the sense of good survival instincts. Being ignored is actually your best possible outcome. If she's interested, if she hurts you, *then* you've made the cut.

There are always questions about why she is the way she is. Well-intentioned (albeit delusional) fans long to pin down the exact moment in time when her mind went awry—so they can tweak her and fix her and ruin my career. More rational readers want me to do the mending. The nicest people ask (beg) for a kinder, gentler Mallory. I politely explain that if I give them what they ask for, I have no book. I'd like to say, "This is crime genre and not a damn soap opera." (In person, I am polite. On the page—not so much.) Each novel was written to stand alone, and reading one out of order will in no way ruin the plot of any other book in the Mallory series—so you won't be charting warm and fuzzy life-affirming changes in the character. However, gaining personal insight here and there creates the illusion of growth in a sociopath who cannot change what she is.

She has a partner named Riker, who keeps a very special rainy-day bullet in the nightstand by his bed, and he sometimes thinks of loading it into his gun. But he never speaks of this. There are no overt signs of his state of mind. And Mallory should be the last person on earth to intuit his suicidal ideation. And yet, there are nights when she parks her car in front of his apartment building and looks up toward the bathroom window and the glow of Riker's plastic Jesus nightlight. When every light but this one has gone out, she drives away.

Perhaps her only clue to Riker's sadness is in the chaos that he calls home. It's best described by a character who once said to him, "You know why you don't have cockroaches? Those genius bugs—they know it's not safe to eat here." Mallory, that neat freak who straightens pictures on other people's walls, once broke into Riker's apartment and cleaned it for him. She dragged her mop and bucket from room to room, stopping on the threshold of the bathroom, where exquisite good taste kicked in, and she wanted to trash that plastic Jesus nightlight. Instead she cleaned it and left it shining so that Riker would not stumble and fall in the dark.

So what's in a name when it comes to dangerous pathology?

The pigeonholes that we make for people like Mallory are only for convenience's sake. We are all special cases. I am sometimes asked, "How does a sociopath differ from a psychopath?" (Here you have to bear in mind that we live in an era of broadcast news that uses authors of techno-thrillers as weaponry experts to explain what's going on in an actual war. And they have other fiction writers on standby if there's a plague coming.) So I respond to the question from my audience. (What the hell. I can't do worse than the amateur expert who sent America to the hardware store one day with the promise that duct tape would protect us from nuclear radiation.) I usually preface my remarks by warning people that the quacks on their favorite television shows cannot agree on this point of mental aberration. However, real doctors seem to have a consensus in their professional journals, which, alas, lack the credibility of the bestseller list.

It appears that there is no longer any distinction made between a sociopath and a psychopath. Based on research, I can tell you that those terms are used interchangeably in academic literature. And a quote from one psychologist of my acquaintance sums up modern policy on this matter: "Today's sociopath is yesterday's psychopath." Putting rational thought to one side for the moment, common usage of these particular words carries more weight with the general public: Many people, with and without television credentials, see a sociopath as someone who can shoot a baby in the head and sleep through the night, and a psychopath as someone who can eat the face off a baby and sleep through the night.

Go with whatever definition makes you the most uncomfortable.

For some readers, Mallory is entirely too real. But I find that letters from mental patients are frequently the most insightful, and I welcome them. In my view, madness is a place. You go. You come back. And I think we all take turns being the mental patient. Without a touch of crazy, literature can be a desolate place. In the current climate of careful speech, even fearful speech, smoke-free film scripts, thought-free songs, and child-proof locks on American minds, the oft-repeated lament of the arts is "Where have all those wonderful madmen gone?"

The strong (and defective) character of Mallory may be what people remember best about these books. However, in a book where character is everything, you have nothing but an essay with no legs. The plot is the animation that runs you at gunpoint from cover to cover, sometimes at a heart-attack pace, a race to the end; and sometimes the plot is crawling, dragging its nails in the dark, coming up behind you . . . and then . . . at the end, you should be startled, and your next reaction should be "Oh, of course."

Most important, the plot has to work with the protagonist. You will sometimes hear the literati say that they have no control over their characters, and they frequently alter a book because their protagonist would *never* do a thing like that. This should not happen in the crime genre, where there are promises to keep. The author must be in control of the material; this is the appeal, the draw, and the covenant with the reader. You should not be subjected to a thousand pages of angst, boring descriptions of the wallpaper, and the added misery of watching the protagonist boil eggs for breakfast. Instead, you are entitled to a sleek plot that will carry you somewhere, a plot with fangs and moving parts, a beginning, a middle, and a solid resolution.

I promise to tell you a story.

Ideally, the setting of every story should be a place that you can inhabit for the duration of a novel, and Manhattan, which figures prominently in most of my books, takes on character status. So this is not the dreaded scenery description; it's character development, and I always aim to make it painless:

> *Riker's binoculars strayed to the surrounding buildings and then down below to the stream of late traffic. Ah, New York, all decked out in city lights like sequins on her best dress—all dazzle and smart moves. He had seen the city in harsher light, and he knew she was really a whore, but that could be fun, too.*

Stone Angel was a departure, a foray into southern gothic and a different kind of setting, a place where nature is no small player and every living thing is running for its life or running for its supper:

> *One osprey flopped its catch onto the grass. The fish struggled under the bird's talons; its silver scales were striped with watery blood. The fish hawk was so intent on tearing flesh from bone, he paid the woman no mind as she drew closer, smiling benignly on the creature and his bloody living meal, nodding her approval of a good catch.*
>
> *If reincarnated, Augusta knew she could depend on coming back to*

the earth with feathers, for she had the ruthless makings of a fine bird, and God was not one to waste talent.

And once I took Mallory on the road—the Mother Road:

The two homicide detectives were soaked through and through. They surrendered, throwing up their hands and then jamming them into coat pockets. Grim and helpless, they watched the heavy rain come down on their forensic evidence and carry it away. There it went, the body fluids, stray hairs and fibers, all flowing off down the gutter. The corpse, washed clean, could tell them nothing beyond the cause of death—extreme cruelty. There had never been a crime scene quite like this one in the history of Chicago, Illinois, nothing as shocking, nothing as sad.

The religious detective made the sign of the cross. The other one closed his eyes.

The dead man at their feet was pointing the way down Adams Street, also known as Route 66, a road of many names. Steinbeck had called it a road of flight.

When strangers on a train or a plane ask what I do for a living, I say, "I kill people." This response makes for a short conversation, no eye contact, and no sudden movement by my seatmate, only peace and quiet.

Rare is the fellow passenger who asks why I do it.

I suppose I got tired of hanging out in a book all day long waiting for a story to begin. I write the kind of novels I want to read. And why the theme of solving murders? Violent death is larger than life. And it's the great equalizer. By law, every victim is entitled to a paladin and a chase, else life would be cheapened.

And the *real* reason I do this? My brain is simply bent this way. There is nothing else I would rather do. This neatly chains into my theory of the writing life: If you scratch an artist, under the skin you will find a bum who cannot hold down a real job. Conversely, if you scratch a bum . . . But I have never done that. (The heart of my theory has Puritan roots: If you love what you do, you cannot call it honest work.)

I love a mystery. And I loathe lectures.

Characters may have their independent issues, but nothing overshadows the death of a human being. I write crime novels, not morality plays—no soapboxes, no scolding. If you fail to wash your aluminum foil before recycling it, I am not gunning for you. If you smoke, I don't care. If you drink too much, I wasn't born to save you by burying a twelve-step program in the chapters. Also, I have no desire to suck all the charm out of your life by adding more green leafy vegetables to your diet. And political correctness has no place in my work.

Mallory never deals with any feminist issues. She doesn't have to. It would not occur to most people, while facing a woman with a loaded gun, to suggest that she might be happier barefoot and pregnant. That's an image of her that never comes to mind on any page of these books. There are no diatribes on bigotry of any kind, which can only come as a relief to people who are really, really tired of being told how it feels to be them. I envision a great dump site filled with broken lamps, the casualties of books being hurled across a room and missing the target of the open window.

Do you walk with a cane or roll in a chair? I don't care.

Because the handicapped populate my city, they are sometimes major players or peripheral characters in my books. (Do I go gently with them? Yeah, *right*.) Informed by observation, I say the halt, the lame, and the blind have the same percentage of ignoble people among them as can be found in the general population. And I never received any hate mail about that poor sightless bastard from *Killing Critics* who had a dead fly pitched into his drink. (Mallory did it.

But he had it coming. This was retribution for an unkind remark to a friend of hers.)

Just before he took a sip . . .

The small group surrounding the blind man wondered, each one of them, if it might be rude or worse, politically incorrect, to mention the dead bug in his wineglass. Wouldn't that call attention to his blindness?

Ah, too late.

(One small deviation on the subject of special-interest politics: As a concession to animal-rights activists, no actual house pets are killed or injured in the creation of these novels.)

A copyeditor once wrote a sweet note on a Post-it and stuck it to the last page of my manuscript. She thanked me for merely wounding a pet this time and not killing it outright. Apparently, I can murder all the people I like. No one minds that. But the first time an animal died (on the first page of my first book), it generated anxious mail.

The dog circled the chair, fear rising up to a human crying. He moved her hand with his nose. Nothing. The hand fell limply to her lap.

The dog wailed.

Soon.

The dog's mind was breaking. Regimentation instilled by pain was falling apart. He was departing from ritual, backing out of the room, terrified eyes fixed on the woman till he was clear of the kitchen. Now he turned and flung himself into the next room, racing across the carpet, passing through the open door and down the long hallway, paws touching lightly to ground in the perfect poetry of a beautiful animal in motion, muscles elongating and contracting, eyes shining with purpose. Now springing, rising, flying, crashing through the glass of the fifth-floor window.

Vermin have no fan base—only dogs and cats do—and a lot of fictional rats had to die so that I could bring you that bit of trivia.

I don't go out of my way to upset social watchdogs. Without even trying, I was once bumped from an interview on a radio show noted for political correctness. (I don't name names. Don't ask. I slaughter a great many fictional people. In real life, my bloodletting pales.) The radio host objected to the first acts of murder in *Killing Critics*, a double homicide. "Gratuitous violence," he said. Evidently, the person who read the book for him failed to explain the context of the New York art scene, where topping the over-the-top is no small feat. The victims were displayed as works of sculpture. Their *objectionable* murder (on the charitable assumption that there is another kind) occurred years before the book began and was first disclosed by Detective Mallory's reconstruction of the event in a bare room— no weapons, no bodies, and no blood on the floor, only dust. (Yet this was too much for him to bear. If he had only put that in writing, I would have included it among the book jacket reviews for the next edition.)

I don't do anything *gratuitously*. Well, yeah, once I did throw an unnecessary pigeon into a scene with an unbalanced character:

They advanced across the flat stones, quick jerking shapes of light and dark, and some were spotted with brown and gray, uniform only in their forward motion, and one of them was insane.

Feet of red and red rings around the bright mad eyes, he was otherwise coal black until he passed into a dapple of sun, and iridescent flecks of green shimmered in the light. The feathers of his head were not smoothed back and rounded. Spiky they were, and dirty, as though a great fear had put them that way, and the fear had lasted such a long time, a season or more, and the dirt of no bathing or rain had pomaded them into stick-out fright, though the bird was long past fear now and all the way crazy. No fear of the human foot. A pedestrian waded through the flock, which parted for her in a wave, all but the crazy one, and it was kicked, startling the pedestrian more than the bird.

The woman shrieked and stiff-walked down Seventh Avenue. The insane pigeon followed after her, listing to one side with some damage from the kick, until he forgot his purpose.

I do not like the Thought Police, modern cousins to D. H. Lawrence's Censor Morons—I *love* these people. I cultivate them. I call them Cannon Fodder.

And I make no apologies . . . except for the gratuitous pigeon.

ROBERT B. PARKER

Robert Brown Parker was born in 1932 in Springfield, Massachusetts, where he met Joan, his future wife, when they were children. They began dating while both attended Colby College and were married in 1956. They separated in 1982 but reconciled two years later and celebrated their golden anniversary in the autumn of 2006. They have two sons, David and Daniel. Parker received his doctorate from Boston University in 1971 with a thesis on the private eyes of Dashiell Hammett, Raymond Chandler, and Ross Macdonald.

Generally regarded as next in succession after the three icons mentioned above, as *the* great writer of the hard-boiled private-detective novel, Parker has averaged nearly two books a year for more than three decades. In addition to his Spenser series, which served as the basis for the popular television series *Spenser: For Hire* in the 1980s, he has written several books each about Jesse Stone and Sunny Randall, two with Philip Marlowe as the protagonist, and such stand-alone novels as *All Our Yesterdays, Wilderness,* and *Double Play.* His fourth novel, *Promised Land,* won an Edgar® as best novel of 1977. The Mystery Writers of America named him a Grand Master for lifetime achievement in 2002.

SPENSER

BY ROBERT B. PARKER

S usan and I sat at a table in the Charles Square courtyard, having a drink in the late afternoon with Susan's friend Amy Trent. It was one of those days in late June. The temperature was about 78. There were maybe three white clouds in the sky. The quiet breeze that drifted in from the river smelled fresher than I knew it to be.

"I'm trying to write a book," Amy said. "The working title is *Men Who Dare,* a series of profiles of men who are strong and tough and do dangerous work. Mountain climbers, Navy Seals, policemen, firemen."

"Amy needs a sample profile to submit with her proposal, in hopes of getting a contract and an advance," Susan said. "I said you'd be perfect."

"Amy's looking for sexual splendor as well?" I said.

Amy smiled.

"Always," she said. "Will you talk with me?"

"Sure," I said.

"Okay, I have a bunch of questions written down," Amy said. "You can answer them, dismiss them, respond to a question I didn't ask, anything you want, I'm interested in what you're like. Okay?"

"Okay."

"Susan, feel free to jump in any time," Amy said. "You know him better than anyone."

"Don't rat me out," I said, "about the sexual splendor."

"Our secret," Susan said.

Amy took a notebook out of her book bag and opened it. She was a professor at Harvard and, faced with that limitation, not bad looking. If she had dressed better, done her hair better, improved on her makeup, and worn more stylish glasses, she might have been good-looking . . . but then the faculty senate would probably have required her to wear a scarlet *A* on her dress.

She studied her notebook for a moment. I looked at Susan. She smiled. Zing went the strings of my heart. Then Amy took out a small tape recorder and put it on the table.

"Okay?" she said.

"Sure."

She turned the recorder on.

"Okay," Amy said. "Just to warm up a little. Why are you such a wise guy?"

"It's a gift," I said.

Susan frowned at me.

"If you're going to do this, " Susan said, "you have to do it."

"You didn't tell me I had to be serious," I said.

"Well, you do."

Amy waited. She had a lot of kinetic intensity about her, but she knew how to keep it in check. I nodded.

"I seem to have an unavoidable capacity for seeing a thing and seeing beyond it at the same time."

"Would you say that you have a heightened sense of irony?" Amy asked.

"I probably wouldn't say it, but it's probably true."

"It is also," Susan said, "a distancing technique. It keeps people and events from getting too close."

"Except you," I said.

She smiled again.

"Except me."

"Besides Susan, are there things that can get through that ironic barrier?" Amy said.

"I don't think so."

"Because?"

"Because if they did," I said, "I couldn't do what I do."

"But if you refuse to care . . ." Amy said.

"I don't refuse to care," I said. "I refuse to let it control me."

"How do you do that?"

"It's a matter of perspective."

"Meaning?"

"There's a line from Auden," I said. *"'The torturer's horse scratches its innocent behind on a tree.'"*

"A poem," Amy said.

"'Musée des Beaux Arts.'"

"Life goes on," she said.

"Something like that," I said. "Though not for everyone."

"And you find that consoling?"

"I find it instructive."

"Perspective," Amy said.

I nodded.

Amy wasn't reading her questions now. She seemed interested.

"In such a world," she said, "do you have any absolutes?"

I nodded at Susan.

"Her," I said.

"Love," Amy said.

I shook my head.

"Her," I said.

Amy frowned. Then she nodded.

"Yes," she said. "I see."

One point for Harvard. The waitress came by, and I had another beer and Susan had another white wine. Amy had more iced tea.

"So why do you do it?" she asked.

"What I do?"

"Yes."

"Because I can."

"That simple?"

"I'm pretty simple," I said.

Amy looked at Susan. Susan smiled.

"He is," Susan said. "And he isn't. That will show itself if you talk with him enough. But I warn you, he's almost never one thing."

Amy nodded and braced herself with another slug of iced tea.

"So you do what you do because you can," Amy said. "You're good at it."

"Yes," I said.

"Do you like it?"

"Most of the time," I said. "It allows me to live life on my own terms."

"Aren't there other jobs?" Amy said. "Ones that allow you to do that and don't require you to carry a gun?"

"Not that many," I said. "And almost none at which I'd be any good."

"You say you want to live life on your own terms; what are they?"

"The terms?"

"Yes."

I thought about it. As the afternoon moved along, more people were coming in for a drink. Maybe several. It was a relatively glamorous crowd for Cambridge. Few if any ankle-length skirts or sandals with socks. I looked at Susan.

"What are my terms?" I asked her.

"He's being cute," Susan said to Amy. "He understands himself very well, but he wants me to say it."

"It's pretty hard for me not to be cute," I said.

Susan rolled her eyes slightly.

"He can learn, but he can't be taught," Susan said. "He can find his way, but he can't take direction. He will do very difficult and dangerous things, but he cannot be ordered to do them. Voluntarily, he's generous and compassionate and quite kind. But he cannot be compelled to it."

"Autonomous," Amy said.

"To a pathological extreme," Susan said.

Amy checked her tape recorder. It appeared to be doing what it was supposed to.

"Can you get him to do things he doesn't want to do?" Amy asked Susan.

"I'm doing this interview," I said.

Neither of them paid me any attention.

"Up to a point," Susan said.

"What is the point?" Amy said.

"I can't change him," Susan said. "I cannot make him cease to be who he is."

"Would you want to?"

"I would prefer he didn't risk his life," Susan said. "In a sense he's risking mine as well."

"Because?" Amy said.

"I cannot imagine a life without him in it."

"Do you try to change that?"

"No. It's part of what he is," Susan said. "He would not be him if he didn't do what he does. And it's the him he is that I cannot imagine life without."

"Wow," I said.

"The syntax is perhaps a little convoluted," Susan said. "But so are you, Ducky."

"You mean I'm not simple?" I said.

"You are and you aren't," Susan said.

"Oh," I said. "Yeah."

"I want to talk more about your relationship," Amy said. "Since it's come up. But I'm not sure I have yet gotten a solid handle on why you do what you do, which would be sort of the heart of my book."

"There are a lot of problems which need to be solved," I said, "and their solution takes the kinds of skills I have. But because of my extreme pathology, I can't solve those problems in a structured context: police work, military, Harvard College. So I do it this way."

"And," Susan said, "you do it because it allows you to state who and what you are."

"So who and what is he?" Amy said.

Susan shook her head.

"It has something to do with honor," she said.

They both looked at me. I looked at Susan.

"*'I could not love thee, dear, so much,'*" I said, "*'Lov'd I not honor more'?*"

She smiled again.

"Oh, shut up," she said.

"Which makes a nice segue," Amy said, "back to your relationship. Why have you never married?"

Susan and I looked at each other.

"I don't really like her that much," I said.

"Yes, you do," Amy said. "You've been together for years. You seem like the kind of people who would marry. Everyone says you are the two most connected people they've ever seen. Why not get married?"

I looked at Susan. She smiled and didn't speak. I was, at least for the moment, on my own.

"What we have," I said, "is a very . . . delicate . . . love affair. We are different at almost every level that doesn't matter. We are very, ah, committed to our own point of view . . . and what we have is amazingly good. I guess we don't want to mess with it."

"Have you ever lived together?"

"We tried it once," I said.

"And?"

"And all the differences that don't really matter, mattered when they were contained in one space."

"You travel together?"

"Sure," I said. "And we spend nights together. But we don't live together."

Amy frowned.

"Do I hear you saying," she asked, "that what you have is too precious to risk compromising it by getting married?"

"Yes," I said.

Amy looked at Susan. Susan smiled and nodded. Amy looked back at me. I smiled.

"Well," Amy said. "All righty then. Let me ease onto simpler ground here. A little history."

"Okay," I said.

"You were born in Laramie, Wyoming."

"I was."

"And your mother bore you, as it were, posthumously."

"Yes," I said. "She died, but they were able to save me."

"So you never had a mother."

"In any but a biological sense, no."

"And your father brought you up?"

"My father and my two uncles."

"You father's brothers?"

"No," I said. "They were my mother's brothers."

"Really?"

"It's how my father met my mother. He was friends with her brothers."

"You all lived in the same house?"

"Yes."

"How was that?"

"Fine," I said. "It didn't seem unusual. It was just the way my family was."

"What did they do?"

"Carpenters, hunting guides, raised a few cattle, broke some horses, used to ride bucking horses in rodeos, used to box for prize money around Wyoming and Montana at carnivals and smokers."

"They sound like tough guys," Amy said.

"They were tough guys," I said.

"Were they tough with you?"

"No."

"Did any of them marry?"

"They all went out with a lot of women," I said. "My father never remarried. Both my uncles married, but not while I was living there."

"So essentially you grew up in an all-male household," Amy said.

"Yes."

"What was the effect of that, do you think?"

"I suppose there must have been one," I said. "But I haven't got a glib answer for you. They made me feel valuable. They made me feel secure. They used to show up at every PTA meeting, all the time I was in school. All three of them, sitting in a row in the back. I'm told they made the teachers nervous."

"Anything else about them?"

"They made me feel equal. I was expected to share the work of the household, which included the work of raising me. If I didn't want to do something, they listened to me, and sometimes I didn't have to do it and sometimes I did. But they were never dismissive. I was always a participant. And they were never unkind."

I stopped and thought back about my family. It made me smile.

"Nobody much crossed them, though," I said.

"Is Susan the fulfillment of a long deprivation?" Amy said.

I drank some beer.

"Absolutely," I said. "But that would be true if I'd had a mother. The time I spent before I met Susan seems aimless."

"They teach you to box?" Amy said.

"Yes. My uncle Nick, mostly. I fought some golden gloves and had some pro fights, and was looking like a comer. But I also got a football scholarship to Holy Cross, and so I went there to play football for a couple of years."

"I don't know much about football, but what position were you?"

"Strong safety," I said. "And I ran back punts."

"Were you good?"

"Yeah, but I didn't like being coached, and college was boring, so I went back to boxing."

"Was it boring because it was Catholic?" Amy said.

"No," I said. "It was boring because it was college."

"You sound scornful of college," Amy said.

"I am."

"But you've read a lot of books, I'm told. You quote poetry."

"Self-educated," I said.

"Remember what I told you about him," Susan said.

"Were you a good boxer?"

"Not good enough," I said. "While I was still fighting, I took the police exam and passed and decided to do that."

"Were you good at that?"

"No, too many rules."

"So you quit," Amy said.

"I did," I said. "I may be unemployable."

"And became a private detective."

I nodded.

"You met Hawk while you were boxing?"

"You know about Hawk," I said.

"Susan introduced us," Amy said.

"Whaddya think?" I said.

"He terrified me, and . . . excited me, I guess."

"Me too," I said.

"I don't believe that for a minute," Amy said. "Hawk told me you bailed him out of a difficult racial situation."

"We conspired on that," I said.

"Do you want to talk about Hawk?" Amy said.

"No. You'll need to talk with him direct. Hawk is what he is."

"Including your friend."

"Yes."

"Why are you so close?"

"We know the same things," I said.

"Like fighting?"

"Like . . . if I were black and Hawk were white, then he'd be me and I'd be him."

"Race makes the difference?"

"I grew up white in a white culture. Hawk grew up black in a white culture. When you're marginalized, you become very practical."

"Marginalized," Susan said.

I shrugged modestly.

"I'm with Harvard grads," I said. "I'm showing off a little."

"Talk a bit more about the effect of marginalization," Amy said.

"You have less room to maneuver about what's right or wrong," I said. "Mostly what's right is what works. Your view becomes pretty up-close."

"It makes him immoral?"

"No, Hawk is moral," I said. "His word is good. He does nothing gratuitously. It's just that his morality is more results oriented. He does what needs to be done without agonizing over it before or after."

"You agonize?"

"Too strong," I said. "I probably think about it more than Hawk. And *right* may have a more abstract component for me."

"Is that a good thing?"

"I don't know," I said.

Amy sat for a moment, contemplating the slowly turning tape in her recorder.

"Do you trust him?" she said.

"Absolutely."

Again Amy thought for a while.

Finally she said, "I guess I don't entirely understand."

I shrugged.

"Best I can do," I said.

"Susan?" Amy said.

"He admires people who can do things." She smiled. "Hawk can do things."

Amy nodded. It was moving on toward supper time. I looked around at the now crowded and lively courtyard. Even though we were right in the heart of Cambridge, there was a heartening absence of Birkenstocks.

"Okay," Amy said. "Let's talk about you and Susan again."

"What is this?" I said. "Men and Women Who Dare?"

Amy smiled.

"I think maybe I can't understand you without understanding you in her context," Amy said.

"Probably," I said.

"How did you meet?"

"I was working on a case, missing teenage boy, up in Smithfield. She was the school guidance counselor. I questioned her about the boy, and she was immediately taken with me."

Susan rolled her eyes.

"What's your version?" Amy asked Susan.

"He was working on a case, missing teenage boy, up in Smithfield," Susan said. "I was the school guidance counselor. He questioned me about the boy and was immediately taken with me."

"There seems a disparity here," Amy said.

"Just say we were taken with each other," Susan said.

"And you've been together ever since?"

"Except for when we weren't," I said.

"Can you talk about that?" Amy said.

"Nope."

Amy looked at Susan. Susan shook her head.

"We aren't who we were," Susan said. "We'd be talking about people who no longer exist."

I could see Amy thinking about how to go further with this. I could see her decide to give it up.

"You were married before," she said to Susan.

"Yes."

"And divorced."

"Yes."

"How do you feel about that?" Amy asked me.

"I don't," I said.

"Don't feel anything about it?"

"Correct."

"No jealousy, anything?" Amy said.

I shook my head.

"A famous shrink," I said, "once remarked, *'We aren't who we were.'*"

"You can put the past aside that easily?" Amy said.

I think she disapproved.

"Not easily," I said.

Susan said, "It's quite effortful."

"But you do it?"

Susan and I said yes at the same time.

"Earlier," Amy said to me, "you said something like *I don't refuse to care; I refuse to let it control me.* Now you say that with effort you can put the past behind you. You, actually both of you, seem to place a premium on, what, will?"

"Yes," I said.

"First you need to understand why you do things that aren't in your best interest," Susan said. "Then, armed with that understanding, you have to stop doing them."

"And that would be a matter of will," Amy said.

"Yes. Given a reasonable level of acumen," Susan said, "most people can be brought to understand their behavior. The hard thing is getting them to change it."

"But some people can change?"

"Yes."

"And you changed?"

"Both of us," Susan said.

"Obviously," Amy said. "Susan, you've had psychotherapy."

"Of course," Susan said.

Amy looked at me.

"Have you ever had psychotherapy?" she asked.

I looked at Susan.

"Every day," I said.

"Any formal therapy?"

"No."

"What would be unacceptable behavior?" Amy said. "A, ah, deal-breaker, so to speak."

"An ongoing intimate relationship with someone else," I said.

"Susan?" Amy said.

"That," Susan said.

"What about a brief and casual dalliance?" Amy said.

"What did you have in mind?" I said.

I think she blushed, though it may have been the angle of the late-afternoon sun. She studied her notebook for a moment, made a little mark in it, and put it down. Then she stopped the recorder, took out the tape, put in a new tape, and started it.

"How about hopes and dreams?" Amy said.

"I'm in favor of them," I said.

Amy shook her head in a faint gesture of annoyance, as if she were shaking off a fly.

"Is there," she said, "anything you wanted to accomplish that you haven't?"

"No," I said. "I am everything I wanted to be. I've done everything I ever wanted to do."

"Nothing else left to do?" Amy said.

"Let no fate misunderstand me and snatch me away too soon," I said.

"Another poem," Amy said.

"Frost," I said. "More or less. I would be pleased to live this life and do what I do and be with her forever. But I have no need to improve on it."

"My god," Amy said, "a happy man."

"Love and work," I said. "Love and work."

"Freud," Amy said. "Right?"

"I believe so," I said. "Though he didn't say it to me personally."

Amy looked at her notebook again and made another small mark. While she was doing that I managed to snag the waitress for another beer. Susan declined a refill, and I don't think Amy even noticed the opportunity. Probably just so much iced tea you can drink.

Amy looked up from her notebook.

"What would you do if you couldn't do this?" Amy said, and smiled. "Whatever *this* might be exactly."

"I would think about international superstar, or maybe retiring to stud," I said. "But if those answers didn't satisfy you, I guess I'd say I could be a carpenter. I like to make things. I know how to do it. I could be pretty much self-directed if I took the right job."

"And if you took the wrong job?"

"I'd quit."

"Like you did the police?"

"Yes."

"Yet you have friends who are policemen."

"They're good at their work, and they probably don't have an extreme pathology," I said. "They can work in a context where I can't."

"A man needs to know his limitations," Amy said.

"He does."

The waitress brought me my beer, and I asked her for the check.

"Oh, no," Amy said. "This is on me."

"Okay," I said. "Bring her the check."

The waitress produced it on the spot and put it facedown on the table.

"I have a sense that the interview is winding down," Amy said.

"Me too," I said.

"Just indulge me on one more subject."

"Sure."

Amy took out a credit card and put it on top of the check. Then she turned back to me.

"Does anything frighten you?" she asked.

"Of course."

"What?"

"Same things that frighten most people," I said. "Death, loss, pain, failure."

"And how do you overcome those fears?"

"Same way most people do."

"Willpower?"

"I suppose."

"But you voluntarily chose to do things that involve the danger of death, pain, failure, and loss," Amy said.

"True."

"What's up with that?"

I smiled.

"I figure those are part of the deal," I said. "If I'm going to do what I do, I have to get around those fears."

Amy waited. I didn't have anything else to say. So I didn't say anything. After an appropriate wait, Amy looked at Susan.

"One of the things you have to keep in mind is that he doesn't expect to fail. And that diminishes the other dangers," Susan said. "He knows intellectually he could be killed. But I think, deep down, he doesn't think anyone can do it."

Amy looked at me and raised her eyebrows.

"You're that confident?" she said.

"So far, so good."

"So," Amy said. "Let's say you are facing a man with a gun. Do you feel fear?"

"Yes."

"What do you do about it?"

"Ignore it."

"And you are able to?"

"Yes," I said. "Otherwise I couldn't do what I do."

"How much does confidence enable you to do that?"

"I don't know," I said. "I know I can shoot. I know I'm quick. And like anybody who used to fight, I'm pretty sure I can win one in the street."

"And that's what gives you confidence?"

"Some," I said.

"I think," Susan said, "that what gives him the most confidence is that he knows he can overcome his fear."

"He has confidence in his confidence, sort of," Amy said.

"He is convinced," Susan said, "that he can do what he has to do."

"And you believe that about him too?" Amy said.

Susan looked at me and smiled.

"So far, so good," Susan said.

RIDLEY PEARSON

Born in Glen Cove, New York, and raised in Riverside, Connecticut, Ridley Pearson was educated at the University of Kansas and at Brown. He was the first American to receive the Raymond Chandler–Fulbright Fellowship at Oxford University in 1991.

He has written nine novels set in and around Seattle featuring police detective Lou Boldt and forensic psychologist Daphne Matthews, and three about Sun Valley sheriff Walt Fleming. He has also written several stand-alone thrillers, including *Never Look Back* (1985), *Blood of the Albatross* (1986), and *The Seizing of Yankee Green Mall* (1987). Under the pseudonym Wendell McCall, he wrote three novels about Chris Klick: *Dead Aim* (1988), *Concerto in Dead Flat* (1999), and *Aim for the Heart* (1990). As Joyce Reardon, PhD, he wrote *The Diary of Ellen Rimbauer: My Life at Rose Red* (2003).

With humorist Dave Barry, he has written two very successful children's series, one about Peter Pan, including *Peter and the Starcatchers* and *Peter and the Shadow Thieves*, and the other set in Never Land, beginning with *Escape from the Carnivale* (2006).

Pearson also plays bass guitar and sings with the Rock Bottom Remainders, a band made up of such successful authors as Amy Tan, Stephen King, and Dave Barry—a band that, according to Barry, "plays music as well as Metallica writes novels."

Pearson divides his time between the Northern Rockies and Saint Louis.

LOU BOLDT

BY RIDLEY PEARSON

Boldt: First, for the record, I want to say emphatically that I've not committed any crime. I've agreed to talk without counsel. Anyone who knows any detective knows he would never speak without an attorney present, not to his own mother if she were accusing him of eating an extra piece of pie. But your accusation is a bit more serious than that, isn't it? And for the record: my mother is dead. So's my father. I have a sister, lives in central Washington. That's what's left of that part of my life. But anyway, I'm innocent of the charges.

Define your relationship with Captain Philip Shoswitz, as well as with Detective John LaMoia.
Boldt: Define it? Have you got a few hours?

We have all the time you need, Lieutenant.
Boldt: First, can I make some observations, Sergeant Feldman? You and Dr. Hainer. I'm guessing you're what, Sergeant? Forty-two? Dr. Hainer's thirty-five, thirty-six? I imagine you slogged your way through beer and coeds and managed a bachelor's degree in pub crawling. Same as any red-blooded kid. Dr. Hainer didn't fare so well. He never left the bottle behind.

Let's keep this to the investigation, shall we?

Boldt: If you don't mind, it's important to the people reviewing this interview that they understand the mind-set of those doing the interview. Very important to me. I'm trained in detection, Sergeant, same as you. And it's important that we know each other. Dr. Hainer looks like a man born for graduate school. Probably lived off the parents' checkbook for as long as possible. Maybe a few years too many. See his clothes? He's worn that jacket a long time. There are stitch marks where he removed an emblem—a college or fraternity emblem, I'm guessing. The bloodshot eyes tell me the good doctor had a very late night last night, or was into something more destructive. The jaundice in those eyes suggests coke or alcohol. The gut he's wearing tells me it's booze. Coke would have left him a rail. And if I'm right, this destructive tendency is the result of marital problems. Note the tan line suggesting a missing wedding band. That's recent, so I'm pretty sure it explains the pain behind the jaundice. I've been there, you see.

She left you, am I right? Possibly in part because you're cheap. You haven't bought yourself a new pair of shoes in what—two years? Same with the shirt. We've already discussed the coat. So I'm sorry for whatever you're going through, Dr. Hainer, but I'm wondering if you're fully qualified to judge my state of mind when your own is in question.

[Dr. Hainer excuses himself and leaves the room]

Feldman: That was hardly necessary.

Boldt: Unless you're sitting where I am. Dr. Hainer's report is going to play significantly in the review of this interview. His state of mind is critical to that review. I question his ability to assess me fairly. That's all. I mean no disrespect.

For the sake of the tape, Dr. Hainer has left the room at . . .
10:37 a.m. Subject remains.
Boldt: For the sake of the tape: he looked a little queasy.

He has a personal matter to attend to. He'll be back shortly.
Boldt: He's going to have a smoke and recompose himself. He smokes
menthols. Did you smell it? Half a pack a day, I think. And he has
a problem with athlete's foot—uses that spray stuff. It's my nose.
[subject points to nose] Best old-factory around. [subject laughs]

Let's start with your relationship with Captain Shoswitz.
Boldt: My relationship? You make it sound as if we shower together.
If you want to understand my closeness to Captain Shoswitz, then
you have to understand my attraction to the job. It started with
my father. He was a drunk. Your friend Dr. Hainer, who just beat a
hasty retreat, he may find this useful. I'm laboring under some kind
of daddy complex, which explains so much about me. We need him.
Bring him back.

Your sarcasm is noted, Lieutenant Boldt, though I'm not sure it
helps your case any.
Boldt: My case? That's rich. My father had some brushes with the
law. By "the law" I mean my uncle Victor. They called him Lightning. Lightning Boldt—get it? He was a blue, like you and me. Victor, I'm talking about. Not my father. He was a drunk. Plain and
simple. The life of a drunk *is* plain and simple. Simple, and difficult, and tragic—which pretty much sums up dear old Dad. And
by "brushes" I mean knock-down-drag-outs, where the two of them
went at it like a pair of Irishmen. This typically followed my father
getting into trouble, and my uncle Vic getting him out. Dad showed
his thanks by offering his fists. Dad liked to hit. [subject makes a

sucking noise between his teeth] Dad liked to hit whatever, whoever, was handy at the time. Ah-ha! Dr. Hainer returns. A glass of water to justify his absence. Yes, have a seat—we were just discussing my effed-up childhood and my *relationship* with my dad. Although he couldn't relate to anything, so it's a misnomer. Yes, by all means take a note. Write that down. It could prove incredibly important to *my innocence.*

You were going to tell us about you and Captain Shoswitz.
Boldt: It's all connected. My uncle Vic started on the beat. Yesler Way and south into what used to be mostly the fish trade. Some rough characters.

No one's questioning your uncle's integrity.
Boldt: No, but you're questioning my integrity. You're accusing me of helping out the captain in a way that violates regs. Twenty-seven years, four months, and this is what it comes down to? You actually think I carried ten grand in cash and put it back into Property? Do you actually think LaMoia was involved as well? And you think I would do all this for Phil Shoswitz, which suggests he took that money out in the first place, which I don't believe. The implication is that he did it because his son was into some bad real-estate deals. More incredible, you say you can prove all this. Has it occurred to *any* of you that this goes totally contrary to my career, to LaMoia's, and to the lieutenant's—the captain's? Isn't it far more likely I've been set up?

To what purpose?
Boldt: I have ideas but no proof. If you'd give me time to track some of this down . . . Instead you've got me in here with you two, and all we're going to do is circle the drain.

You were going to tell us about your relationship with Captain Shoswitz.

Boldt: I was going to tell you that my uncle Vic moved on to form the first SWAT squad this department ever had. Worked with Jerry Fleming from the Bureau. Jerry had run the D. B. Cooper case. Remember that one: guy hijacks a plane and jumps from a jet with eighty grand? Jerry's the real thing. His son, Walt, too. He's the sheriff over in Sun Valley. And Uncle Vic and Jerry set up a response squad—special weapons and tactics. That's when Vic got into the interesting work. Over the next few years, he and his squad saved sixteen lives. Hostages. Attempted suicides. You name it. And he might have left this department with his chin up and a chance at a private-sector job if some TV crew hadn't scared a jumper off the I-5 bridge back in the '80s and made it look like Vic had screwed the pooch. It wasn't Vic that lost that guy—but the video made it look that way. And that was the end of Vic. That's what you guys are. Do you see that? You're the TV crew in my career. Twenty-seven years, and you're going to make it look like I did this thing. And I did not.

Captain Shoswitz.

Boldt: *Sergeant* Shoswitz recruited me for a vice sting on the canal. A gaming room in an abandoned vessel. Maybe he took me for my size, maybe because he owed one to Uncle Vic. But I got the call. I was riding in Freemont mostly. Watching the grass grow between the cracks. Not a lot of work in Freemont. A stolen salmon maybe. A buoy snatching. Lowball stuff. And Shoswitz calls me onto a vice sting. I don't think I slept the night before that. I was pretty wound up. Vice. That was the real stuff. This is the late '70s. I was a young buck. The wharves and the canals were full of prosts and dealers. Coke and weed. Some H. AIDS hadn't arrived yet. Vice was *the* place to be. When you love this job, you love it. I think my uncle Vic understood that about me: he knew I had something to prove. That I wasn't my father. That I wasn't going to go down a bottle and that I wanted to fix things instead of screw them up. That Crosby, Stills and Nash song. You ever hear that one: "Teach Your Children"? I'm a jazz guy myself, but that song pretty much sums up the first part of my life. The second part, once I was wearing that uniform, was going to be different, and the sergeant understood that about me.

So you owed him.
Boldt: I did. I do. Yes, absolutely. You know the way it is. Show me anyone who doesn't owe somebody something. Nuns owe it all to God. For Lance Armstrong, it's the bike. Gimme a break. It's all connected. That's what makes investigating—and some of us actually investigate crimes before throwing around charges—so much fun.

That connection between you and Captain Shoswitz ... Why don't you explain it to me?
Boldt: The thing about you guys in I.I. is you lose your trust. You lose your faith. You spend too much time investigating your fellow blue and you lose perspective.

Philip Shoswitz received a favorable bank loan from your wife. You want to tell us about that?
Boldt: Am I supposed to be impressed that you did your homework? Listen, it was a *car* loan. It was back in the Stone Age. He got the loan well before I ever met Liz. She and I tell people we met in college. We've told that so many times maybe even we believe it. But it's not right. We met in a bank. Across a loan desk in a bank. Romantic, huh? The lieu had taken out a bank loan on a new car—some kind of Buick, I think. He told me about it. Incredible rate. An incentive thing, you know? Back when interest rates were obscene. But if you opened a checking and savings account then, they shaved a bunch

of points off the car loan. It was this all-in-one thing. A promotional thing. Best deal in the city. So I went, and the loan officer . . . Well, you know: one of *those* stories. A year later we were hitched. I was never great with math. I don't handle the money at the house, guys. So you implying I handled money here . . . that's just plain wrong.

We've implied nothing.
Boldt: You've charged me. Excuse me. You've charged me with . . . let me get this straight . . . placing ten thousand dollars cash—in bills twenty dollars and less—*back* into the property room. Not stealing, but returning. Isn't that right? So the charge is, what, *not* stealing?

You know what the charges are.
Boldt: Not really.

Your wife, Elizabeth. You may have met her in a bank, but it was her recruitment of you that led to your relationship. It's that kind of fudging the line, Lieutenant, that ultimately will work against you.
Boldt: You have as long on the job as a guy like me, and you expect people to come after you. The reputation gets too big. The department doesn't like any officer getting bigger than the badge. But listen, that hasn't happened here. I'm *well aware* of my limitations and shortcomings. I have a lot yet to prove, cases to close. If you're trying to pressure me off the force, this is a hell of a convoluted way of doing it.

Dr. Hainer: Your wife's neighbor was having problems with her husband. Tell us about that. She asked you for some help with that.
  Sergeant Feldman: You can't take on that kind of employment while carrying the shield. It's moonlighting. It's not permitted.
Boldt: This was fifteen years ago.

You were off-shift. You put a man in the hospital with a broken collarbone and a dislocated elbow.

Boldt: The guy beat his wife on the bottom of her feet with a length of garden hose filled with bird shot. He performed acts—sexual acts—that she did not consent to. Repeatedly. He withheld food from her and drugged her against her will. It's true he took a swing at me and I defended myself. It's also true he got the short end of that stick and ended up in need of medical attention. How I got there that night . . . there is no record of that. What you're citing is rumor and hearsay. Unsubstantiated nonsense.

It was that incident that brought you and your wife together.

Boldt: You see: it's that legend thing again. Rumors. I never asked for that mantle. People who get that, they never ask for it. It just arrives one day. And believe me, it's a damn uncomfortable thing, that kind of label. What good does it do anyone? I maintained an 80 percent clearance rate for the better part of eight years on homicide. That's luck. Plain and simple. I'm not a super-cop. You're ginning up stories that have little or no basis in fact. If you're going to pretend to do your homework, check your sources. You gotta always check your sources: first rule. Besides, what business is it of yours what brought Liz and me together? How could that possibly have any bearing on—

[Interrupts] Because it solidified and defined the relationship between you and Captain Shoswitz.

Boldt: Not true! You are way off base. Stick to the facts. You're not paying attention to the facts.

And the facts are?

Boldt: Okay. [subject looks between the two interviewers] You want this from my side? [subject clears his throat] You allege that ten thousand dollars went missing from Property, that the missing money was discovered in a random inventory. You neglect to figure into this—somehow—that the discovery was kept secret. Neither I nor anyone else below the chief, I assume, was made aware of the missing money. You then suggest that I somehow divined the money was missing, recovered the money, and returned it in order to protect Phil Shoswitz, who you claim stole it in the first place. Throughout all of this, you fail to give any credence to the idea that the initial inventory was inaccurate, that someone made a mistake on the front end of this thing, and that all of this is just a horrible accounting error.

That's what you'd like us to believe.
Boldt: I'm telling you my impression of the events.

Shoswitz moved you along with him at each and every promotion. That suggests more than just a bond of friendship or camaraderie.
Boldt: Do not go there.

It suggests a tie between the two of you. A debt. A street debt. Something that creates the kind of bond we all know happens on this job. Happens more frequently than is acknowledged. You moved from Vice to felony investigation, Major Crimes, and Homicide. Each time Shoswitz moved, you followed six months later.
Boldt: Maybe he valued my abilities.

Dr. Hainer: You did the same for the career path of Barbara Gaines.
Boldt: Is that what this is about? Payback for me bringing the first woman onto Homicide? Aren't we beyond that?

Dr. Hainer: Did you or do you have a sexual relationship with Barbara Gaines?

Boldt: I did not. That would be fraternizing. And just for the *record,* Dr. Hainer, you are precariously close to losing your front teeth and most of your face as you know it.

Sergeant Feldman: For the sake of the record, let it show that Lieutenant Boldt's threatening remark was aimed at Dr. Hainer.

Boldt: We're on video, Sergeant. I think they can see where I'm looking. And yeah, it's at Dr. Hainer. *For the record,* I have never had anything but a fully professional and platonic relationship with Detective Gaines, not that it pertains to this case in any way.

Sergeant Feldman: But it does. Gaines is part of this investigation. [pause] So shocked? Didn't you know? You, LaMoia, Gaines, and Matthews. You're all to be questioned.

Boldt: [subject is restless in the chair] You're after my entire squad? My lead unit? What kind of a witch hunt is this?

Each person on your lead squad holds some kind of debt to you. The way you do to Shoswitz, or Shoswitz to you—we don't know which. This department doesn't run that way anymore. You're old-school, Lieutenant. It may give you a hell of a clearance rate, but it has complicated this investigation.

Boldt: The only thing complicating this investigation is the limited scope of the person running it. Face it: you want me out. Now you have the chance to use someone's incompetence to try to take me to the mat. Why don't you just say it? But let me tell you something. I'm not going. I'm not done. And I'm sure as hell not leaving the job like this. You picked the wrong way to go after me, Feldman. Why isn't it mentioned anywhere that each time I was promoted, you were up for the same promotions? Where's that in all your paperwork? Why don't we stick to the evidence, the way police work is supposed to be handled?

While we're on the topic of professional conduct, why don't you tell me about how Daphne Matthews fits into this?
Boldt: Ms. Matthews is a civilian. She serves in a professional capacity as an employee, a consultant to the department. By "fits into this," do you mean homicide investigations? I think even you should be able to understand how the services of a criminal psychologist might be of use to a homicide investigation.

You brought her into the department.
Boldt: Exaggeration.

As I understand it, she approached you for an interview.
Boldt: Okay, now I'm impressed. There aren't many who know that. Well done, Sergeant.

About your uncle Vic's jumper, wasn't it?
Boldt: I've been on the job for twenty-seven years. I'd like to think I've touched a lot of lives, hopefully in a good way. You can throw Matthews into that, I suppose.

You allowed the interview. You don't often allow interviews, do you, Lieutenant? In your twenty-seven years of service, how many interviews—press or otherwise—have you agreed to?
Boldt: She was interested in the psychology of the case. Both sides. That impressed me. She was a graduate student at the time. When she was degreed, I consulted her on a case. Her insight proved valuable. Six months later, I turned to her again. By then she'd applied for a position, I believe. I might have that wrong. But at any rate, along came the Cross Killer. Ms. Mat-

thews was a critical piece of the investigation, and that of the copycat killings that followed.

And you became close.
Boldt: I'm close to LaMoia too, so watch your implications.

I wasn't implying anything.
Boldt: Nice try.

And how did Ms. Matthews fit into the property room switch? How was she involved in that?
Boldt: Let's talk about the video camera and log book. I'm told you have both LaMoia and me on tape and in the book signing into the property room that night. Never mind that we were called out on a case. Gaines? Do you have her? Why aren't you looking at who might have the ability to substitute videotape? Why haven't you used a forgery expert to check the signatures in the log? Let me ask you something, Feldman: you see my right foot? [subject extends right leg] You see what I'm wearing? It's a sandal. A Birkenstock. A hippie shoe. Because I got problems, big problems, with the pinky toe on my right foot. Check with my podiatrist. I've been in this sandal for the past eight months. Now, you go take a look at your security video. I haven't *been* to the property room in *eighteen* months. I'm a lieu, not a sergeant. I have no reason to go down there. You check my footwear. Ten to one, I'm not wearing a sandal. That's because someone took some older footage of me using the property room and performed some video magic and changed the time code. Moved it from twenty-ought-six to twenty-ought-eight. Something like that. But it's Sonny and Cher: "It Ain't Me, Babe." All that precious evidence of yours is part of a scheme to frame me and my best unit. If you'd done your homework, we wouldn't be here right now. You're wasting both my time and yours. It's a shame you don't know what you're doing.

[Sergeant Feldman is summoned to door. Pauses interview. Heard from door: Feldman: ". . . so have a look at the damn video." Feldman returns to table.]

Boldt: You want a break, we can take a break. You don't look so good, Feldman.

You're not the one running this interview. [pause]

Boldt: [whispers, but is caught on tape] I am now.

[Clears throat, takes sip of water] Matthews is ambitious. She used you to advance her name in criminal psychology, to build a career where she's now one of the highest paid consultants in the nation.

Boldt: I wouldn't know anything about that.

Wouldn't you? Oh, come on! Define your relationship with Ms. Matthews, please, Lieutenant.

Boldt: Have you been listening? It's incumbent upon the interviewer to actually listen to the subject.

You were separated from your wife for a time. This was just after the Cross Killer investigation, about the time copycat crimes surfaced. You and Ms. Matthews worked closely *together during this time, did you not?*

Boldt: I've explained that Ms. Matthews's contributions to both investigations were instrumental to the clearance of those cases. That's all I need to say.

She is currently living with Detective LaMoia, as I understand it.

Boldt: Fraternization is not permitted by this department and you know it. It can lead to nepotism. Ms. Matthews is an expert witness and a consultant used by many units in this department. I don't track her personal life.

Not what I hear.

Boldt: [leans across the table, then returns to chair] You and I . . . [subject sits back down] Go check your video evidence, Sergeant. I can wait. And while you're at it, check the logs and compare the signatures. When all that is done, you might want to explain to someone that you served for three years on Vice's video surveillance tech squad. You moved from there to I.T. for a couple years. Isn't that right? So let's take a long, hard look at who in this room is qualified to mess with video evidence. The only thing I know about a mouse is you feed it cheese. You could give me every computer book in the world, and I couldn't do a thing with video evidence. And yet, here you are, with me in your sights, and I'm telling you that you picked the wrong guy. I get a guy like you. I understand that kind of patience, that anger at being passed over for promotions. Matthews could explain how a guy like you . . . how that kind of obsession festers. It goes bad. It makes you sick. And it's no secret that I'm nearing the end of my run. Nothing a guy like you would rather see than me going down in flames or being forced out. I know all this, and I believe I may be able to prove it. But you took care of that: the one guy who might challenge this absurdity of an investigation is the one guy you took care of by aiming it at him. My only hope is that since Internal Investigation tapes are reviewed, someone watching this, listening to this down the line, will at least bother to look at the evidence with a less jaundiced eye.

This is ridiculous.

Boldt: Which is what I'm saying. We're saying the same thing. So why are my accusations ridiculous, and yours are not? Hmm? You want to explain that? You made a mistake, Sergeant Feldman, by coming after me. You doctored those tapes. You got someone to forge a couple of names in the log book. But you didn't do your homework: you didn't know about my bum foot and the sandal. The Sandal Scandal. The sandal [subject extends leg] is going to turn this all back onto you.

We're done here.
Boldt: One of us is.

This interview is over. [Detective Feldman quotes date and time, and closes session]
Boldt: I'd get a lawyer if I were you. A good lawyer at that.

———

Two days later, Boldt met LaMoia in Carkeek Park. Boldt big. LaMoia long and narrow and, it was apparent, strong and quick. A steady wind blew in their faces, enough wind to prevent any long-range microphone from picking up anything said. They faced the whitecapped waters of the strait, the lush islands, distant and low, like green jewels on gray cloth. LaMoia's mustache and goatee shook with the stiff breeze. His nose ran and he constantly mopped it with a handkerchief that he also held over his mouth as he spoke.

"What was that like?" LaMoia asked.

"Like when we do it, only the other way around. It got messy."

"Are you okay with it?"

"I don't like being accused of things. They wanted to bring you and Daphne and Bobbie into it. They hammered away on my friendship with Phil. They tried to make a case that we'd done this together."

"Jeez."

"You better get her things out of the loft. They accused you two of fraternizing."

LaMoia chewed on his lower lip till the skin turned white. "Shit. And the other thing? The prop room?"

"Feldman's seen *Murder on the Orient Express* one too many times. His theory is, if I read it right, that each of us returned a few thousand until we got the cache back up to ten grand. I think they realized no one person entering Property empty-handed could have carried the full ten grand."

"How creative of them."

"Seriously." Boldt looked past LaMoia at a ferry plowing through the chop. A water bug on a breezy pond. "Can you imagine coming up with a plan like that? Who could think of such a thing?"

"Certainly not a criminal psychologist with a love of old movies."

Boldt reprimanded LaMoia with a sharp look.

"And the videotape?" LaMoia asked. "Did they hit you with that?"

"They'll figure it out. Someone will. Feldman was called to the door by someone looking on. I wouldn't be surprised if it had to do with the video. They're going to realize that tape of me is nearly two years old. When they do, I think it'll be Feldman sitting in that chair I was sitting in."

"And if not?" LaMoia said.

"What are the chances that any four or five cops would risk their careers for one person? Phil Shoswitz or no Phil Shoswitz. Never mind that Phil was drunk when he allegedly took that money— never mind that it was his one and only gaffe in all those years of service. Are you going to tell me that four officers would put themselves at risk like that?"

"I'm not."

"Because it's absurd. Feldman's on drugs."

"But he took the case."

"Of course he took the case. He'd give anything to bring me down. Had to be him."

"And if it hadn't been?"

"But it was. No one else in I.I. had the personal motivation he did."

"But if it hadn't been?" LaMoia pressed.

"You let me know if they contact you. I don't think there's much chance of that, but I need to know the minute you hear anything."

"Will do."

"I'm going to your place now. I need an hour."

LaMoia looked at Boldt, but the lieutenant only stared out at the chop and the ferry's slow progress.

"How often does it feel like that?" Boldt asked. "Push like hell, get nowhere."

"Name of the game."

"You going to ask me why?" Boldt asked.

"You and her? No. Should I?"

"Most guys would."

"And since when am I most guys?" LaMoia asked.

They both watched the ferry's effort.

"Listen," LaMoia said. "It's a three-legged dog at the moment. Her and me. And the kid. I could lie and tell you otherwise, but that's the truth. If I was a betting man . . ."

"And you're telling me this because?"

"Because I'm not stupid, Sarge."

LaMoia had called him that for too long to switch. Boldt would never be a lieutenant in his eyes.

"You two . . ." LaMoia said. "Liz must feel the same way I do at least some of the time."

"And how's that?"

"Like I'm watching from the sidelines."

"That's absurd."

"No, it's not," LaMoia said. "She's gotten me into those old movies. And the one thing I've come to understand is that some actors have this chemistry, this *thing* between them. You feel it, whatever it is. It's like a magnetic field or something. Like some kind of light the camera doesn't actually catch, but it's still there." He paused to wipe his nose and clean his mustache. "You two are like that."

"That's B.S."

"It's not. Maybe you don't feel it the way I do. Maybe neither of you do. Maybe you've lived so long with it that you're used to it. How should I know? Maybe you're hosing me. I sure as shit hope not, because I'd hope by now the two of us have more respect for each other than that."

"I've got to tell her things, John. I've got to explain things, including the possible fraternization charges. I think this mess . . . I think something just kind of popped in me that some things have got to be explained," Boldt said.

"The two of you live in no-man's-land. I don't know how you do it. She's with me. Sort of. But she's never left you."

"She was never *with* me."

"Try telling her that."

"You and her. It's been, what? A year. More than a year."

"And we're happy. We're friends. Good friends. Absolutely. But best friends? Listen, I'm infatuated. Hook, line, and sinker. Honest to God, I could take some cabin on a lake with her and never come back. I'm in. All the chips. And of course it's the one and only time I've felt like that—and of course it's never going to happen. I think, when you've had my kind of history with the opposite sex . . . I think something like this is bound to happen."

"It's called irony, John."

"It's called bad luck, Sarge. You go to her. You say whatever you have to say. But I'd be less than honest if I told you it'll sit all right with me. Because it won't. The kid's in play. We come up for review on that pretty soon. My gut says we won't be allowed to keep the kid, but my heart—and this is me talking, don't forget—wants it more than anything."

"Kids don't hold a marriage together. If anything they challenge it in ways you can't imagine."

"But I can imagine. It's been a year, like you said. I'm not expecting miracles."

"They asked me about my past," Boldt said. "They made me relive all sorts of stuff that I'd forgotten. Phil. Daphne. You and Bobbie. How it all came together."

"And how it damn near came apart."

"And something about that made me realize I had to speak my piece. To each of you."

"You call this speaking your piece to me?"

"You? No. I'm not ready for you."

"There's some kind of order? A line?" LaMoia looked around at the grass blowing all around them. "That's precious."

"In my head there is."

"I always wondered what was in there," LaMoia said. "Lines, huh?"

Boldt stopped a smile from forming. He checked the ferry again, surprised at how steadily it moved across the strait. It had made great progress.

"Do what you gotta do," LaMoia said.

"It isn't what you're thinking. It's nothing like that. It's about explaining the past, not making up a future."

"And that's the first time I've breathed in the past five minutes."

Boldt couldn't stop the smile; it exposed him. "I'm going to the Joke later. Play some piano. If you come by, drinks are on me."

"Are we celebrating?"

"Feels like we should, don't you think?"

"What would we be celebrating?"

Boldt said nothing.

"What if they dig up that Gaines studied film for two years of college? What if they find out that what that really meant was two years of working in video?"

"Do you really think anyone would ever believe that four officers would all risk their careers for any one person?" Boldt asked again.

"That would be stupid."

"Incredibly stupid."

"Ridiculous."

"Absurd."

The ferry was nearly out of sight. A small speck spitting a trail of white foam.

"Beauty is in the eye of the beholder," Boldt said.

"Do you love her?" LaMoia asked. His eyes were moist as he blew his nose again.

Boldt wondered if the wind was doing that to his eyes. He placed a hand on the shoulder of LaMoia's deerskin jacket and gripped firmly. LaMoia continued looking out across the water. He would not turn his head.

Boldt squeezed once more, then headed toward the Crown Vic, fighting off a chill he couldn't seem to beat.

ANNE PERRY

Anne Perry was born in 1938 in Blackheath, London. She endured several illnesses while young and was unable to attend all but a few years of school. Largely educated at home, she was aided by a deep affection for reading. She has lived in various parts of the world, including the Bahamas, a small island off the coast of New Zealand, and Southern California. She took the name of her stepfather, becoming Anne Perry—not a pseudonym but her legal name. Her first book, *The Cater Street Hangman,* was published in 1979. In addition to the novels featuring Thomas Pitt and his wife, Charlotte, Miss Perry has produced a bestselling series featuring William Monk, novels set during World War I, Christmas novellas, and several stand-alone works. The author of more than fifty books, she lives in northern Scotland.

CHARLOTTE AND THOMAS PITT

BY ANNE PERRY

I would like you to tell me as much as you can about Thomas Pitt," Naylor said respectfully.

"Really?" Lady Vespasia Cumming-Gould raised her silver eyebrows in surprise. She had considered the possibility that Naylor might come to her, and then dismissed it. She did not often make mistakes. She had survived Victorian society dazzlingly, as one of Europe's greatest beauties and, far more important, as a woman of passion and courage who dared to say what she thought. She had reached an age that she no longer cared to name in this year of our Lord 1912.

"And why is that, Sir Peter?" she inquired.

"Matters in Europe are becoming most grave," Naylor replied. "We need a man of extraordinary abilities at the head of our Intelligence Services in this country. The prime minister is considering Mr. Pitt, but there are those who speak against him, primarily the king himself. We cannot afford to be wrong, now of all times."

A flicker of amusement moved Vespasia's lips, but it was not untouched by sadness. She knew quite as well as Peter Naylor how darkly the future loomed.

"Thomas Pitt has been one of my friends for thirty years. Do you trust me to have an unbiased opinion?" she asked.

"I trust you to tell me the truth, Lady Vespasia," he replied. "You understand human nature, and the politics of Europe, therefore you know what must lie ahead. And if you are fond of Thomas Pitt, then you will not wish to see him in a position of leadership for which he is unqualified. It would be not only a disservice to your country, it would be a tragic end to his, so far, highly distinguished career. And I do not use the word *tragic* lightly or melodramatically."

"I know," she answered him. "It may be offensive to underrate a man; it is the ultimate cruelty to overrate him. What is it you wish to know? I assume you already have a history of his cases?"

"I do, for what it is worth. The details are open to interpretation."

"And you have spoken with Pitt himself?"

"Of course. That is why I need your estimation all the more. The man is an enigma to me, a Gordian knot of contradictions."

She waited for him to continue, sitting motionless in her ivory silk gown, her back still straight, a cascade of pearls almost to her waist, her throat and wrists masked in lace. There was a gold lorgnette on the small table beside her, but either she did not require it in order to see him or she was not sufficiently interested in the details of his appearance to use it.

Since she was apparently not going to prompt him, he continued. "He sounds like a gentleman, his diction is perfect and his vocabulary wide, yet he looks . . ." He hesitated.

"As if he had dressed in the dark, in someone else's clothes," she supplied. "And quite obviously not found a hairbrush. And yet I have never seen him unshaven."

"Quite. Can you explain it?"

"With ease. His father was a gamekeeper on Sir Arthur Desmond's estate. Desmond's own son was young Thomas's age, a charming boy but lazy. Sir Arthur decided to educate them together, as a spur to his son, at least to exceed the gamekeeper's boy in academic achievement, if not in sportsmanship."

Naylor smiled. "And did he?"

"No. I believe in neither respect. Pitt excelled beyond young Desmond in intelligence, and lagged behind him in athleticism, and barely knew or cared about one end of a horse from the other. However, he was a good shot, I believe."

Naylor smiled again. "All that would explain his speech and his apparent education. Still, he has never forgotten his humble origins, to judge from his manner, and a certain . . ." He stopped, clearly not wishing to offend her.

She allowed him to fumble. She was quite aware of what he meant, but she was not going to assist him.

"Attitude of mind, an ordinariness," he finished lamely.

Naylor knew she was amusing herself, but he also knew that she would not let him leave without all the information he needed, honest to the last word and beyond, even to the unsaid implication.

"Part of him never left the servants' quarters," he said, watching her face. "And yet it is not a lack of ambition which holds him there. And I am certain beyond any doubt whatever that it is not an innate respect for those who might consider themselves his 'betters.' Will you tell me what it is, or do I have to guess?"

The amusement was there on her face again. "His father was accused of poaching—not on Desmond's land but on that of his immediate neighbor. He was found guilty, wrongly, Pitt believed. So did Desmond himself, but there was nothing he could do. It was an old feud, and Pitt's father paid for it. He was transported to Australia. It was the time when we still did that."

"I see." Naylor nodded, tight-lipped. "Yes, that explains much. His passion for justice no doubt stems from that time. And perhaps a knowledge that it does not always prevail. Yes, that would explain why he worries a case to the last degree. He may see in every accused man the shadow of his father."

"You are being too clever, Sir Peter," Vespasia corrected. "As a young man that may have been true. He is in his sixties now, and has seen too much of life to be so full of dreams. He knows that very little is so simple as that would suggest."

"I thought him something of an idealist." He was not quite contradicting her, but he was certainly questioning her estimation.

"A man with ideals," she corrected him mildly. "It is not the same thing. He is a realist who has never lost hope, a man who has made enough mistakes to forgive those of others, knowing that a great many of them will inevitably be repeated."

Something in Naylor's face pinched with a shadow of disappointment. "A compassionate man," he observed. "Others said that of him."

"Compassionate," she agreed. "Not indecisive, Sir Peter. What I believe you are asking me is, will he have the strength to make harsh and unpopular decisions, or act against those he may still pity. Are you afraid that he is too eager to please his social superiors to risk making a decision that will displease them? Or perhaps he is like the man driving one of those new motors towards the cliff edge, so balanced in judgment that he can see the virtues of turning to the left so equally with those of turning to the right that he cannot choose for either and ends in going into the abyss. He is of the servant class by birth, Sir Peter, and far too practical for such a piece of stupidity."

"Yes, I suppose so," he conceded. "But servant class, all the same. Might that not make him too easily swayed to give respect where regrettably it is not due?"

This time she laughed outright, a rich, happy sound of pure delight. "My dear young man"—he was close to fifty but seemed very young to her—"if you imagine that our servants are blind to our faults or our weaknesses, then you are utterly naive. I'm sure your valet treats you with the utmost respect, but do not forget that he has seen you at your most vulnerable and most absurd." She ignored his blushes, although she may have been well aware of the kind of incident he was recalling with such embarrassment. "He may be very fond of you," she continued. "But it is not a blind affection. On the contrary, it is probably more clear-eyed than that of your wife. And you may be certain she thinks a great deal that she is far too tactful to say."

At this point he felt very young indeed, and at a considerable disadvantage. Had he not been directed by the prime minister himself to obtain this information from Lady Vespasia, he would have excused himself stiffly and left.

Vespasia was still smiling at him. "It was Pitt's very painful decision in a certain matter some years ago which rescued His Majesty when he was still Prince of Wales. It was a situation which might well have cost him the throne—indeed have cost England its monarchy. Instead it earned Pitt the undying enmity of the king. Queen Alexandra will confirm what I say. Thomas Pitt may agonize over a decision, but he will make it according to his conscience, not according to orders, favors, or threats. That is something you may wish to consider both for him and against him. But he will place his duty to his country first, which I believe is what you are asking me?"

"Yes," he said reluctantly. "I suppose I am. But he is fallible!"

"Of course," she agreed. "And occasionally stubborn. He knows a good painting when he sees one, from his time in the Metropolitan Police when he investigated the thefts of art from the homes of the wealthy. He is particularly fond of land- and seascapes, and pictures of cows. That is because he has a deep love of the land. He was too close to it in childhood to be sentimental about it. He knows it is full of little deaths; he chooses not to think of them.

"He loves poetry, because he loves language and ideas, but he might as well have ears of cloth as far as great music is concerned. I have watched him suffer a form of torture, having no choice in courtesy but to sit through an entire ballet and pretend that he was not bored to tears by it. It is to his credit that he almost succeeded. The transfixed look on his face was mistaken for rapture. He was invited to go again, and I was obliged, out of pity, to rescue him."

"His manners are not of concern to us," Naylor admitted graciously. "And we will do something so he does not look as if he has dressed out of the ragbag."

"I doubt that," Vespasia replied. "His wife has tried for a quarter of a century and not made the slightest difference that I have observed."

"Ah, yes, his wife. I shall come to her in due course. The clothes may be addressed later, if necessary. To more delicate subjects." He looked at her gravely. "All men have weaknesses. Please do not be evasive out of kindness, Lady Vespasia. I ask because I require to know. I cannot protect a man—and believe me, he will have enemies—unless I know where his vulnerabilities lie, the points at which he may be betrayed from within, manipulated by the unscrupulous, or threatened by the ruthless. The safety of our nation may come to lie in his hands."

"I am quite aware of why you ask, Sir Peter," she told him. "His family is his greatest strength and his greatest weakness, which is perhaps true of all of us. We can be reached most wildly and dangerously through what we love."

Naylor bit his lip. "He has a son, Daniel, and a daughter, Jemima, I believe. Daniel is at university, studying medicine, and Jemima has just married an American." He raised his eyebrows questioningly.

"If you are considering that that may be a problem," she answered, "then you know something unfortunate of Anglo-American relations that I do not. Many of our great families have married Americans, to their benefit. The Churchills and the Astors, to name but two."

He sighed and sat back. "Tell me something about the man, so I feel as if I know him better than a casual encounter at the club, if you please."

"You will not encounter him at your club," she replied, as if the very notion entertained her. "Or at anyone else's. He would greatly prefer to be at home by his own fireside or, better yet, in the kitchen. It is an extraordinarily agreeable room. The floor is wooden and frequently scrubbed, as is the large table. I like the smell of clean wood, perhaps just a trifle damp still, do you not?"

He was taken aback.

"I . . . I've never thought about it," he admitted. "Did he tell you this?"

"Of course not." She was dismissive. "I have observed it. There is a Welsh dresser against the wall, with blue-and-white ringed china on it, and some with painted butterflies and wild grasses, drawn extremely well. There are copper kettles and pans on the wall, and more often than not, clean linen on the airing rail, which hangs from the ceiling. The aroma of that brings back to me memories of laughter and friendship, of desperate battles against evil fought side by side, and good people who are no longer with us. Perhaps that is why he has no wish to move from Keppel Street, even though he could well afford to. The house is full of the past, of triumphs and disasters that have both been enriching." Her eyes seemed far away for several moments, then suddenly she returned. "And you are not entirely correct about the untidiness. He has always loved good boots, ever since his sister-in-law, Emily, gave him his first pair. So far as I know, it is his only extravagance, the very best boots."

"And his indulgences?" he asked.

She did not hesitate an instant.

"Cider, and steak-and-kidney pudding, the proper sort with mushrooms in, and even oysters, and of course a suet crust. That is absolutely imperative. And black currant jam, preferably on toast. Dark marmalade, sharp enough to bite back at you, but then anyone with any taste at all likes that. Must be made with Seville oranges, of course, obtainable only in January. But you must know that yourself. I apologize for telling you. Pockets full of string, paper clips, pipe cleaners, penknives, stubs of pencil, mint humbugs, and anything else which might conceivably one day be useful . . . or not."

"I begin to like him," Naylor remarked.

"Good. Although it is irrelevant."

"A very different kind of man," he observed.

"Very," she agreed with a smile, as if she knew much that she would not say.

"That brings me to Charlotte Pitt." He leaned forward again. "A somewhat unconventional woman, one might even say 'meddlesome.'"

"Unless one were being unhelpfully tactful, one would definitely say 'meddlesome,'" she agreed. "Usually to excellent effect."

He tried to hide a smile, and failed. "Might she be his greatest weakness, Lady Vespasia? His Achilles' heel?"

"Socially?" The idea appeared to amuse her. "She comes from a good family, Sir Peter. Not top drawer, but perhaps second. Her sister Emily married very well indeed. Her son is Lord Ashworth. She is now, of course, Mrs. Jack Radley."

"Member of Parliament. Yes, I know. He is definitely a great supporter of Pitt," he acknowledged. "He did not conceal the relationship. Not that I imagine he could have, or wished to. But Emily Radley is perfectly respectable. That does not mean that her sister is the same. It is a matter not only of blood but of behavior."

"Of course it is. I have known women who could scarcely name their parents and who were so respectable they could barely speak at all for fear of saying something unconventional, even to an opinion on the suitability of the curtains." Her eyes widened. "And, thank heaven, I have also known duchesses who could be outrageous, and frequently were. I hope no one has ever said of me that I was respectable?"

Now it was his turn to be amused. "Never, Lady Vespasia, I swear. Beautiful, brave and wise, charming and of devastating wit, always fashionable, because if you wore something it automatically became fashion. I cannot recall anyone even hinting that you could be . . . tedious."

"Thank you. I am very relieved. I hope to die before I risk becoming sanctimonious and predictable."

He leaned forward again. "I have heard that Mrs. Pitt is unpredictable. Is that a fair thing to say?"

"I sincerely hope so."

"Lady Vespasia . . ."

She raised an elegant hand only a few inches.

"Yes, yes, I understand. You need the truth. Charlotte was the second daughter of Edward and Caroline Ellison, well-to-do gentry. Her eldest sister, Sarah, married Dominic Cord, who is now a dynamic and rather outspoken . . ."

Naylor was startled. "*The* Dominic Cord? Really? Some of his views are a trifle unorthodox. And his wife is certainly extraordinarily outspoken. I believe she has offended the archbishop of Canterbury himself!"

Vespasia did not attempt to hide her admiration. "So I heard," she said enthusiastically. "I hope profoundly that it is true. It is very good for the mind to be upset every now and then, rather as taking a brisk walk is good for the constitution. It sets the blood flowing."

"You were telling me about Sarah Cord. I assume she died, or Cord himself could not have married again?"

"To be more precise, she was murdered," Vespasia corrected him.

"Good God!" The color fled from his face.

"It was nothing to do with the family," she assured him. "A number of very respectable young women were murdered in the area at the time. She happened to be one of them. She was doing nothing amiss whatever. That was the case in which Charlotte met Thomas Pitt. Naturally her mother had intended her for a more socially fortunate marriage, but she had the wisdom to allow Charlotte to follow her heart. And she has been very happy ever since. It cost her her social standing, and of course a great deal of money. However, she learned to live on a policeman's salary and keep house with the assistance of one all-purpose maid. She had to reduce drastically the size and quality of her wardrobe, which is never easy for a handsome woman, but she managed. I do not believe she has ever regretted her choice, and that is more than most women can say."

He looked a little startled.

"She is happy, Sir Peter," Vespasia repeated. "She does not look back with question or regret. She does not envy anyone. And possibly that does not make her the right wife for a man seeking high office. She knows both sides of society. She can dance with a duke, but she never had the art of making trivial conversation or flattering to please. And so far as I know, she never made the attempt to hide her opinions on subjects about which she cared."

"What subjects might they be?" he asked warily.

"Right and wrong," she replied. "Justice and injustice, prejudice, intolerance, self-righteousness, cruelty, hypocrisy, and the building and destroying of dreams."

"Are you sure we are speaking of Charlotte Pitt, my lady, and not perhaps a little of yourself?" His voice was gentle and a trifle wry.

She sighed, her gaze far away. "Maybe I see in her what I wish to, but I think nevertheless that I am accurate. Charlotte was never as beautiful as I, so she had not the confidence in herself, nor perhaps the arrogance. Nor had she the title or the wealth, which both bound and freed her. But she married the man she loved, and she always knew in her heart that he loved her. That gave her a different kind of confidence, and an inner peace which few of us ever know."

Naylor said nothing, touched by a sort of truth deeper and possibly more painful than anything they had said before.

"She is also capable of rubbing elbows with the washerwoman," Vespasia went on, "and speaking sensibly to her of home and domestic duties, of poverty and good ways in which to save money. That she learned first from Pitt, then from experience. She does not belong completely to either one world or the other, which leaves her lonely at times. She is impetuous and given to acting before she fully considers the possible outcome. But then, too much thought, too much awareness of the pitfalls and the losses ahead, would rob us all of the courage or the passion to act. We can creep cautiously to death from inertia, and expire safely in our beds of old age and spiritual paralysis. We can look back on an unblemished career of never having said or done anything wrong—or anything right either. We could pass through the world without having left a mark."

He said nothing, an abyss of emptiness opening up before his mind.

"No one will say that of Charlotte," Vespasia continued. "She is a person one would remember for her vitality, the strength of her feeling, not always wise, certainly, but always honest. She is lukewarm about nothing."

"I have not met her," he admitted. "She sounds rather daunting."

"I think you would like her," she told him. "She is very attractive, both to look at and to speak with. She is fairly tall, but Pitt himself is of good height and has a certain artless grace of movement. She, of course, moves excellently, as do all girls brought up by a strict mother who has ambitions towards a good marriage. She practiced the customary walking while balancing books on her head, sitting with a straight back and shoulders, speaking with perfect diction, and knowing how to address everyone correctly, from the archbishop to the cook, and saying something pleasant and innocuous to all of them."

"That is not what I have heard of her," he said dubiously.

"She has good features and very beautiful hair," Vespasia continued, ignoring his interruption. "And perhaps too handsome a figure entirely for her own good. She has drawn much admiration at times, even if her strength of character has alarmed some people."

He was curious, both interested and now concerned. "Are you try-ing to say that certain men have been . . . attracted to her?" he asked.

She gave him a withering look. "I know of three or four who were unquestionably in love with her. What I do not know is if she herself was aware of it. She has my considered respect if she was and man-aged never to show it. It must have made difficult situations a great deal easier for the men in question."

"Who were they?"

"How indelicate," she reproved him. "Since I am quite certain that nothing improper took place, I do not think it is your concern."

"It does not leave this room," he promised. "Either in word or deed. But the knowledge may affect my decision. Who were they?"

"General Brandon Ballantyne and Victor Narraway," she replied. "Among others."

"Indeed!" He was truly surprised. "I know them both. Neither are men of easy passion. I begin to look at Mrs. Pitt in a new light. She must have more depth of character and more integrity of purpose than I had supposed."

Vespasia smiled. "You saw her as meddling in Pitt's cases out of boredom, mistaken idealism, the kind of arrogance that assumes abilities it does not possess and lacks the imagination to see what harm the well-meaning but ignorant can do?"

He blushed. "I had not thought of it quite so cruelly, but I suppose that is more or less what I had supposed. Pretty women sometimes are led to believe that charm can overcome any deficit in intelligence or experience."

"I can hear Charlotte's laughter in my mind as you say that," Ves-pasia responded. "She is very observant of small things, as women often are. She notices tone of voice, the way people stand, look at each other, the expressions on faces when they imagine themselves unobserved. But of course she would be far too wise to tell you what she had seen—at least she would now."

"And earlier?"

"That was a different matter," Vespasia admitted. "If one's mistakes are dramatic enough, one does not repeat them."

"You alarm me, and intrigue me," he said. "I shall most certainly meet Mrs. Pitt. Tell me, do you think she will wish him to take this position, should it be offered him?"

Vespasia thought for several moments. "Oh yes, she will wish him to accept it. She was never a coward. But she will not be blind to its costs. She will know that the decisions he has to make will at times be dangerous and painful. He will make mistakes, because we all do, and he will grieve over them. He will lie awake wondering how he can spare people, knowing there is no way and yet still laboring to find one. He is a man born poor, who understands the poor, the ordinary, and the fearful. He will speak to the common man as an equal. He will at times be something of a prude and offend the aristocratic, as he has offended the king. He will not always know when to laugh and when to keep silent. But sooner or later he will earn their respect, because they will come to know that they can trust both his judgment and his kindness. That is a lot to say of any man, Sir Peter."

"And Mrs. Pitt?" he asked.

"Oh, you may trust her to be shocking, charming, disastrously frank, and utterly loyal. You will like her, whether you wish to or not, because you will not be afraid of her. She is impractical only in the things that do not matter at all, except to people who have no sense of proportion." Her face tightened fractionally. "A sense of proportion is going to matter in the times ahead, I think. We will need to know with great certainty what it is we value, what we are prepared to give our lives to preserve. Yes, Sir Peter, the prime minister should offer this position to Thomas Pitt. He is the essential Englishman, rooted in the soil of his ancestry, willing to live and die for the common decencies of life, the honor and tolerance, the kindness and the absurdities.

"You will be happy to sit at the kitchen table with him and drink tea with a slice of cake at the end of a long case, and know that you have done your best."

He rose to his feet. "Thank you, Lady Vespasia. I shall recommend to the prime minister that we overrule His Majesty's misgivings and do exactly that. I appreciate your candor. I believe that I now know more of Thomas and Charlotte Pitt than anyone else could have told me."

She inclined her head and smiled, with a faraway, dreaming look of long and happy memory.

DOUGLAS PRESTON and LINCOLN CHILD

Douglas Preston was born in Cambridge, Massachusetts, in 1956. He graduated from Pomona College in Claremont, California, where he studied mathematics, biology, chemistry, physics, anthropology, geology, astronomy, and English. He worked at New York's American Museum of Natural History for eight years as writer and editor of the in-house publication, eventually writing the nonfiction book *Dinosaurs in the Attic* for St. Martin's Press, where his editor was Lincoln Child. They formed a friendship that resulted in their coauthoring the bestselling FBI Agent Pendergast series and other novels.

Lincoln Child was born in Westport, Connecticut, in 1957. He graduated from Carleton College in Northfield, Minnesota, majoring in English. He took a job with St. Martin's in 1979 and, after editing more than a hundred books and founding the company's horror division, left in 1987 for a position with MetLife as a programmer and systems analyst. His first collaborative novel with Preston, *Relic,* was published in 1995.

Preston and Child have collaborated on thirteen novels, nine about Pendergast and four stand-alones: *Mount Dragon* (1996), *Riptide* (1998), *Thunderhead* (1999), and *The Ice Limit* (2000).

On his own, Child has written the thrillers *Utopia* (2002), *Death Match* (2004), *Deep Storm* (2007), and *Terminal Freeze* (2009).

Preston's solo works are *Dinosaurs in the Attic* (1985), *Jennie* (1994), *The Royal Road* with José Antonio Esquibel and photographs by Christine Preston (1998), *Cities of Gold* (1999), *The Codex* (2004), *Tyrannosaur Canyon* (2005), *Blasphemy* (2008), and *Monster of Florence* with Mario Spezi (2008).

ALOYSIUS X. L. PENDERGAST

BY DOUGLAS PRESTON AND LINCOLN CHILD

Douglas Preston

My first job out of college was as an editor at the American Museum of Natural History in New York. It was over a quarter mile from the front door of the museum to my office, way in the back, and it took seven and a half minutes to make that walk (I timed it). I had to pass through the great African Hall, with the elephants, a series of smaller halls, the Egyptian Alcove, the Hall of Man in Africa, the Hall of Birds of the World, the Precolumbian Gold Hall, and the Hall of Mexico and Central America. It is one of the largest museums in the world, and I found it an amazing place to work.

Part of my job was to write a column about the museum in *Natural History* magazine. I wrote about the Copper Man, about the Ahnighito meteorite, about Meshie the chimpanzee, about the dinosaur mummy, and the Star of India.

One day, I got a call from an editor at St. Martin's Press. He had been reading my columns in the magazine and wondered if I would do him the kindness of joining him for lunch at the Russian Tea Room to talk about a possible book.

I said I would certainly do him that kindness, and I rushed down to the Salvation Army to buy a jacket so I could get into the Russian Tea

Room. When the appointed day came, I showed up expecting to meet an éminence grise from St. Martin's Press. Instead, waiting for me at a table in the back was a kid even younger than I was: Lincoln Child.

Lincoln Child

I had been a fan of the museum ever since coming to New York as a dewy-eyed college graduate. I loved nothing better than taking the behind-the-scenes tours and seeing the cubbyholes where real-life Indiana Joneses hung their pith helmets. After each such tour I would leave the museum thinking, "What an amazing old pile! When I retire I'll have to write its history." Then one day I realized: "You dolt! Why go to all that work when you can pay some other poor scrivener to do it?" After all, I was a book editor, and it was my job to find new projects for my house to publish. I found Doug's articles in the museum's magazine, and I invited him to lunch. He was exactly the kind of person I was looking for: young and hungry looking (note to Preston-Child readers: imagine Bill Smithback). I pitched the idea of an informal history and armchair tour of the museum, to be written by him. He immediately jumped at it: he was more than ready to graduate from articles to full-length books. And that was the birth of what was to become Doug's nonfiction title *Dinosaurs in the Attic*.

During the writing of the book I was always pestering Doug for a *real* behind-the-scenes tour, not the two-bit one that the tourists got. But he was afraid to do it, because I didn't have the appropriate security clearance and he wasn't able to get it for me. But finally he hit on a plan: it would be a *midnight* tour, when presumably nobody would be around to check our credentials. Doug had a special key that would get us into many odd places and storage rooms full of strange things. So it was that, one midnight, Doug snuck me in for a personal guided tour. And what a tour! I saw flesh-eating beetles, whale eyeballs in formaldehyde, rooms full of dinosaur bones as big as VW Bugs. We ended up on the fourth floor, in the (then-named) Hall of Late Dinosaurs (no pun intended). There was a terrific storm outside, and flickers of lightning from the ceiling skylight illuminated the huge, ancient T. rex towering over us. I don't know what possessed me, but I turned to Doug and said, "This is the scariest building in the world. Doug, we have to write a thriller set in a museum like this."

He turned to me, eyes shining with emotion—or maybe it was just that last wee nip of Macallan making an unwelcome reappearance.

And then a guard making his rounds surprised us. I don't know who was more scared: us, the guard, or the T. rex. But that's a story for another time.

Doug

No, let's tell that story now. When the guard surprised us, I thought, *now I'm in deep shit.* But Linc's brilliant wit saved us—the first of many such rescues. As the guard inched into the dark hall, shining his light around, anxious voice booming out, *"Who's there?"* Linc came up with the perfect reply. He cried out, "Thank God, you've finally found us! We've been wandering around for *hours* looking for the exit! How in the world do you get out of this place?"

The guard escorted us out the security exit, never knowing I was a rogue museum employee conducting an undercover tour.

Linc and I began discussing our novel, set in the museum, which we had decided to call *Relic*. One evening, Linc and I were sitting on his porch in Westchester County, sharing a bottle of good single malt. Between tipples of malt and discussions of what fine fellows we were, what rare geniuses, and how we would take the literary world by storm, we managed to hash out the plot to *Relic*. I agreed to take a crack at the first few chapters.

In the meantime, I had moved from New York City to Santa Fe,

New Mexico, and the calls began coming. How were the chapters going? Fine, just fine! I would reply. After a year of this, Linc's patience began to wear thin. He is not normally the kind of person who employs vulgar language, but I do recall him telling me one time, "Doug, just write the fucking chapters already."

So I finally did. To my great surprise, I enjoyed the experience. I had always thought of myself as a serious writer, in line for a Nobel Prize, but I found I enjoyed writing a novel about a brain-eating monster loose in a museum a lot more than I expected.

I sent the first few chapters to Linc. He called me and said he liked them very much, except for one thing. I had two New York City cops, partners, who were the investigating officers. "Doug, they're both the same character," Linc said.

"What do you mean?" I was immediately furious at this slight to my literary talent.

"You got this one guy, Vincent D'Agosta, ethnic New York City cop, rough on the outside with a heart of gold. And then you've got his partner—exactly the same, except he's Irish."

After profoundly damning Linc's contemptible literary taste, I finally came around to seeing his point.

"What we need," Linc said, "is a detective no one's ever seen before. A real fish out of water. Someone who will act as a foil to D'Agosta and to New York City itself."

"Oh, God," I said, "not another 'unique' detective, please! What, you mean like an albino from New Orleans?"

There was a long silence and then I heard Linc say, "An albino from New Orleans . . . Intriguing . . . *Very* intriguing . . ."

Linc

The thing one has to keep in mind is that we wrote *Relic* as a lark. Don't get me wrong: we had high opinions of our writing skills and our ability to craft an interesting story. I'd edited dozens, hundreds, of novels, and Doug has always had a far deeper knowledge of literature than most English professors could boast (and he himself has taught writing at Princeton). What I mean is that we wrote the story to amuse ourselves rather than others. A lot of first-time novelists try to write what they think other people want to read, or cynically attempt to write a novel that will have the broadest appeal. Not us. We wrote—for want of a better word—irresponsibly. We created eccentric characters and put them in extravagant situations. Having two of us in on the job improved—or exacerbated—the situation. I'd read something Doug wrote, would be hugely amused, and would then expand on it. If he wrote a scene of a terrified mob stampeding past an upended table of free hors d'oeuvres, I'd add a gratuitous bit about a huge bolus of pâté being ground into mud beneath the running feet. And then Doug would have some character knocked to the ground, landing face first in the pâté, and so on, each trying to top the other.

It was into this hothouse atmosphere that Agent Pendergast first stepped. In those days Doug frequently wrote four out of every five new chapters, while I did significant rewriting and produced the outlines for the chapters to come. So one day I received, via 2,400-baud modem (don't laugh; it was the Pony Express of its day), what would eventually become chapter fourteen of *Relic*. It was an exciting rough draft. Among other things, in it Lieutenant D'Agosta is so revolted by a particular sight that he vomits his breakfast of scrambled eggs, ham, cheese, and ketchup all over a museum courtyard. This happens moments after Agent Pendergast makes his very first appearance. (The two events are unrelated.)

What is remarkable is that even in this first chapter, Pendergast displays some of the traits that go on to become his defining attributes: touchstones that readers return to again and again like mantras. For example, the first word out of his mouth: "Excellent." Or, when discussing certain personal flaws: "A very bad habit, but one that I find hard to break."

Doug had put the initial touches on a character that, I saw immediately, had the potential to be deeply cool. He was cultured and cultivated. He was unabashedly eccentric. He could take in a crime scene with a single heavy-lidded glance . . . though you wouldn't comprehend the depth of his perspicacity unless he chose to reveal it to you. He could descant at length, and with extensive learning, on the beauty of a particular painting—and then point out in an offhand way the fresh bloodstains that had recently marred it. This was exactly the kind of character I could sink my teeth into. So I was quick to add my own eccentric touches. As I did so, I had several antecedents in mind: Sherlock Holmes (of course), Futrelle's Thinking Machine, and (perversely) Christopher Walken's character in *The Dogs of War* (from whence came the many references to Pendergast's feline grace). But for me, the single biggest influence was Alastair Sim's insouciant portrayal of Inspector Cockrill in the obscure English mystery film *Green for Danger*.

Still, perhaps the strangest thing about the creation of Pendergast is that neither Doug nor I can articulate with any precision what each of us ultimately brought to the character. It's as if Pendergast told us what to do, rather than the other way around. Even, say, my recollections of the name are probably apocryphal. I think Doug had initially spelled it "Prendergast" and at some point I dropped the first *R*. But this may well be completely wrong.

Doug

In this way, Pendergast just sprang out of our heads, fully formed, like Athena from the forehead of Zeus. The strange thing about Pendergast is that we don't know him very well at all. We didn't even know his first name for the first five years of our writing partnership.

In a strange way, Pendergast created himself. He came into being in a completely different way than all the other characters we've created.

I'll give you an example: Corrie Swanson, Pendergast's sidekick in *Still Life with Crows*. First we picked her name. Then we gave her an age, eighteen, and a style, Goth. But we decided she wouldn't be a typical Goth; she'd be a smart Goth. A non-drugged-out Goth. A misunderstood person who loved reading, father gone, mother an alcoholic, Corrie lived in a trailer in a tiny Midwestern town and prayed someday to get out. And so on and so forth. We made lists of what kind of music she listened to and even compiled a CD of her favorite tunes. We made lists of the books she'd read and diagrammed out all her friends and enemies at the local high school. We gave her a minor criminal record, undeserved, and a bad relationship with the local sheriff and his son.

We built her from scratch. We knew more about her than would ever go into a novel. We created her the way we created all the other characters in our novels.

Except Pendergast.

When we were done figuring out who Pendergast was, we never wrote him a backstory. We never gave him a family. We didn't know where he went to school, what he did before becoming an FBI agent (beyond a few juicy rumors), what kind of books he read. Even though we knew exactly who he was as a *character*, we knew absolutely nothing about his *history*. No personal details.

This is, oddly enough, exactly how Pendergast would want it. He is a secretive soul, reticent, an enigma. *He* knew all these things, and that was enough. *He* would reveal them to us in time.

It was only after writing half a dozen books that we have begun to piece together his backstory. We learned his first name began with *A* in the third novel, and learned in the fourth what that *A* stood for. We still don't know what his middle initials—X. L.—stand for. Some say *L* is for "Leng." But we don't know that for sure. Just the other day, Linc and I had an argument about that. I said it couldn't be "Leng" for a number of obscure Talmudic reasons. Linc disagreed. E-mails went back and forth. And we still don't know.

Linc

A few years ago, our audio publisher asked us to write up an interview with Pendergast. . . . They thought that having us "interview" Pendergast in our own voices (and having René Auberjonois, the voice talent, "be" Pendergast) would make a nice extra for the audiobook version of *Brimstone*.

So Doug and I dutifully sat down and began work on the interview. We did this in the way we frequently work (and, in fact, the way the very piece you are reading was created): one of us will make a start, then lob the work-in-progress through the virtual ether to the other. In time, with enough back-and-forths, the work will grow, through accretion, into a lustrous pearl (or an inert lump, as the case may be).

As usual when it came to Pendergast, the interview basically wrote itself. Pendergast took the reins and led the conversation in his own direction. And when it was complete, Doug and I were quite surprised by some of the things he had revealed. In particular, I was struck by Pendergast's lack of appreciation for our chronicling of his exploits. You would think every Johnson would appreciate his Boswell, but not Agent Pendergast. He was not only ungrateful, but he seemed to have a distinctly low opinion of our talents.

Although Pendergast's disapproval of our efforts might be galling, the amount of enthusiasm and support our readers have shown has had precisely the opposite effect. We're surprised and delighted by how vigorously people have taken our special Special Agent to their hearts. There are websites devoted to the most obscure Pendergast arcana; there are online forums in which readers recount (sometimes rather shockingly) their personal Pendergast fantasies (including one site called Pendergasms, which we shall not explore further in these pages). There are even Pendergast bumper stickers rumored to be seen in the wild!

Doug

Many people have asked us why Pendergast was cut from the movie version of *The Relic*, which was released by Paramount Pictures in 1997 and became a number one box office hit.

I remember well receiving a series of drafts of *The Relic* screenplay. In each successive draft, Pendergast's role withered until, in the last one, he had vanished completely. I asked the producers why. I got various explanations, which boiled down to this: he was too complex, too eccentric, and too scene-stealing a character to be in a movie. The screenwriters were having a lot of trouble with his personality, voice, and manner. He was a character who had rarely, if ever, been seen before on the silver screen, and he was not a Hollywood "type." They could not write him and they could not cast him. To Hollywood, he was "a riddle wrapped in a mystery inside an enigma," to borrow a phrase from Churchill. They couldn't get a handle on him. On the other hand, Pendergast's sidekick, Vincent D'Agosta, was very much a Hollywood type, the tough-talking Italian-American cop with a heart of gold. So D'Agosta became the star of the movie, played by Tom Sizemore, cast alongside Penelope Ann Miller as Margo Green, James Whitmore as Frock, and Linda Hunt as the museum's feisty director.

Linc

One thing we've particularly enjoyed is doling out—in maddeningly small amounts—Pendergast's backstory. Certain of our readers are desperate to learn more about him. And his natural reticence is the perfect foil for our scattering little hints and trace clues like gold dust throughout the stories.

What started as relatively uncoordinated and spontaneous asides has now morphed into a cohesive history, replete with certain mad and half-mad relations (Aloysius is not only the last of his line, but one of the few to be born compos mentis). We meet, or hear about, relatives of his—Great-Aunt Cornelia, Comstock Pendergast, Antoine Leng Pendergast—who have decidedly perverse and criminal minds. Even the Pendergast family mansion, the Maison de la Rochenoire, once a famous landmark on Dauphine Street in New Orleans, was ultimately burned to the ground by an angry mob.

Certainly the most memorable of Pendergast's relatives to date has been his brother, Diogenes, who became the antihero of his own trilogy: *Brimstone, Dance of Death,* and *Book of the Dead.* (We had intended it to be a single book, but it basically "ran away" into something much bigger than we'd planned, not unlike the Castle Bravo thermonuclear test.) Diogenes first surfaces—if you can call it that—in our third Pendergast novel, *Cabinet of Curiosities.* I wrote a chapter in which Pendergast takes a mental journey through a purely intellectual reconstruction, a memory palace, of his childhood house. (Please don't ask; read the book and you'll understand what I mean.) As he walks down the upstairs corridor and passes his brother's room, he observes that the door is locked and chained, *and would always remain so.* There was no reason for me to add this other than sheer perversity; I knew this tantalizing tidbit would set our readers frothing at the mouth. But as with so many things in our books, it essentially took on a life of its own. Once he'd trodden the boards, Diogenes refused to leave the stage; and we began adding increasingly frequent allusions to his dreadful past and shocking misdeeds. It wasn't long until he demanded—and got—his own trilogy.

Doug

It was only through the introduction of his brother, Diogenes, into the series that Pendergast's character reached completion. We conceived Diogenes as a twisted Mycroft Holmes, brilliant, perverse, refined, and utterly criminal. His name alludes back to two sources: the Diogenes Club of London, where Mycroft Holmes lived, and the Greek philosopher Diogenes himself. The real Diogenes was a cold, unforgiving fellow who wandered the streets of Athens by day with a lantern, searching for but never finding an honest man. When Alexander the Great paid Diogenes a visit and asked the reclining philosopher if there was anything he could do for him, Diogenes waved his hand and replied that he could step aside and cease blocking his sunlight.

This seemed a perfect name for our über-villain.

The two brothers complete each other: one a top FBI agent, the other a brilliant criminal. Between them, the date of a perfect crime and a challenge: stop me if you can.

Slowly, bit by bit, as we wrote the trilogy, the full dimensions of Aloysius Pendergast's life began to emerge. It was as if *he* were finally revealing himself to *us*. By this time, Pendergast had become a *real* person to us—more real, in fact, than many flesh-and-blood people we know. Living with this strange and enigmatic man for so many years, spending hours with him every day, watching and recording his every movement, had turned him into a real human being. I am sure we're not the first novelists who have had this experience, but it is certainly peculiar when it happens.

The really odd thing is, it turns out we don't like Pendergast very much. He is cold, haughty, judgmental, and unforgiving. He himself likes very few people—and those he does like are not often aware of that fact, since he is so reticent with his feelings. There is a kind and gentle side to him, but it is deeply buried in the eternal snows of his personality. You could not have a jolly dinner with Pendergast, a casual conversation, a lighthearted exchange of pleasantries. You certainly could not "hoist a few" with him.

I am afraid Pendergast reciprocates these chilly feelings toward us. Pendergast finds me a bit dull, slow on the uptake, of conventional morality and habits. He would not care to visit my house, where the chaos of children would disturb his peace. He would find my conversation charmless and most of my friends idiotic, vapid, uncultured, and middle-class. He would despise my interests in the outdoors, skiing, horses, and boats. And he would be horrified at the fact that I live in a small town in rural Maine where there are no restaurants, theaters, concert halls, museums, or even a decent grocery. Pendergast and I have little in common beyond a love of fine food, wine, art, music, and the Italian language.

I daresay he wouldn't like Linc much better. Certainly he would find Linc more congenial than I, wittier and more charming, the effect marred by an unfortunately low and vulgar turn of mind. He would find curious Linc's acquisitiveness, as evidenced by his collections of rare pens and books. He would shake his head in dismay at Linc's suburban lifestyle, the Mercedes and Range Rover in the garage, the Dalmatian in the backyard, and the neat flowerbeds and manicured lawns of his New Jersey neighborhood. He would, however, enjoy Linc's connoisseurship of green tea, and he would approve of both his library and his reclusive impulses, and no doubt they would have a great deal to talk about when the subject turned to Dr. Samuel Johnson and eighteenth-century English poetry.

Linc

Most of all, Pendergast would consider our obsessive chronicling of his life utterly useless and a colossal waste of time—not to mention annoyingly intrusive.

I should add that while we may not like Pendergast very much as a person (in the way that we like, say, Bill Smithback), we most certainly admire his mind and relish his eccentricities.

How better to conclude this portrait than with a transcription of the original version of the one and only "interview" I mentioned earlier on? It took place—we like to think—at Pendergast's apartment in the Dakota, Central Park West and 72nd Street, New York City, on August 31, 2004.

Pendergast: Gentlemen, welcome. Would you care for a sherry? I have a fine Amontillado aging in a back room.

Child: Why, that would be very kind—

Preston: Linc, remember what we talked about . . . ?

Child: [Sighs] No, thank you, Agent Pendergast.

Pendergast: As you wish. I hope we can keep this short. I have neither the time nor the inclination to bandy civilities with a couple of writers, even ones as distinguished as yourselves [mordant smile].

Preston: We'll try to keep it short. Let me begin by asking a fairly simple question: why do you always wear a black suit?

Pendergast: That kind of vapid query is precisely why I eschew interviews.

Child: Agent Pendergast, a lot of our readers are curious about your background and the history of your family. Can you tell us something about your parents, your childhood and later education?

Pendergast: I would prefer to keep the questioning on a professional level. Suffice to say I was born and raised in New Orleans to an old family of French ancestry. After the loss of our family home by fire, in which my parents were killed, I attended Harvard University, from which I graduated summa cum laude in 1982.

Child: We never knew you went to Harvard.

Pendergast: There is much you two don't know, despite all your pretensions to the contrary. And much you will *never* know.

Preston: What did you major in?

Pendergast: Anthropology.

Preston: That doesn't seem like an obvious major for a future FBI agent.

Pendergast: On the contrary.

Child: You did graduate work, didn't you?

Pendergast: Yes, at Oxford University. I have a dual PhD in classics and philosophy, and I took firsts in both.

Preston: And then, I believe, you went into the Special Forces? We've heard rumors that you were engaged in a number of black ops.

Pendergast: If I was, I could hardly be expected to discuss them, could I?

Child: Getting back to your childhood, we know the Pendergast mansion was burned by a mob. Why?

Pendergast: [Long pause] The Pendergast family was, shall we say, *eccentric,* and not at all popular with the local folk—but it was my great-aunt Cornelia who was the proximate cause.

Child: Cornelia? The one in the Mount Mercy Hospital for the Criminally Insane?

Pendergast: That is correct.

Preston: What did she do?

Pendergast: She was a chemist of no small talent, which is all I am going to say on that subject. I believe I've already made it clear that I would prefer to avoid personal topics. Mr. Preston, would you care to be questioned about that streak of mental instability in your own family? For example, I understand that your brother Richard—

Preston: [Loudly clearing his throat] The interview is about you, not me.

Pendergast: Quite.

Child: Moving on, I wonder if you would tell us about some of your more interesting cases.

Pendergast: Other than the ones which you have so regrettably sensationalized in your books? On a personal level, the most remarkable case I worked on was in Tanzania—the attacks of the red lion.

Preston: The "red lion"?

Pendergast: It was, according to the local tribal legend, a monstrous lion that attacked only at night; it had an unquenchable hunger for human flesh. And it was of a color never before seen. The killings flared up while I was on a bushbuck hunting trip. Over the space of five evenings, twenty-four people were killed, their livers eaten.

Child: How horrible. But I assume—since you call it a "case"—the murderer turned out to be human?

Pendergast: More or less.

Preston: More or *less?* What does that mean?

Pendergast: There are degrees of humanity, Mr. Preston. The two of you wrote up my recent case in Medicine Creek, Kansas; you should know that. In any case, the chief presented me with a brace of elephant tusks by way of thanks. [He nods to a doorway] They make a rather dramatic entrance to my study, don't you think?

Child: Was this the same hunting expedition on which your wife accompanied you? Where you were charged by the Cape buffalo?

Pendergast: Yes. In fact, my wife was instrumental in working out some of the highly peculiar psychological aspects. It was our last case together.

Preston: If you don't mind me asking, what happened to her?

Pendergast: [Stiffly] That question lies outside the bounds of this interview. Earlier, I said there are many things about me you will never know. The fate of my beloved wife is one of those. Now, gentlemen, if you don't mind, this interview is over; Proctor will see you out.

IAN RANKIN

Born in Fife, Scotland, Rankin went to the University of Edinburgh, majoring in English. Writing profusely, he sold several short stories and then a slim novel, *The Flood* (1986), which had a very small print run. In 1987, he wrote his first John Rebus novel, *Knots and Crosses,* which also had a modest printing. After a spy novel, *Watchman* (1991), he returned to Rebus with *Tooth and Nail* (1992) and continued to write about the Scottish policeman until 2008, when Rebus took his last case in *Exit Music*. Rankin also wrote three novels as Jack Harvey in the early nineties: *Witch Hunt, Bleeding Hearts,* and *Blood Hunt*.

In 1991, he received a Chandler-Fulbright Award, with a substantial cash prize that had to be spent in America, which he then toured with his wife, Miranda.

Rankin's breakout book was *Black and Blue,* which won the British Crime Writers' Association Gold Dagger as the best novel of 1997. In 2005, he was given the highest honor bestowed by that organization when he received the Cartier Diamond Dagger for lifetime achievement. He won the Best Novel Edgar® in 2004 for *Resurrection Men*.

A television series based on the Rebus character began in 2000 with John Hannah in the title role; Ken Stott took over in 2005.

Achieving unprecedented success in the UK, Rankin still holds a Guinness world record for simultaneously occupying eight of the top ten spots on the Scottish bestseller list.

Ian Rankin lives in Edinburgh with his wife and two sons.

JOHN REBUS

BY IAN RANKIN

I

"Male hero (a policeman?)"

That was my first note to myself, dated March 15, 1985, about the character who would eventually become Detective Inspector John Rebus. I was twenty-four years old and a postgraduate student at the University of Edinburgh. I was living in a shared apartment with two other (female) postgrads in Arden Street. I'd been in the city six and a half years, and still I couldn't fathom the place. My doctoral thesis was concentrating on the novelist Muriel Spark, and through her I was beginning to investigate the Edinburgh of the imagination. In Spark's most celebrated work, *The Prime of Miss Jean Brodie,* Miss Brodie is a descendant of William Brodie, a real historical character. Brodie was a deacon of the city, a councillor, cabinetmaker, and a man who lived a double life. Respectable and industrious by day, he led a masked gang into the homes of his victims by night, robbing them of their valuables. Brodie was trying to fund his lavish lifestyle (including a couple of demanding mistresses), and had diversified into lock-fitting, meaning he had little trouble gaining unlawful entry. When caught and found guilty, he was hanged on a scaffold he had helped to modernize as part of his day job.

Deacon Brodie provided the template for another great character from Scottish literature, Robert Louis Stevenson's Dr. Henry Jekyll. Muriel Spark was a huge fan of Stevenson, and my research took me to *The Strange Case of Dr. Jekyll and Mr. Hyde*. The idea of the doppelgänger had been explored before, however, in James Hogg's *Confessions of a Justified Sinner,* so I had to read that book too. At the same time, I was becoming fascinated by contemporary literary theory, enjoying the "game-playing" aspect of storytelling. Eventually, I would name my own fictional detective after a type of picture-puzzle, and the mystery in his first adventure would be solved with the help of a professor of semiotics.

That's the problem with *Knots and Crosses* (and one reason I find it hard to read the book these days)—it is so obviously written by a literature student. Rebus reads too many books and even quotes from Walt Whitman (a writer whose works he really shouldn't have known). He is overly literate, perhaps because I didn't quite *know* him. I was twenty-four and knew little enough of life outside the confines of academia. I certainly didn't know what it would be like to work as a cop. The plot of *Knots and Crosses* demanded that Rebus be a seasoned pro, so I made him forty years old. He's separated from his wife and has a young daughter. Really, this guy was unlike me in so many ways, and our one resemblance—that love of literature—made him less than realistic.

It seems to me now that I wasn't interested in Rebus as a person. He was a way of telling a story about Edinburgh, and of updating the doppelgänger tradition. *Knots and Crosses* was self-consciously based on *Jekyll and Hyde,* just as a later Rebus novel, *The Black Book,* would use *Justified Sinner* as its starting point. The thing is, I'd always been a bit of an outsider, always tried to present several faces to the world. I'd grown up in a fairly tough neighborhood—in a town of seven thousand inhabitants—which had existed only as a hamlet and a couple of farms until coal was discovered at the start of the twentieth century. That's when my grandfather shifted the family east from the Lanarkshire coalfields. Homes were constructed quickly (and cheaply) to house the new labor force. There wasn't even time to think up names for the streets, so they just got numbers instead. My dad (the youngest of seven) didn't work down in the mines, but all his brothers did. By the time I came along, however, the coal was running out. The klaxon that signaled the start of each new shift fell silent one day, and that was that. Not that I took much of this in, being too busy living a completely separate life inside my own head.

There was another world in there—a fantastical world filled with spaceships and soldiers and constant thrilling adventure. In winter, I'd pretend that my bed was an Arctic encampment—which wasn't so far from the truth. There was heating only in the living room downstairs, and in the winter months I'd wake up to a thin film of ice on the insides of my windows. But even that ice seemed strange and wonderful to my young imagination. I'd be under the thick blankets with a flashlight and a good supply of comic books—British and American. Soon I was even making my own versions, folding sheets of paper and slitting the edges to make little eight-page booklets that I would cover with doodles and drawings—more spaceships, more soldiers. I think I remember showing one of my creations to my mum, who seemed bemused. Maybe she'd spotted something I hadn't: an absolute lack of artistic ability.

Not that this mattered, because by the age of twelve I was moving from comic books to music. I'd started buying chart singles and reading pop magazines. I was decorating the walls of my room with posters. A friend's older brother opened my ears to Frank Zappa, Jethro Tull, and Led Zeppelin. My mother agreed to buy me a Hendrix album for my birthday, although this meant a terrifying sortie to the "hippie" record shop in nearby Kirkcaldy. As with comic books, however, I wasn't interested in being a mere bystander—I wanted a band of my own, and created on paper what was impossible in real life. My alter ego was vocalist Ian Kaput, and he was joined by guitarist Blue Lightning and bassist Zed "Killer" Macintosh (plus a drummer with a double-barreled name, but I forget now what it was). The group was called the Amoebas. They started off playing three-minute pop hits but eventually graduated to progressive rock—their masterpiece lasted twenty-six minutes and was called "Continuous Repercussions"—and I was with them all the way, writing their lyrics, designing their record sleeves, planning their world tours and TV appearances. I'd make up a top ten (albums and singles) each week, which entailed the creation of another nine groups, and so it went.

I'm conscious now that what I was doing was "playing God," reimagining my world and making it more exciting and evocative than the reality. It's what all writers do, and already I was starting to feel like a writer. My parents weren't great readers, and there were few books in the house, but I was drawn to stories. I would haunt the town's library and soon started borrowing "adult" titles, meaning books whose films I wasn't old enough to see at the cinema. At age thirteen, I was reading Mario Puzo's *The Godfather* and Anthony Burgess's *A Clockwork Orange*. By fourteen it was *One Flew Over the Cuckoo's Nest*. I also came across Ernest Tidyman's Shaft books (and would eventually give Rebus the forename John as a nod to "black private dick" John Shaft). I checked the TV schedules to see if there were any programs about books and would watch them, deciding that I really needed to read this guy Solzhenitsyn (I ended up struggling through volume two of *The Gulag Archipelago*). Later on I would fail to finish Dante's *Inferno* but be thrilled by Ian McEwan's first book of short stories.

My best subject in high school was English. I always enjoyed writing essays (which were in effect short stories). One was called "Paradox" and concerned a man who seemed to be president of the

United States but turned out to be an inmate in an insane asylum. My teacher liked it but wondered why I'd chosen that particular title. It was the name of a Hawkwind song, I told him, and I just liked the sound and look of the word.

"And no, sir, I've no idea what it means."

For another essay, we were given the phrase "Dark they were and golden-eyed" and told to use it as our starting point. I wrote about two parents searching a house filled with drug addicts, seeking their errant son.

Words were a passion of mine. I would do crosswords and flick through the dictionary, noting interesting words (including, after the exchange noted above, *paradox*). And those song lyrics for the Amoebas had become poems, one of which I entered for a national competition. It was called "Euthanasia" (another of those great-sounding words) and was runner-up. When my success was noted in the local newspaper, my parents learned for the first time that I was writing poetry. I hadn't dared tell anyone until then. (Later, I would learn that Muriel Spark's first publication had also been a prize-winning school poem.)

I'd always been a successful chameleon, playing the part of fitting in. I played soccer (badly) and had a bicycle. I hung around the street corners with the tough kids. But when a rumble started, I'd be on the periphery of the action, taking it all in without getting involved. When I went home, I'd head for my bedroom and write poems about the fights, the booze, the first sexual fumblings, and then my notebook would go back underneath my bed, hidden from view.

II

Okay, so I'm seventeen now, and I want nothing more than to be an accountant.

See, nobody in my family has been to university, but it seems I'm brainy and it's expected I'll go. And if you're working-class, you go to university to escape your roots—to get a good career: doctor, lawyer, dentist, architect . . .

I had an uncle in England, and he owned his own house (unlike my parents) and had a flash car (neither of my parents could even drive). Our summer holidays were spent at seaside resorts in Scotland and England, or in a cramped trailer twenty miles north of my hometown. My uncle always seemed to have a tan from foreign holidays. He was the most successful man I knew, and I wanted the same for myself.

Problem was, I wasn't very good at math. And I was growing to be ever more in thrall to books and to writing. I'd cranked out a couple of "novels" (probably twenty pages long, scribbled on jotters stolen from my school). The first was about a teenager who feels misunderstood so runs away from home and ends up in London, where he is ground down by life before eventually committing suicide. The second was a retelling of *Lord of the Flies,* set in my high school. It was starting to dawn on me: why the hell was I thinking of going to university to study a subject I had no real interest in? I broke the news to my parents and watched their shoulders sag. They were in their late fifties by this point, not too far from retirement. What, they asked, would I do with a degree in English? It was a fair question.

"Teach" was all I could think to reply.

I started looking at possible universities. St. Andrews was the closest, but I liked reading modern American and British novels, and "modern" at St. Andrews meant John Milton. I knew this because I'd asked. Edinburgh, however, had a course in "American literature," so I applied there and was eventually accepted. How well did I know the city? Hardly at all. I'd lived all my life about twenty miles north, but the family seldom ventured that far. I remember being taken there to see a stage version of *Peter Pan,* and my mother once took me to the castle and a children's museum. In my last couple of years at high school, I'd made occasional Saturday-afternoon forays with friends. But we would always stick to the same route, taking in all the available record shops, one radical bookshop (where porn, under the guise of "art books," could be perused), and a couple of pubs where the bar staff had decided we weren't underage enough to pose a problem.

Arriving in the city in October 1978 as a student was terrifying and exciting. The university had been unable to provide me with accommodation, so I was sharing a room with a school pal in a motel on the outskirts. I was quick to join the poetry and film societies; quick, too, to discover new pubs, live-music venues, and strip bars. I also joined a punk group (as singer and lyricist), so found a new outlet for my stanzas. And I was on the receiving end of a slew of rejection letters from magazines and newspapers.

The poetry society held weekly meetings. Hormonally charged young men (all the poets seemed to be male, the audience fifty-fifty) would recite odes of love lost, love unrequited, love from afar. My poems were a bit different. A typical opening might be:

> *Mutated machine-guns patrolling the subways*
> *While glue-sniffing kids hang themselves in lift-shafts . . .*

I had another poem called "Strappado" (a form of torture) and yet another telling the moving story of a husband who strangles his young wife on their honeymoon. Where was this stuff coming from? Why was I writing lyrics about addicts and killers and crucifixion? I can't find anything in my early life to justify this apparent interest in the bizarre and the demonic. I even had an alter ego, a drifter called Kejan, who cropped up in several poems and who would usually be drinking absinthe in Paris or traversing the stews of Alexandria:

A foreign body in the bloodstream of Berne,
Kejan tips the remnants of tobacco
From the pack onto the paper,
His breath scattering the flakes
Onto the floor
To lie wriggling in the draught.
Kejan needs some air . . .

None of this, it goes without saying, was helping me get laid.

But I did get to meet a lot of "real" writers for the first time in my life. The poetry society had funding to bring one professional poet to do a reading each week, and afterward we would all go for a drink or nine, during which time the poets would attempt to sell us copies of their books and pamphlets while we'd be asking questions such as "How do I get published?" I soon learned that most poets don't make a living writing but have to supplement their income with other work. I wondered if the same was true of fiction writers.

My poems were far from the Wordsworthian ideal of "emotion recollected in tranquillity." They were narratives. My characters went places and did things, or things happened to them. (There were always consequences.) I started writing short stories, influenced by Ian McEwan, Jayne Anne Phillips, and anyone else I happened to be reading at the time. I was trying to find out two things: what I wanted to write about, and how to do the actual writing. It took me a while to realize that the thing I really wanted to write about was enveloping me and embracing me every step of the way and with each and every breath I took.

It was Edinburgh itself.

III

This is a haunted city. For centuries it was haunted by the memory that it had once been a thriving capital before signing that status away to London. It's a city rife with ghost tours. Its cemeteries teem, and there are myriad streets, tunnels, and caves just below ground level. It's a city that hides itself away from the world. In the past, whenever invaders called, the denizens would scurry underground, emerging once the triumphant armies had tired of taking possession of what appeared to be a ghost town. The city the tourist sees, even today, is far from the whole story. Edinburgh is also home to a bloodstained history. Burke and Hare were serial killers who posed as grave robbers, slaughtering at least seventeen victims before being brought to justice (after which Burke's skin was crafted into a series of gruesome souvenirs, some of which can be viewed in the city's museums).

There were stories of well-respected citizens who had confessed to devil worship, of a coach driven by a headless horseman, of covenanters executed and witches burned. By night, the teenage Robert Louis Stevenson used to creep from his home to consort with harlots, poets, and ruffians in the seediest bars he could find.

The more I looked at Edinburgh, the more I learned. The city is geographically divided—the mazy Old Town to the south of Princes Street, the rational and elegant New Town to the north. The journey the young Stevenson took from one to the other was the journey of Dr. Jekyll toward Mr. Hyde. But was that particular Edinburgh a city of the past? Not really. In October 1977, a year before I'd arrived as a student, two teenage girls had vanished after a night out. Their last sighting was in a bar called the World's End. Their bodies were found the next morning. For more than two decades, their killers went undetected. Edinburgh's students knew that there really was a "bogeyman" out there; we didn't need the frisson provided by ghost tours and the like.

Contemporary Edinburgh and the city of the past collided in my imagination. I was living in the 1980s but reading about Miss Jean Brodie (set in the Depression years of the 1930s), Jekyll and Hyde, and the Justified Sinner. The Edinburgh I walked through by night seemed to have changed very little. There was a heroin problem, a housing crisis, and HIV was on the horizon. There was bitter rivalry between the city's two soccer teams, spilling over into weekend violence. Go-go bars would eventually be replaced by lap bars; we all knew that Leith had the red-light district but that the saunas were also more than they seemed. I'd started listening to a lot of music that would later be classified as "goth": Throbbing Gristle and Joy Division and the Cure. My imagination was darkening all the time. I was sleeping till noon and staying up until four a.m. I was writing, reading, writing, reading, and then writing some more. My short stories had titles like "The Suffering," "Confession," "The Violation of Mr Paton," "Pig," and "Isolation." I'd finished my degree but applied to do a PhD with Muriel Spark as the subject. Her stories were filled with supernatural elements, gothic settings, harsh satire, and devilry. But she was such an elegant, subtle, and concise writer that often critics chose not to notice the darkness lying just below the shimmering surface of her prose. I was learning from her too.

One day, I got a letter telling me I'd won second prize in a short-story contest run by the *Scotsman* newspaper. They would print the story and give me some cash. It was called "The Game" and concerned the last day in the life of a shipbuilding yard. (I've no idea where *that* came from either.) Around the same time, another story was accepted for publication by *New Edinburgh Review* magazine. Two more were taken by the BBC to be broadcast on radio. A story about a cop patrolling a soccer game was going to appear in a collection called *New Writing Scotland*. In August 1984, I won a story contest organized by a local radio station. Peter Ustinov presented me with my prize.

Bloody hell, I thought. It could only be a matter of time before my first novel found a publisher.

Ahh, my first novel. It was called *Summer Rites* and was a black comedy about a hotel in the Scottish Highlands. It never did find a publisher, but I was already busy with my next book, *The Flood*. Taking to heart the adage "write what you know," I set this new book in a (thinly disguised) version of my hometown. It did find a publisher, a small press in Edinburgh that printed a couple hundred hardback copies and maybe seven hundred paperbacks, many of which went unsold and were pulped.

The same week I signed the contract for *The Flood,* I got the idea for yet another novel, set in Edinburgh this time, the gothic Edinburgh I'd been reading about at university, but very much in the present and featuring:

"Male hero (a policeman?)"

On March 19, 1985, I recorded in my diary that "I've not written any of it yet, but it's all there in my head from page 1 to circa page 250." On March 24, I wrote the first four pages and decided to give it the working title *Knots and Crosses*. By July 4, the first draft was finished, but for some reason I didn't start the second draft until September 18. I'd typed out the first couple of revised pages when, again according to my diary, my flatmate at the time, Jon Curt, suggested a trip to the pub where he worked. The pub was called the Oxford Bar: "splendidly uncontrived and open until 2:00 a.m." It would be a few years before the Oxford Bar appeared in a Rebus novel (I thought bars, streets, etc., had to be fictional in a work of fiction), but I was glad to have made its acquaintance.

From the above, it seems I've been guilty of a protracted lie. For years I've been telling people that I wrote *Knots and Crosses* in that apartment in Arden Street, right across the road from where Rebus still lives. But I vacated Arden Street in the summer of 1985 and moved in with two undergraduate students (Jon being one of them) in a place way over on the other side of the city. This means that *Knots* is even closer to *Jekyll and Hyde* than I'd guessed, having been written partly to the south of Princes Street and partly to the north.

Because my novel *The Flood* had been accepted for publication, an agent had come to ask if I was working on anything else. She decided that we should send copies of *Knots and Crosses* to five London-based publishers: Bodley Head, Collins, Century-Hutchinson, Andre Deutsch, and William Heinemann. Eventually, we'd get the thumbs-up from only one—Bodley Head. But that was all we needed, and I was especially thrilled that I would have the same publisher as Muriel Spark—at least for a short while.

My final diary entry for 1985 ends: "Year after year, there's improvement."

When the book was finally published, however, on March 19, 1987, I noted that it seemed to receive less publicity than its predecessor. Working with a publicity budget of zero, Bodley Head ran no advertisements and secured no interviews with newspapers or magazines. The book came and went without anyone really paying it any attention at all. It failed to make the short list for the Crime Writers' Association's first-novel award (won that year by Denis Kilcommons), though the CWA asked me if I wanted to join them anyway. It was at this point that I realized the awful truth: while trying to write "the Great Scottish Neo-Gothic Novel" I had somehow become a crime writer. Not that this gave me too many sleepless nights. I had said farewell to the character called Rebus and was moving on to a spy novel called *Watchman*. It would be another year or two before my editor cleared his throat and asked me what had happened to John Rebus.

"I liked him, and I think there's more you can do with him. . . ."

I think his clearing of the throat was a way of telling me that he didn't expect *Watchman* to do any better than *Knots and Crosses,* but that maybe the crime genre was worth another try.

This editorial musing was, in retrospect, invaluable, but the gods also seemed to be looking favorably upon Rebus. A TV producer had shown some interest in that first novel. He had formed a new

company with an actor (known for his role in a popular soap) and was looking for a promising project. If successful, the action of *Knots and Crosses* would have been moved to London (to accommodate the actor's English accent), and that might have been the end of my creation. However, my agent disappeared halfway through negotiations, and the deal fizzled out. (Don't worry, she reappeared some years later.)

Hide and Seek gave me a second bite at Rebus's cherry, if you'll pardon the expression. The name Hyde is implicit in the title—in fact, the book's working title was *Hyde and Seek*. I followed it up with a novel in which I dragged Rebus to London (where I was living at the time) so he could hate it as much as I did. By then the damage was done: three books down, I had produced a series. And for as long as Inspector Rebus proved a satisfactory vehicle for my investigations into contemporary Scotland, that series would continue. I just hoped a readership would eventually follow.

IV

So where *did* Rebus come from? Well, from my subconscious, obviously, from a young man's brain, filled with stories and strategies. But also from the books I'd been reading, the city I'd made my home, and the blood that had soaked into its pavements and roadways. Yet it still seems to me that he appeared as a bolt from the blue. I've looked at photos of myself in my student room in Arden Street, and have pored over my diaries from the time, seeking clues. The notes I jotted down prior to starting the novel shed very little light. I saw the book as "a metaphysical thriller" but spent very little time delineating Rebus's character. I wanted the story to contain lots of "puzzles and wordplay," wanted it to be "a very visual piece," and decided it should be written in the third person: "Don't need to go too far inside the main character's head." Rebus was to be a cipher rather than a three-dimensional human being. From a rereading of *Knots and Crosses,* I think it's true to say that the reader feels more distanced from Rebus in that book than in any of the others that followed. There was a good reason for this: I wanted Rebus himself to exist as a potential suspect in people's minds. Hence the momentary flashbacks, the hints of something awful in his past, and the "locked room" in his apartment. He also at one point almost strangles a woman who has invited him into her bed.

Nice.

Through sheer force of will, however, Rebus stuck around and grew into someone more fully formed, to the point where fans are now worried about his health and find when they meet me that I fall disappointingly short of Rebus himself. I'm just not as damaged as he is, as complex, or as dangerous to be around. I'm only the bloke who commits his stories to paper. What became obvious to me early on was that a detective makes for a terrific commentator on the world around him. He has access to the highest in the land and the lowest, the politicians and oligarchs, as well as the junkies and petty thieves. In writing books about Edinburgh, I could examine the city (and the nation of which it is capital once more) from top to bottom through Rebus's eyes. I was lucky too—there was no tradition of the crime novel in Scotland, so I could make my own path. And back then there were no crime novels set in contemporary Edinburgh, meaning that for a little while I had no competition.

I've been lucky also in that Edinburgh and Scotland continue to change in interesting ways, giving me plenty of plots while delivering up their secrets and mysteries only very slowly. I've been living in this city now for almost thirty years, on and off, and it continues to surprise me. Underground streets and chambers are still being discovered. Archaeological digs at the castle bring new truths to the surface. Exhibits long forgotten in the various museums turn out to have their own tales worth telling. As a subject, the city seems inexhaustible. This is, after all, a city of words. Where else in the world would you find the main railway station named after a novel (Waverley) and a vast edifice in the city center celebrating that work's author (the Scott Monument)? Robert Louis Stevenson brought his own imagination to bear on his hometown. Arthur Conan Doyle was born here. Muriel Spark grew up here. Robert Burns made his name here. James M. Barrie was a student here. Not to mention the likes of Carlyle and Hume. Right up to J. K. Rowling, Irvine Welsh, and Alexander McCall Smith in the present day.

Rebus, too, is composed of words—millions of them—so you might think that by now I'd have got to the heart of what makes him tick, but he continues to surprise me, which is perhaps only fitting for a man whose name means "puzzle." For twenty years now, he's been living inside my head, but sometimes it feels as though I'm the one living in *his*. When a psychoanalyst interviewed me at a book festival a while back, he wondered if Rebus represented the brother I never had, or maybe the life of adventure I was never going to allow myself to lead. Both my parents served in World War II (my father in the Far East). One of my two sisters married a Royal Air Force engineer and spent much of her life thereafter traveling the world. As a kid, I once wrote to the army asking for information on joining up. But I was resolutely bookish, and all my adventures took place inside my head.

Maybe the psychoanalyst had a point; maybe Rebus really is an extension of my own personality—doing all the dangerous stuff I'd be too scared to do, breaking rules and conventions, getting into fights and scrapes, and even coming up against the occasional deadly force. Some commentators have decided that *Dr. Jekyll and Mr. Hyde* is a book about the creative process and the division between our rational mind and the darker fantasies we keep hidden from view. In which case, Rebus would be my Hyde, acting as a force of nature, saying the unsayable, doing things I could never bring myself to do—even though I could (and can) all too readily imagine myself doing them.

Sir Winston Churchill once called Russia "a riddle wrapped in a mystery inside an enigma." I've found the same to be true of Scotland and Edinburgh.

And of Detective Inspector John Rebus.

ALEXANDER McCALL SMITH

Alexander McCall Smith is a Scotsman born in Bulawayo, Rhodesia (now Zimbabwe), in 1948; he studied law at the University of Edinburgh, where he is now emeritus professor of law. A highly respected expert on medical law and bioethics, he is the former chairman of the British Medical Journal Ethics Committee, the former vice chairman of the Human Genetics Commission to the United Kingdom, and a former member of the International Bioethics Commission of UNESCO. When his writing career became a full-time commitment, he discontinued his involvement in these areas.

His series about Precious Ramotswe of the No. 1 Ladies' Detective Agency, which began as a series of short stories for a small Scottish publisher in 1998, have become enormous international bestsellers (and the basis for a popular television series), as have his other books, notably the six volumes about Isabel Dalhousie of the Sunday Philosophy Club (*The Sunday Philosophy Club*, 2004; *Friends, Lovers, Chocolate*, 2005; *The Right Attitude to Rain*, 2006; *The Careful Use of Compliments*, 2007; *The Comforts of a Muddy Saturday*, 2008; and *The Lost Art of Gratitude*, 2009). He has also written three novels in the Portuguese Irregular Verbs series, five in the 44 Scotland Street series, and three short-story collections, all of which are told with a gentle charm that cannot help but captivate readers. He has also written nineteen children's books. Professor McCall Smith lives in Edinburgh with his wife, a doctor; they have two daughters.

PRECIOUS RAMOTSWE

BY ALEXANDER McCALL SMITH

1

My entire childhood and youth were spent in Africa, in a bewitchingly beautiful but somewhat unhappy country then called Southern Rhodesia. The rest of my life, the greater part of it, has been spent in Scotland. I consider myself a Scot who has had one foot in Africa, which is a continent I love. Most people who have lived for any time in Africa are affected by it profoundly. It is a part of the world with which it appears to be very easy to fall in love. It claims the heart, and often breaks it—again and again.

That is why I write about it.

2

In 1980, I went to work for six months in Swaziland, a small country sandwiched between Mozambique and South Africa. I worked at the university there, and I lived in a house that had magnificent views of the mountains about which Rider Haggard wrote in *King Solomon's Mines*. I had not been in Africa for a long time and I found many memories came flooding back. I was there in the rainy season, and once again I experienced that extraordinary sensation—the smell of rain on the wind. I saw birds that I remembered seeing as a child. Outside my window was a great bougainvillea bush of the sort that grew outside my window when I was a boy.

The nearest town of any size was a place called Manzini. This was reached by a road that ran first past a hospital and then past a hotel called the Uncle Charlie Hotel. The Uncle Charlie Hotel had a dining room with a mural painted all the way round the top part of the wall, above the picture rail. This mural showed African animals—cantering giraffes, a pride of lions, scattered zebras—against a background of wide savannah. At one end of the picture there was a lake, and in front of the lake was a tiny flagpole with a painted Union Jack fluttering in the breeze.

I used a fictional hotel a bit like this in a short story I wrote many years later, "He Used to Like to Go for Drives with His Father." In the story, the owner of a hotel in Swaziland has a mentally handicapped son and a bored tennis-playing wife. He is very proud of a Mercedes-Benz car that he has, in fact, stolen and had repainted. The boy loves going for drives in this car, but the wife is determined that her husband should be punished for stealing it, and takes drastic action.

Swaziland struck me as an eminently suitable setting for such a story. I believe in the existence of a literary continent called Greeneland, so called because the places within it are exactly the sort of places where Graham Greene set his stories. Greene never used Swaziland, but he would have loved it. There was just the right sense of being caught at the wrong end of history; and the lives led there by outsiders (and most of Greene's characters are washed up from somewhere else) seemed to me to have that air of desperation, of dislocation, that makes a Greene novel so haunting.

I was still single then, and time at weekends hung rather heavy on my hands. On Sundays I would sometimes drive up to Siteki, on the ridge of the Lebombo Mountains, and have lunch in the Siteki

Hotel, an old colonial hotel that appeared to have changed little over the years. They served Brown Windsor soup, a heavy beef-based soup that was popular in Britain until the 1950s, and the tables were covered with carefully starched white linen. It was extraordinary that such a place should have survived.

When I had rather more time—a break of three or four days—I would travel through South Africa, across what was then the Transvaal, all the way to Botswana. I had friends who lived in Mochudi, a village to the north of the capital, Gaborone. I would stay with them for a few days and then travel back to Swaziland.

The road to Botswana ran unswervingly across dry plains of red earth, taking a breather every fifty miles or so in some depressing little agricultural town of neat, soulless bungalows and shops with wide verandas. As one approached these towns, the sun would glint off the silver spire of a Dutch Reformed church like a sharp sliver of Calvinist disapproval. And all about there was a feeling of things having stopped, of waiting for something that was expected but had yet to materialize.

Then, after a God-forsaken town called Zeerust, the road turned north and headed for a final seventy miles or so to the Botswana border. Something happened now; the landscape changed, became more wooded; hills appeared, abrupt protuberances in the land like islands rising out of the sea. And as the landscape changed, so, too, did the atmosphere. Suddenly, as one neared and then crossed the border into Botswana, it seemed as if a weight of oppression lifted off one's shoulders.

3

There are places that immediately impress the visitor with some special quality, a quality that has nothing to do with what you see about you—the landscape, the buildings— but has everything to do with what one might call spirit of place. Arriving in Botswana, I felt that I had come to, quite simply, a good place. I have felt something like that on other occasions, if not so markedly; conversely, in other places one may pick up an atmosphere of sadness and loss, as on the site of a great battlefield—Culloden, for instance. In Botswana I felt a peacefulness that was redolent of social harmony, of human decency. It was very striking, and it continues to resonate with visitors to that country. It is not imagined; it is really there. This was a place where human values were respected, where people lived together without fear, where kindness might be encountered.

How can it be that what happens in a particular setting can remain in that place? Marconi espoused the theory that sound waves never die away but simply become fainter and fainter. If this is true, then all the sounds ever made persist and, had we the instruments, we could indeed hear everything ever said, all the music ever played. Would a place of conflict, then, be a place of faint, agonized cries; a place of peace one of gentle singing?

Such resonances seem inherently unlikely, but there are still places that somehow reflect the contentment and peacefulness of those who have lived there. Whatever lies behind this phenomenon, Botswana seems to be such a place.

4

My friends in Mochudi were Howard and Fiona Moffat. Howard was then the doctor in charge of the small hospital there. His wife, Fiona, had been a librarian. They had two children, John and Claire, who went to Maru-a-Pula School in Gaborone.

I had known Howard since boyhood days. He is the great-great-grandson of the famous Scottish missionary Robert Moffat, who set up the mission at Kuruman in the Northern Cape and whose daughter, Mary Moffat, married David Livingstone. Robert Moffat was the first person to render the language of those parts, Setswana, into written form. He was a great friend of the king of the Matabale people, Mizilikazi, and went on several long trips up into Matabeleland, where Mizilikazi had his capital at Bulawayo. I had spent my boyhood in Bulawayo, the city of Cecil John Rhodes, the arch-imperialist of Victorian times.

Howard worked all the hours of creation in Mochudi Hospital. He was much appreciated by the people there—a good, kind doctor. When he took me round the hospital, small children came up to hold on to the white coat he wore. There are many places in Africa where, in the midst of suffering, one sees love in action.

5

On one occasion when I was staying in Mochudi, Fiona and I went down into the village to see a woman who had said that she wished to give us a chicken we could cook for lunch the next day, which was the anniversary of Botswana's independence. Botswana had been a British Protectorate until 1966, when it ceased to be Bechuanaland and became Botswana under the presidency of that great and good man Sir Seretse Khama, paramount chief of the Bamangwato people.

As a young man studying in London, Seretse Khama had met a secretary, Ruth Wilson, with whom he fell in love and whom he married. This marriage was very much opposed by the British government and by the tribal authorities back home. The British government, under strong pressure from the nationalist government in South Africa, exiled Seretse from his homeland. He returned home, however, and triumphed over those in the tribe who had opposed his marriage. Ruth Khama proved to be very popular. Eventually Seretse Khama went into politics and led the party that took Botswana to independence.

In spite of the shabby way in which he had been treated by the British government, Khama was not one to nurse a grudge. He set the moral tone of the new country, insisting that nonracial democracy was the only way forward. Under his government, Botswana prospered. Diamonds were discovered, and the revenues from this were put to good use. Whereas in many other African countries mineral wealth was pillaged by dictators and their retinues, in Botswana such funds were used for the benefit of the whole society.

The Mochudi woman who that day was to give us the chicken lived in a small house with a beautifully kept yard. The sweeping of the yard is one of the most important symbolic tasks women in Botswana traditionally perform. A house with a well-swept yard would be a well-run establishment. An unhappy, chaotic house would not have a well-swept yard.

I remember the woman greeting us at her gate. She was wearing a red dress and had the naturally courteous manner one finds so often in that country. Walking about in the yard, blissfully unaware of the fate that awaited it, was a chicken.

After a few niceties had been exchanged, the woman started to pursue the chicken, which ran here and there, squawking in alarm but unable to escape. Once she had caught it, she dispatched it with a flick of the wrist and handed it to Fiona. I remember thinking: *What a remarkable woman.* And then I thought: *I wonder what her history is?* And finally I thought: *One day perhaps I should write a story about a woman like this who lives in this village.*

That was the beginning of the story of Mma Ramotswe.

6

The following year I went to work in Botswana for a period of about eight months, having been allowed to do so by the University of Edinburgh, where I lectured. The University of Botswana had requested that I be seconded to them to set up their law program. I was happy to do this, as I had very much enjoyed my time in Gaborone the previous year and I rather liked the idea of spending more time there.

I went out and was allocated a house behind a garage, not far from the Tlokweng Road. The garden was bare, but I was approached by a young man who wanted me to take him on as my gardener. In Botswana, as in other countries in the region, it is very much expected that one will contribute to the local economy by employing staff one does not really need. In Swaziland I had given a job to a young man called Simon who spent most of his time tending to the strawberries that were already growing in the garden. Then he ate most of the strawberries himself. It was a satisfactory arrangement—from his point of view, at least.

Now I employed a man called Felix, who unfortunately revealed on the first day he worked for me that he had a very severe cough. I became suspicious and took him up to Mochudi to be seen by Howard, who confirmed that Felix was unfortunately suffering from tuberculosis. Howard admitted him to the hospital and cured him within three months or so. Felix returned to work; in many other countries in Africa, where health budgets are much more pinched, the outcome might have been different.

One day Felix came to me and complained that somebody had whipped him very badly. He took off his shirt, and I saw the skin covered with weals. I asked him who had done this, and he replied that it had been the supervisor at a local mission. I drove with Felix to make a complaint to the missionary, who interrogated the supervisor. The supervisor agreed that somebody had whipped Felix, but said that this was because Felix had gone round the mission station biting his enemies.

There was not much I could do, but I was reminded of a lesson that I was subsequently to make use of in the Mma Ramotswe books: Informal solutions are very common in African countries, and one has to be careful about interfering if one is an outsider. Mind you, I do not know quite what Mma Ramotswe would have done in this difficult situation.

7

I returned to Scotland. Each year, though, I would go back to Botswana, where I was still involved in a number of projects, including writing a book on the criminal law of the country. I imagined that one day I might write something about Gaborone and the people I had met there, but I did nothing about it. I had other things to work on and was kept fairly busy with them. But in 1996, I sat down one day and wrote a short story about a woman called Precious Ramotswe who uses the inheritance she received from her father to start a little business—a private-detective agency. All the odds are against her, but she succeeds.

I wrote the short story in the space of an hour or so. I do not remember the circumstances in which I wrote it; most of us, I suspect, do not know at the time that some apparently insignificant act will change our lives. Perhaps there are some authors who, when they put pen to paper, say to themselves: *Now, this is something that is going to change everything for me*. I have never done that, even if I occasionally remember where I was and what I was doing when an idea came to me.

I do remember, however, where I was when I wrote most of the novel that followed. My wife and I had arranged a house exchange with a couple from a small village outside Montpelier in the south of France. The house we were in had a study on a mezzanine floor, and it was here that I sat as I wrote *The No. 1 Ladies' Detective Agency*. I wrote in the early morning, and then at lunchtime we would drive off to a picnic place near a river to take the children swimming. I remember finishing the book, but I do not remember thinking that it would be likely to have much of a life beyond an initial small print run.

I gave the book to the publishers who had brought out my previous collection of short stories, *Heavenly Date*. Stephanie Wolfe Murray, who then ran the firm, read the manuscript while she accompanied a truckload of relief supplies to the Balkans. She said that the book would be published, and I waited to hear more. Then the publishing firm ran into difficulties and was bought by somebody else. Stephanie, one of Scotland's great publishers of the twentieth century, was no longer in charge. I suspect that I was too non-hip for the new owners and so, realizing that my face did not fit, I took the manuscript to another publisher. This firm, Polygon, was then owned by Edinburgh University Press, and the commissioning editor was Marion Sinclair (God bless her). She and Alison Bowden (God bless her too) saw the book through to publication in 1998. I will remain forever in their debt.

They printed fifteen hundred copies. At the time of publication I was spending six months as a visiting professor at Southern Methodist University in Dallas, Texas, a private university in a plush part of that remarkable and most unusual city. I was happy there, although I found that Dallas was a city that required a bit of work to get to know. I made friends amongst my new colleagues at SMU and began to study the saxophone under an African American instrument repairer and jazz player who took me to blues clubs in Dallas that I would never have been able to find had it not been for him.

Another set of very good friends in Dallas were Joe and Mimi McKnight. Joe, who is a well-known Texas legal historian, was a Rhodes Scholar and is a great devotee of Oxford, where he and Mimi spend part of each summer. Mimi is a bibliophile, an authority on the ways of cats, and sings in the choir of a high Episcopal church in Highland Park. They held a launch party for the book in their house in Dallas. My friends from SMU generously came to this party, but nobody, including me, thought that this book would go anywhere in particular. Who would be interested in reading about the life of a woman in Botswana, a country that relatively few people then knew anything about?

8

The book was published in Scotland and was given a very encouraging review in the *Daily Telegraph* by Tony Daniels, who is an accomplished essayist and the author of a number of highly entertaining and thought-provoking books. Rather to my surprise, the first print run sold out and additional copies were printed.

I wrote a sequel to the first book, and another book after that. After their publication in Scotland, these books were offered to large London paperback publishers but were consistently turned down. My agents pointed to the generous reviews, but this would not sway those publishers. Why? The impression I had was that they wanted *edge;* they expected violence and dysfunction, especially from a Scottish writer. We were all meant to be gritty and in-your-face.

In the United States the books were initially distributed by Columbia University Press. They sold them into a number of independent bookstores, where they slowly started to get a word-of-mouth following. Eventually there were four in the series, and that was the stage at which the series was picked up by large publishers in New York, Anchor Books and Pantheon. Suddenly it became very successful. Foreign editions were sold, and today the books are published in some forty-five languages. Mma Ramotswe had arrived.

It was the Americans who discovered Mma Ramotswe. I owe everything to my American readers, who bought the books in large numbers. Like any country, the United States has its faults, but at heart Americans are a kind and generous-spirited people, and the country remains a beacon in the darkness of this world.

9

But who is she, this woman from Botswana who has somehow succeeded in speaking to so many very different people?

Her name is Precious Ramotswe, and she is called Mma Ramotswe. Mma is the honorific for a woman and is pronounced *mar,* with a slight emphasis on the *m* sound. She is the daughter of the late Obed Ramotswe, a miner who went from Botswana to work in the gold mines in South Africa. Her mother died when she was very young, and Precious was brought up by her father and a female cousin of his. She does not remember her mother, but she remembers her father very well and thinks of him constantly. "Not a day goes past," she says, "not a day but I think of my late daddy, Obed Ramotswe, miner, citizen of Botswana, and a great judge of cattle."

Obed Ramotswe was a good man. In his daughter's mind he represents the old Botswana values—those of integrity and concern for others. She remembers his moral example and his love for her. He was proud of his daughter, just as he was proud of his country.

People sometimes say to me that I rather overstate the pride people in Botswana feel for their country. I do not think I do. The Batswana are immensely proud of their country and of what it has achieved in the forty or so years since independence. They have built a prosperous country, brick by brick. They have done so by their own efforts. They have avoided getting into debt. They have been consistently democratic and they have observed the rule of law through all those four decades, even when they have been surrounded by countries in conflict. They have every reason to be proud.

A few years ago I had a conversation with a man in Botswana about his country. Our conversation was being filmed by the BBC for a television show. I asked him, "Are you proud of your country?" and he replied, "Yes, I am very proud of Botswana. I am proud to be a Motswana." And then I saw that tears had come into his eyes.

10

Precious Ramotswe stayed at school until she was sixteen and then she had a series of smallish jobs. She met a handsome trumpeter called Note Mokoti, and she married him. It was a terrible mistake, of the sort that any young person can make when confronted with glamour or good looks. Note was a bad husband and he was violent toward her, hurting her.

She had a baby, who lived only a matter of hours. She was able to hold this small scrap of humanity until death took the child from her. Note did not even come to the funeral. Her father, Obed, took her back when Note left. He did not gloat, although he had seen Note for what he was; he simply took her back into his home.

In due course Obed himself became ill. The mines had ruined his lungs, and the damage that they had done caught up with him. Part of Mma Ramotswe's world ended when Obed died. Part of Botswana, this country she loved so much, seemed to wither and recede into the past.

11

She sold a number of the cattle her father had left her and set up her little detective agency near Kgali Hill, on the edge of Gaborone. She had no idea of how to be a private detective, but she managed to get hold of a manual by one Clovis Andersen. This book, *The Principles of Private Detection,* became her main guide, even if a lot of the advice it gave struck her as being merely a matter of common sense. Incidentally, I am often asked by readers where they can purchase a copy of *The Principles of Private Detection.* I reply that the book does not exist, which I think causes them disappointment. Perhaps I shall write It myself. Certainly, in a future book I shall write about a visit that Clovis Andersen makes to Botswana. Mma Ramotswe will meet him and will, with her characteristic kindness, do something to help him. I see Clovis Andersen as a bit of a failure; he may be able to write about being a private detective, but I suspect that he will never have been very good at the job.

Mma Ramotswe acquired an assistant, Mma Makutsi, a graduate of the Botswana Secretarial College who, in the final examinations of that college, achieved the hitherto unheard-of result of 97 percent. That 97 percent is of immense importance to Mma Makutsi, and she often refers to it. She represents all those who have had to battle to get anywhere in life. She comes from a poor background in the north, and she has had to make do with very little in the material sense. She is a resourceful and intelligent woman, however, and in the later books she finds a kind and wealthy fiancé, Phuti Radiphuti, the proprietor of the Double Comfort Furniture Store. Mma Ramotswe likes Phuti. She sees him as an entirely suitable husband for her assistant.

Mma Ramotswe's husband is Mr. J.L.B. Matekoni, the owner of Tlokweng Road Speedy Motors and the finest mechanic in all Botswana. He is a good man, but he has certain minor failings, one of which is indecision. It took him a very long time to get round to marrying Mma Ramotswe. Indeed, it was not until the fifth book that this happened, and prior to that I had received many letters from readers inquiring as to why the engagement was proving to be such a long one. But they did eventually get married, in a ceremony performed at the Orphan Farm, with the children singing the hymns and the women ululating with pleasure.

The newly married couple moved into Mma Ramotswe's house on Zebra Drive. They are extremely happy: Mr J.L.B. Matekoni running his garage and she helping people to solve what she calls "the problems in their lives." These are often minor personal issues, although every so often something more serious crops up. Mma Ramotswe does not deal with significant crime, however; she is concerned with minor instances of bad behavior, and she usually deals with the offender by getting him or her to promise to behave better in future.

Is life really like that? Do people turn over new leaves and reform simply because they have been shamed into doing so by a woman like Mma Ramotswe? Probably not. One has to be realistic about human nature, which is often quite perverse. At the same time, Mma Ramotswe understands that you do not get people to be better people simply by punishing them. Those to whom evil is done do evil in return. W. H. Auden knew that and expressed the thought rather effectively in one of his poems.

Mma Ramotswe believes in forgiveness. "I am a forgiving lady," she says in one of the books. Again, she is very wise. Forgiveness is a great virtue, which unfortunately we may sometimes lose sight of when retribution holds center stage. But we really should be readier to forgive people than to hate them or seek to harm them. Forgiveness allows us to look to the future rather than concentrate on the past. Forgiveness heals.

One of Mma Ramotswe's great heroes is Nelson Mandela. Mandela, perhaps more than any other figure in the twentieth century, showed us all how forgiveness can bring an unhappy chapter to an end. Mma Ramotswe understands that. So we should not be surprised when she lets people off. That does not mean that she condones what they have done or underestimates its impact. It is just that she sees the sterility of pure retribution. She does not believe that we are helped by inflicting further suffering where there has already been significant pain and distress. I think she is right.

12

Is she a paragon of virtue, some sort of saint? Certainly not. Mma Ramotswe is very human and has her weaknesses. This humanity, I think, is why people respond warmly to her. They see that she, like the rest of us, has those temptations that she finds very difficult to resist.

One of these is cake. She very much enjoys the fruit cake served by the matron of the Orphan Farm, Mma Silvia Potokwani. And as a result of this sort of enthusiasm, she is what she calls *traditionally built*. This means that she is pretty fat, but she believes that a better way of describing it is *traditionally built*.

I am often thanked by people for inventing the term *traditionally built*. The people who give me thanks for this are often traditionally built themselves.

13

Mma Ramotswe has never been out of Botswana, other than to make a couple of very short trips into South Africa, next door. She has never seen the sea, which she sometimes dreams of seeing. She likes to imagine the sound the sea would make, which she believes is like the sound of wind in the leaves of eucalyptus trees.

In spite of never having traveled, she has a profound understanding of human nature. She knows all about the weaknesses of men, but she does not condemn men for them. She understands how hard it is to be a man. She disapproves of boastful talk. She is modest. She is generous. She has a very soft heart for those who are heavily burdened.

In one of the books she goes to Mokolodi, a small game reserve near Gaborone. There she sees two American women sitting together. She realizes that one of them looks very emaciated—she is obviously ill. Her friend confirms this. They are doing a final journey together. Mma Ramotswe embraces the sick woman and comforts her. Then she says good-bye to her in Setswana, because that is the language that her heart speaks. She turns away and weeps.

Mma Ramotswe would have time for all of us. She would comfort any of us in our sorrow.

14

It is apparent to anybody reading these books that I have affection for Botswana. That is true. I admire the country greatly. I admire the many fine values that one can find in so many people in that part of the world, and also in other countries in Africa. People must not think that Africa is a disaster, that it is a broken continent. It is not. There is still a great deal to be admired and cherished there.

Some people have described these books as a love letter to a country. Yes, they are. They do amount to a love letter, and it is a love letter to which I am proud to sign my name.

COPYRIGHT ACKNOWLEDGMENTS